STARLIGHT

A memoir by

Ida Pollock

Visit us online at www.authorsonline.co.uk

An Authors OnLine Book

Text Copyright © Ida Pollock 2009

Cover design by Ida Pollock and James Fitt ©

ISBN 978-07552-0491-5

Authors OnLine Ltd
19 The Cinques
Gamlingay, Sandy
Bedfordshire SG19 3NU
England

This book is also available in e-book format, details of which are available at www.authorsonline.co.uk

ABOUT THE AUTHOR

Born in Kent, Ida Pollock began writing novels and stories while still at school, setting her first publication, *Palanquins and Coloured Lanterns*, in 1920's Shanghai. Having worked in London through the Blitz, in 1944 she married Hugh Pollock, the glamorous soldier and publisher who had previously been married to Enid Blyton. After the war Ida started writing again and soon she had acquired five publishers, nine pen-names and a million readers worldwide.

FOREWORD

When I was growing up I realised my mother was not quite like other people. I also thought her the most rational being on the planet, my father coming second. She never seemed irritable or depressed and when the going got tough, as it must have done often, she steered her family and her life with the skill of a mariner battling stormy seas.

Many people feel there is some kind of torrent raging between them and whatever it is they want or need. If they follow my mother's example they will just keep going until they find a bridge, and once they have started to cross they won't even think about looking down.

Rosemary Pollock

We are all in the gutter, but some of us are looking at the stars

Oscar Wilde

I

I was born on a Sunday morning in April. It should have been spring, but there was snow on the ground and perhaps this had its effect on the attendant nurse. Or maybe she just didn't like the sight of a delicate looking woman, separated from her husband, giving premature birth to a 'rabbit' of a baby. Whatever the reason, three days later she placed a pillow over my face and if my mother had not, in the nick of time, spotted what was going on, there might have been remarkably little to be said on the subject of Ida Crowe.

If such a thing happened today the police would be called, there would be column inches in the Press and there would almost certainly be 'compensation'. On that far off April afternoon they simply ordered Nurse Hill out of the house, and my mother was left to stare at her new baby. And ponder, no doubt, on an uncertain road ahead.

My mother - M, as I'll call her - had been the much loved youngest daughter of John Osborn, a talented Victorian architect who tended to find his five other children disappointing and a bore. Strikingly attractive – 'they called me the beautiful Miss Osborn' - she turned down a number of marriage proposals, then one evening, at a ball in Greenwich, she danced with a Russian duke ('Russian dukes,' said my grandfather, 'are ten-a-penny'). That night the Russian, a cadet from the Royal Naval College, saw her home, and so began a story that seems eventually to have resulted in me. Three or four years after that first meeting my grandparents died within months of each other, and as life turned upside down M found herself marrying a widower old enough to be her father. Arthur Crowe came from a solid Norfolk family, a race of merchants, lawyers and clergymen, but he had been born with a congenital heart defect and perhaps because of this had squandered money, got into various difficulties and quarreled with his relations. He had a fine singing voice, and had sung in the choir of

Norwich Cathedral. He also possessed striking blue eyes and white-blonde hair, and he was 'a gentleman'. On the basis of these slender credentials his proposal was accepted, and the marriage took place at St. Alphege's Church, Greenwich. The bride, still in mourning for her father, went to her wedding clad in unrelieved black, and as they left the church she apparently longed to tear the ring from her finger and throw it away. I have no details because on this one subject my mother was always vague, but a year or so later the young Russian put in a brief re-appearance and it's then that the mischief, as it were, seems to have been done. Looking at my black hair and slightly slanting eyes, a doctor once asked M if her husband had connections in the East, and years later an Army officer observed that every time he looked at me he thought about the Uplands of Shan. Though I love England, I have to say I have never really felt English, and on the whole I have what might be termed a Russian temperament. But M never even told me the name of her Russian, and it would be hard to trace him. So I have let him go.

Several weeks before her baby was due, M walked out and went to stay with one of her brothers. When I was a month or two old the couple seem to have got together again, but their re-union did not last long. For one thing there was not - never had been - any kind of physical relationship between them. There must have been some feeling, on one side at least, and given a chance the marriage might have worked as such marriages often do, but on top of everything else Arthur Crowe had begun to drink heavily. When he was in a bad temper his years in the choir came back to him, and he sang hymns, predominantly *Fight the Good Fight*. . . not the stuff of mental cruelty, perhaps, but in the circumstances it can't have helped. I know that my supposed father did take some interest in my existence. He chose my first name, Ida - because it would be difficult to shorten - and on one occasion is said to have remarked that he 'wished I loved him too', a tragic observation or a self-pitying one, depending on the way you look at things.

When I was about six months old my mother finally left, taking me with her. Her Old English Sheepdog was also in the party - whatever else she might have decided to leave behind, it wouldn't have been the dog - and that night the three of us stayed at a small lodging house. To deter the dog from attempting to join us on our bed, M tethered it to a wash-stand which it proceeded to drag about all night, but in the morning we sorted ourselves out and went to stay with my Aunt

Dolly, who lived in Lewisham. Aunt Dolly had a little boy, Reggie, who was four years older than I was, and for more than half a century Reggie was to be my best friend in the world.

We all lived together for several years, and on the whole it was an arrangement that worked. Aunt Dolly's husband, a musician, had died before their son's birth and she had been obliged to cope by producing fine woollens for a top London department store - my grandfather, a free-spending *dilettante*, had left little or nothing to anybody. With M looking after the house and the children things probably worked fairly well, but money was always tight and both sisters were tortured by worry. If she hadn't been burdened by me M might have done all sorts of things, but I existed and had to be put first. And then a possibility seems to have arisen. It wasn't something M will have relished, in fact it must have caused her a lot of distress, but at that particular moment it may have seemed like the best option available, at least from my point of view. On an April morning, soon after my fifth birthday, I found myself being put into a railway carriage and sent to stay with one of M's wealthy Osborn cousins, a person known as Uncle Bertie.

Uncle Bertie lived near the Surrey town of Weybridge. He had a wife and three sons, and together they occupied a large, sumptuously furnished house which was surrounded by lawns and tennis courts. To me this stockbrokerish splendour was mystifying, and I couldn't have felt more confused if I had found myself in the City of Oz. There was a nursery, and an elderly nurse called Louie who was expected to look after me. Uncle Bertie's wife, Aunt Ginny, was kind enough in an abstracted sort of way, but she had nothing whatsoever to do with my everyday well-being, and most of the time I wandered about the house like a lost sprite, wondering forlornly if I would ever get out of this prison and find my way home again. Feeling Aunt Ginny might just possibly be the person to approach about this I followed her one day to the doorway of her bedroom, but she didn't seem to notice me and I hadn't the courage to speak. I can see that bedroom now - lavender coloured curtains drifting in the breeze from an open window, and a vast dressing table smothered with pretty bottles. I liked that room, despite my distress, and many years later I put it into a book.

April passed, and May. Soon it was summer, and one day the boys, whom I had always viewed with suspicion, were ordered to take me out on the river. This they interpreted as an instruction to let me follow them on to a boat. As we set out my spirits were lifted, a little, by the fact that I was wearing a rather nice straw hat - something M had acquired for me - but as I sat in the stern of the boat a river breeze whipped the hat from my head and I was forced to watch as it drifted away behind us, bobbing on the water like a demented duck. I never mentioned this incident to anyone, and I'm not sure anyone mentioned it to me. It just seemed to be one of those things. Life was something that happened to you, and there was nothing you could do about it.

Then something positive intervened, a miracle, in fact. My mother arrived. Speechless with joy, I imagined we would be leaving immediately, and was disappointed to find she intended to stay for a night or two. She was *there*, though, and that meant I could put up with anything. I didn't realise I would not be going away with her, not until she was just about to leave, and even then I didn't display my torment; but that night I was violently sick. Through a blur of misery I saw Louie fussing round me - they even called Aunt Ginny. By the next day, however, I had got myself together again. I existed through the rest of the summer, until one day I stood silently in the doorway of Aunt Ginny's bedroom, watching as she checked through a stack of small garments - dresses and skirts and socks and underwear, all designed to fit a little girl just my size. Absently, I wondered who all these things could be intended for. Not that I really cared. Then suddenly M came back again. This time she stayed just one night, and when she left I went with her.

Of course, I was to have been adopted. Aunt Ginny wanted a daughter, and tormented by the belief that I would be 'better off', my mother had sent me to Weybridge for a trial visit. Arriving after an interval to find out how I was settling in she had decided, sadly, that I seemed content. It had been a moment of grave danger, but mercifully in the end she had not felt able to part with me. Not till years later did I understand how close I had come to the abyss.

Anyway, it was over now and a new solution had been discovered. Aunt Dolly had a brother-in-law, a widower who needed someone to look after him. He was prepared to pay, though not a great deal, and could offer a comfortable home in nearby Lee Green, which was a sort of suburban village close to the edge of open countryside. He didn't object to me, and from the start my mother knew she could not afford to refuse his offer, but there was one significant drawback. Because 'Uncle George', as I was told to call him, was not a blood relation, and because his dwelling was too small to provide separate quarters for a housekeeper, there were certain to be raised eyebrows. For a woman as sensitive as M this can't have been easy to accept, but she had already discovered that life is rarely easy; so she gritted her teeth and we moved in with Uncle George.

I began attending the nearby school, and life settled down to a pattern. M was an excellent cook and she had also discovered an aptitude for looking after people - if she had been stronger physically she would have chosen to become a nurse. Soon she was known as someone who could always be turned to in a crisis, particularly when a sick child was involved. Looking back, I can never quite understand how she coped, especially as that year, and the three or four that followed, must have been difficult for a whole variety of reasons. For one thing she was still a very attractive woman, and there isn't much doubt that Uncle George was aware of the fact. She could not have married him, even if she had wanted to do so, because she was already married and divorce was out of the question, but it's fairly certain this *impasse* did not prevent him from getting ideas. One evening I was lifted out of my warm bed, dressed and bundled downstairs into a street filled with cold, brilliant moonlight. For perhaps half an hour or so my mother and I walked up and down. Then we went home, and I was put to bed. Nothing of the kind ever happened again.

And I was happy. School, even, was all right, if one set aside the fact that I didn't quite understand what I was supposed to be doing there. I never seemed to learn much and nobody noticed me either, not that I minded that part, I just wanted to keep my head down and avoid attention. After a time I did begin making one or two friends, but I didn't want to get involved in things, not in the way that other girls did. I didn't belong, and that being the case had no particular interest in following the local customs.

When I was out, alone, I stared up at the sky and the scudding clouds and I ran, faster and faster, usually until I fell over. On summer mornings I sat among the waist high sorrel in the field beyond the railway line, all alone with my thoughts and a bottle of home-made lemonade, and on summer evenings I leaned out of my bedroom window, watching the stars until the lamp-lighter came. I liked the stars better than the moon. They were such a long way away, nothing to do with earth, and when the sky was clear they shed just enough light to steep everything in mystery. I thought it would be fun to travel by starlight, but you had to be grown-up before you could do things like that. After I had gone to bed I frequently lay awake, weaving a story in my mind, a serial story in which I was the central

5

character. In this other life I had an older brother, a dashing Army officer who spoiled me and kept an eye on me. Somewhere I *had* a father, I knew that, so I didn't need to invent one of those. Anyway, you couldn't depend on fathers. They had a habit of going away and not coming back. What I needed was a brother, someone on whom I could always rely. Who wouldn't disappear without trace.

Aunt Dolly, who had gone into private nursing, came to see us a lot and by this time I was firm friends with Reggie, who treated me like a younger sister, which helped me to regain a feeling of stability. But it was to be a long time before I could see my mother go out of the house, without me, and not feel uneasy. The memory of that uneasiness is with me to this day, and the fear of being alone.

Meanwhile, things were happening in the world. In 1914 a war had started and for those who were grown up nothing was ever going to seem quite the same again. The dreamy world of my mother's youth was on the point of disappearing forever. It was a different kind of war, too. For the first time, people in or near London stood a chance of looking up and seeing the enemy's airborne weaponry – doodlebugs – lumbering above their heads. I don't remember picking up any sense of fear or panic, but I do recall the police officers who cycled through our streets shouting 'take cover', and – oh, yes, the female neighbour, a glamorous lady who shopped in the West End, fainting dead away and requiring to be resuscitated by my exasperated mother. Where there was sadness, and there must have been a good deal, I think it was expressed mainly through silence. One of M's nephews had enlisted at the age of fifteen – lying about his age – and with his regiment had been sent to what is now Israel, where he was killed outside the gates of Jerusalem. After the war was over, his mother travelled to visit his grave. Not once, but three times.

My most vivid memory is of an evening in January 1917. Reggie and I had been sent to collect something from a shop, down near the river. I don't know what we were collecting, but I do know that as we turned to leave the shop something happened. A blind that had been covering the window suddenly shot up, and there was an earth-shattering explosion. Outside the sky seemed to catch fire. We rushed out into eerie brightness, only to find no-one about. . . Just silence. Slowly the world began steadying again, and we heard some running footsteps, shouts and cries. We didn't run, though, we just walked rather quickly, Reggie keeping a firm hold of my hand, and when we got close to my home M came rushing to meet us. Panic stricken, she had left the house without pausing to grab a coat.

At the time many people seem to have imagined there had been some kind of enemy attack, but the truth was almost worse. At Silverstone on the northern bank of the Thames, an emergency munitions plant had been set up. Housed in what seems to have been an inadequate structure it was probably an accident waiting to happen, and that night several van loads of TNT had caught fire, triggering what is still described as the worst explosion ever to occur in the London area. Seventy thousand buildings were damaged or destroyed, seventy-three lives lost. While every death was obviously a tragedy, the toll would have been much higher had it not been for one miraculous factor - the explosion happened just before seven pm, a time when most day workers had left, while the night shift had yet to arrive.

The Silverstone explosion was heard as far away as Southampton on the Channel coast. Reggie and I had been no more than five miles from its centre. I can't say it has ever haunted my dreams, but sometimes at the height of a thunderstorm – just for a second or two - I am back in that January night, with the river smell in my nostrils and the earth catching fire around me.

I was fairly healthy - too healthy, in my opinion, other people got far more time off school - but I grew with painful slowness and was also subject to occasional blackouts, incidents that must have been terrifying for M, though they didn't seem to have any lasting effect on me. Our doctor was sure I would grow out of these phenomena, and by the time I was twelve he had been proved right. There is an accepted medical explanation for such attacks, but in my case I can't help feeling they must have had something to do with the attempt that had once been made to suffocate me (all my life I have suffered from an extreme form of claustrophobia).

Though my school career was undistinguished, I had no difficulty in learning to read. The only problem was, I didn't want to *do* any reading. My mother, a voracious bookworm, found this disappointing and efforts were made to obtain books that might catch my imagination, but nothing seemed to work. It was as if I had been placed in front of a brand new computer and shown how to operate it, but someone had forgotten to turn the power on, then one day, I think it was raining, I picked up a grown-up novel set in the old West of America, and the power came on. That book was very long, but I hardly put it down until every word had been digested, and I knew I had discovered something of huge importance. Books were a bridge to that other world I had always known existed but hadn't been able to reach; and they were also something I didn't have to share with anyone else. It struck me that writing books and stories must be a wonderful way of holding on to all those things that otherwise slipped away from you, and I even tried it. Just a few lines at first, the beginning of what was supposed to be a story, then I got through a page or two and M was impressed. At school, I won an award for composition. Considering I was getting quite a bit of practice this probably wasn't surprising, but I remember being astonished, at the time.

I had one or two friends and there was always my cousin, but generally speaking the people I trusted, felt closest to, were usually adults. They stood around me like a guardian circle: my mother, Aunt Dolly, my Sunday School teachers. And Uncle George's family. Uncle George had a brother and three sisters who lived together a short distance away from us. The sisters were middle-aged spinsters, a species that has since died out. They were also civilised, carefully educated women. One had a trained soprano voice, another was an accomplished pianist, the third produced exquisite needlework, and when they weren't doing anything else they all cooked and baked and preserved, filling their small house with delectable scents. They were pillars of the Church, but this did not mean they were narrow-minded or dry or humourless. They were endlessly kind to me, and they were extremely fond of M, whose position worried them. We often went to see them on Sunday evenings. Even in those days most people of my age would have been bored out of their minds, but I adored those visits. It wasn't just the home-made sweets, the pots of strawberry jam or the shilling coins wrapped in tissue paper – '*I expect you can find a use for this*' - though all were acceptable. There was a kind of tranquillity in that house, and there was music, and I craved both of these things.

There was something else, as well. Uncle George's brother, Will Savage, was away a lot on business and for this reason it was probably some time before he and I got to know one another, but eventually an extraordinary friendship developed between us. Will had read a very great deal, so much that it sometimes seemed there was nothing he had not read, and he was in the habit of going to concerts and the opera. He had travelled all over Europe, and spoke a number of languages. And he talked to me.

Normally tongue-tied and inhibited, I always relaxed with Will, and I don't suppose there were many things we never thought about discussing. We went for long walks through Blackheath, making our way along streets with magic names - Blessington Park, Grey Ladies, Love Lane - before cutting across the heath itself, and all the time we talked. About the Alps, which he loved, about China which interested him, about the rival merits of Wagner and Rossini, who otherwise wouldn't have been much more than names as far as I was concerned. He was a bachelor in his forties and I was just coming into my teens. It was an odd relationship and some people might say it was undesirable, but those walks and those discussions were absolutely innocent. They gave me an understanding of the world and a large store of knowledge - as I struggled to dredge readable stories out of my restless imagination, it could be an enormous help to know what the sunset *really* looked like from a Swiss mountainside. And that wasn't all. Because Will took an interest in me, I began to believe in myself. Of course my mother had always tried to give me confidence, but she was my mother. 'Uncle' Will represented the great, sophisticated world, and he thought that I was worth something. I owe him a lot, for that.

Slipping into the muddy waters of my teens I could have begun to experience problems, but so far as I can recall there was nothing traumatic. For one thing I wasn't particularly interested in the opposite sex, not, at least, in the specimens I saw around me. I knew there were attractive men in the world because they turned up in books, and because my mother talked about them - though it had always been impressed upon me that men in general were to be treated with caution. They *might*, sometimes, be glamorous, romantic, interesting, even admirable, but they were at the mercy of their own baser instincts, and not to be trusted an inch. Weighing this up in my mind I decided there could be a touch of exaggeration involved, but on the other hand M's view of most things tended to be reliable. Anyway, I just hadn't encountered any really interesting men, and so far as I was concerned boys of my own age didn't exist. One day, when time had removed their acne, they might, I supposed, turn into something more or less civilised, but looking at one or two I couldn't really imagine such a metamorphosis occurring. I loved my cousin, of course, but then he was my cousin, and that was something else again.

Just once, I remember wondering whether life would ever change, panicking because there was so much I wanted to do and see and I couldn't imagine any of it happening. Most of the time, though, I was content to wait for the future. And change wasn't long in coming.

When I was fifteen years old an important bank ran into difficulties, and Uncle George was affected. He lost his home, his business, his money and his way of life. I witnessed no scenes of panic, nor did I hear talk of breakdowns or whispers of suicide. I knew that my mother looked anxious, and sometimes I heard long, murmurous discussions; but none of it affected me. Not, at least, until the house was sold. . . then to my inexpressible delight I learned we were moving down to Hastings, which was said to be on the Sussex coast. Uncle George's family, it seemed, were helping him to buy a property in this enticing place. On a cool, bright spring day we left Lee Green and moved down into Sussex. I don't believe my mother's relationship with Uncle George had ever changed dramatically, but by this time we seemed like a family, and like a family we settled into our new home.

Our house was one of a cluster that huddled together near Emmanuel Church, just above the town and quite close to a strip of open cliff-top. The cliff top was a miraculous expanse of tussocky grass and scented thyme and just beyond, moody and challenging, was the cold, bright, restless Channel. I had never been near the sea before, I didn't know its smell or its feel, but now I made up for lost time. I spent hours hanging round the lonely ruins of Hastings castle, and more hours just staring at that sea. At last, I was on the edge of Life.

* * * * *

II

When I was seventeen, I started writing in earnest. No-one had suggested I should think about getting a job and consequently the idea hadn't entered my head, but then I knew what I was going to do, and so did my mother. I was going to write novels and I was going to be a sensation, like Ethel M. Dell. For several hours every day I sat at the dining-room table scribbling, struggling to reproduce on paper the ideas that revolved in my head. It was hard work, and a lot of my thoughts were still confused and incomplete, but I loved what I was doing, and I had masses of ideas. . . too many. For a long time, I seemed incapable of bringing one single item to completion.

M had faith in me, though. Not only that, she brought me cups of tea, put flowers on my work-table, protected me from interruption and every day gave her opinion on my efforts - usually this tended to be reassuring, but if she felt there was something wrong she could be relied upon to let me know. Uncle Will, who like his sisters came to stay at regular intervals, gave me all the advice he could, and that was important, because I knew I could trust his judgement. Then there was Aunt Dolly. Now possessed of a wealthy second husband, she earned my unending gratitude by buying me a typewriter. I've never forgotten that first portable typewriter, or the delicious experience of learning to use it. I completed my first full length novel, and Aunt Dolly's husband - probably with tongue very much in cheek - submitted the manuscript to a publishing firm called Constable. It's difficult to imagine what this prestigious company actually thought about my offering, but they did write a very encouraging little note, and Uncle Tom put a clause in his Will to the effect that when he died I was to receive quite a large sum of money - the idea was that this generosity should enable me to undertake a complete trip around the world, an adventure which would enlarge my mind and so advance my literary career.

I completed several short stories, and started sending them away. One, I remember, concerned a Japanese beauty who never strayed beyond the confines of a garden. In the end, she used her own waist-length hair to strangle her lover. . . . I called this piece *The Woman*. It came back and so did the others, so I sent them away again. They came back again. I wrote more stories, and they came back, but I knew that I had to keep going. I was meant to be a writer, I was *going* to be a writer. Sometimes the discouragement was hard to live with, but it didn't stop me. Some day, like Alice breaking through the looking-glass, I would force myself through into that magic world inhabited by published authors. The moment might still be some distance off, but I could wait.

And it occurred to me that possibly, just possibly, I needed something in the way of training. I knew I had talent, but I did understand that talent by itself was not always quite enough. There were things I was uncertain about, wrinkles I probably needed to pick up. I had seen advertisements for the London School of Journalism, and dear Aunt Dolly paid for me to embark upon their Correspondence course for Creative Writers. Though flattered by a tutor's observation that I didn't seem to need much instruction, I did my best to work my way through the course, and though some of it may have been a waste of time it taught me things I have remembered throughout my working life, among them the point that no work of fiction should be without at least one genuinely sympathetic character. Human nature being what it is, readers need to get involved, to care what's happening, and that isn't easy if there's no-one to care about.

I finished the course, got my diploma, and was summoned to London for a meeting with one of the School's advisors, a very distinguished writer called Sir Max Pemberton. Sir Max's best-selling novel *Kronstadt* had won huge critical acclaim, and as I prepared to enter his office I felt as if I might be about to faint, but he was very kind. He had read my work and claimed he found little to criticize.

'Don't,' he advised, 'expect to get very far until you're about forty. But as long as you carry on the way you're going, and avoid purple patches, I think you're heading towards the top.'

Well, it might be nice, getting to the top, but I was sensible enough not to let my head be turned. Before I could even get started on the nursery slopes I would need to begin selling some stories, and so far that goal seemed elusive. I wrote to the popular novelist Ruby M. Ayres, and with amazing generosity she invited me to have lunch with her at the Piccadilly Hotel in London. Arriving in a chauffeur-driven Bentley, she gave me a few useful tips, then concluded encouragingly: 'Just do what I've done! I've made *pots of money'*.

Pots of money. That would be nice, too.

In the meantime, I read everything I could get my hands on. Pierre Loti, Rosita Forbes - at that time a noteworthy woman explorer - Joseph Conrad. I loved the travels of H.V. Morton, and I was captivated by Jeffrey Farnol's eighteenth century England. I was fascinated by Farnol's heroes, too, particularly their habit of possessing rather beautiful grey eyes, fringed, of course, by startling eyelashes. Among novelists, though, my favourite was and always has been Charlotte Bronte. *Now, if I could only meet a Mr Rochester. . . .*

In the meantime, I liked the place where I lived. If I chose I could give the library a miss and spend some time hanging round the smart shops in the middle of the town, now and then stealing a glance at the glamorous Queen's Hotel, where royalty stayed. I could stroll up over the cliff-top, wondering as I walked about all those things that went on beyond the sea - looking back, on a crisp October day, to that other October long ago, when grim wooden ships had come out of the sunrise and changed England forever. In Hastings Public Library, at that time, there was a large sculpture that depicted Edith of the Swan Neck - King Harold's girl-friend, according to Tennyson - bending over her lover on the field of battle. It was a white, shining, beautiful thing, and the story it told, of high romance and great happenings, dominated that library just as distant and long ago images dominated my mind. The last time I visited Hastings I went to look for Edith and Harold, but they had gone long since. I'm not sure where they went, but I hope they're being looked after.

Tragically, after only six months Aunt Dolly's second husband died. I had liked him very much. Unfortunately for me his last Will had remained unsigned, but there was some kind of consolation. Aunt Dolly decided to buy a house not far from Hastings, and her son Reggie, now in his early twenties, came along too.

Reggie liked girls, women of all ages, and they returned the compliment. He also liked cars, and having had a wealthy stepfather was able to afford a string of the latest sporting models. His romantic adventures were innumerable, but he and I were still great friends and when he took a girl out for the afternoon I quite often went along too.

In those days girls and young men tended to go about in groups rather than pairs, and a female cousin came in rather handy, especially one who was in a permanent state of abstraction.

I enjoyed those outings, and they have never left me. Reggie, at the wheel of his latest Vauxhall or Ford, churning up the dust along a quiet downland lane. Sleepy Sussex woods and hedges crammed with Queen Anne's Lace. . . Mary Mason's Yew Tree tea-room. Cream and scones and Dundee cake, fan-tail pigeons and a breeze just rustling the elm tops. While Reggie and his current girl-friend gazed at one another I relaxed into my own world, and by the time we left, in the cool of the evening, I was probably walking on the Great Wall of China. There was one summer in particular, a green-and-gold time full of village fetes and shadowy pubs . . . .

In pubs, though, my lingering distaste for alcohol was frequently an embarrassment (*'I can't keep asking for tomato juice'*). And I could be awkward in other ways. Once I was supposed to be having a driving lesson, but the current girl-friend got in first and by the time she had dumped us all in a ditch my interest had somehow started to evaporate. As far as I could see, the accelerator and the brake were a good deal too close together, and I never again thought about driving a car.

If these excursions sometimes involved young men, other than Reggie, I didn't particularly notice them, but around this time there was someone, a boy called Leslie. He was loosely attached to our set - Reggie had been in love with both of his sisters, whether consecutively or concurrently I can't remember - and he was rather pleasant, with gentle brown eyes. My mother liked him, but the problem was that he and I inhabited different planets. He sent me several letters and presented me with a rather nice row of pearls, which I handed on to M. I think the whole thing puzzled me, rather. Love affairs, boy-and-girl get togethers, were not for me. Romance to me meant distant lands. Colour-washed palaces. Palm-fringed islands.

Anyway I had other things to think about, because there had been a development on the work front. Our Vicar, the Reverend Gordon-Duff, was a powerful preacher whose church was usually crammed to capacity, and he also took an interest in his parishioners. On one occasion he had asked to see one of my stories, and within a few days it had been sent on to a friend who just happened to edit the popular

Sunday Companion magazine. A fortnight or so went by, then I received a note asking me to call and see the Vicar.

Another rejection. My legs turned to jelly, but I ran straight round to the Vicarage, and as I entered his study Mr Gordon-Duff smiled. He had a piece of paper in his hand, and he waved it at me. 'Good news!' he said.

The *Sunday Companion* had accepted my story, and had sent me a cheque for three guineas. Moreover, they had asked to see further examples of my work.

I felt vindicated, and a surge of joy swept through me. I ran home to tell M, and her excited reaction was all and more than I could have hoped for. I sent more stories to the *Sunday Companion*, and they were accepted, then at Mr Gordon-Duff's suggestion I tried the monthly *Sunday Stories* and also the *Christian Herald*, with similar results in both cases. (*Sunday Stories* paid ten guineas). I was a published writer, and could begin to hold my head up.

And then something startling happened. Will Savage asked me to marry him.

Will had been coming to visit us rather a lot, and even in my abstracted state I had begun to understand that these days he saw me in a new and more interesting light, but his proposal still surprised me. It came in the form of a letter, and as I did with everything I took the letter straight to M, who weighed up the pro's and con's. Will was thirty years my senior and of course I wasn't in love with him, but he was *very* well off, and he took an interest in my work. It might be the sensible thing. . . . M, after all, knew better than anyone how life could punish you for failing to do the sensible thing. But she had no intention of pushing me.

I probably thought the idea over for about a day and a half. In some ways, I suppose, I was such a child that I had no powerful feelings one way or the other. I wanted to marry Prince Charming, if he could be found, and get myself carried off over the rainbow; but on the other hand I was fond of Will, and I did know I would be safe with him. As his wife, too, I would be free to pursue my career in comfort, following my star without any need to worry about mounting bills. The proposition had its tempting aspects and very briefly, I think, I was tempted, but only briefly. The whole of life, the whole world was in front of me. If I married Will I would be locking myself into a small grey cage.

I wrote and turned him down. It wasn't until long afterwards that I realised how badly my rejection hurt him.

One day around this time I wandered into a Roman-Catholic church. After looking round I sat down for a moment, and an elderly nun appeared. I explained that I had really been heading somewhere else – that I wasn't a Catholic – and she put a hand over mine.

'Stay with us for a while,' she suggested. 'Come and talk.'

I didn't, of course, I simply went my way, but I have often regretted that hasty decision. I admire the Catholic Church and see nothing wrong with its pursuit of souls – something other churches might do well to emulate. I have often wished I had its strength flowing through my life, and though I have never found the courage to do anything about this I still feel the powerful grip of those persuasive fingers. I wish, very often, that I had that moment back again.

By this time, quite a number of my short and medium-length stories had been printed by the *Sunday Companion, Christian Herald*, etc. It was an encouraging start, and in today's terms had already netted something like several hundred pounds, but still this was not the same thing as being a novelist. I wanted, desperately, to see my name on a book, and also - for myself, for my mother and even for Uncle George - I wanted to make money. My early efforts had mostly been put aside, as early efforts sometimes need to be. Not because I was ashamed of them, privately I thought they were rather good, but because I had to start being more commercial. *The Woman* might be all right in her way, but she was never going to sell in quantity, even if she found a publisher. For a long time, M had been urging me to write something 'pretty', something a little bit closer to Charles Garvice - her own popular favourites were Ouida, Marie Corelli and Hall Caine, but she knew it was important to be realistic, and I had to acknowledge that her instincts in this direction might be sound.

Of course I had read and been told that the golden rule for any aspiring novelist should always be 'write what you know', but if I had felt obliged to abide by such depressing advice I would have gone out and sold my typewriter. I decided to work by a rather different principle – 'write what *intrigues* you'. And what intrigued me most, at that time, was the Far East.

With all the determination I could summon up, I sat down and produced a novel about a spoilt, wealthy English girl being kidnapped in Twenties Shanghai. I had read a good deal about China - enough, I thought, to avoid any horrendous mistakes - but by the time I had finished I was beginning to feel some niggles of uneasiness. In those days, much more than now, it was vital to get your facts straight. It would be awful if my careful work were to be shipwrecked upon some trivial error about the number of rickshaws normally to be seen in the Bubbling Well Road, or the average rainfall along the banks of the Y'angtse. Help was at hand, though, and from an unexpected direction. Reggie's latest girl-friend, later to become his wife, knew a solicitor who had spent some time in China, and at her suggestion the typescript was handed to him. Though I told myself I was perfectly confident I awaited the solicitor's verdict with trepidation, but I needn't have worried. My Chinese background, according to him, was sound; he could find no serious mistakes. It has occurred to me, since, that he might have been urged to err on the side of diplomacy, but on the whole I tend to agree with the American author Henry James, who believed that some fiction writers possess the ability, having swallowed a few facts, to visualise accurately and in detail places and civilisations about which they have no personal knowledge or experience.

Anyway, I now had to select a publisher for *Palanquins and Coloured Lanterns*. There were then, as there are still, a vast number of firms listed in the Writers' and Artists' Year Book. Which one, though. . . ?

After a lot of careful thought I picked on George Newnes, a good general publishing company with a sound reputation and a comfortably large output.

*   *   *   *   *

III

And so one day I found myself standing before the portal of George Newnes Ltd. I had a novel under my arm, and a horrible feeling that once I got inside that building I was definitely going to lose my nerve. In spite of a firm belief that bulls should always be grasped by their horns, I never did have much real confidence.

At that time Newnes' publishing empire was considerable. Apart from anything else, they produced a number of popular magazines. It was their book division, though, that interested me, for it had become the chosen imprint of several very successful authors, among them Edgar Wallace, Richmael Crompton - creator of *Just William* - and even the politician Winston Churchill, though I doubt if Mr Churchill was uppermost in my mind just then.

Summoning up all my courage I passed through the outer door of the building, and a short time later found myself deposited inside a small, square room. I supposed it was a sort of waiting-room, if publishers had such things, but there didn't seem to be any chairs. There wasn't any other furniture, either, if one discounted what appeared to be a large, cumbersome looking safe, positioned in one corner.

Struggling against the urge to flee, I waited alone by a window, and around twenty minutes later was joined in my isolation by a very large gentleman in pin-striped trousers. We stared at one another, and I noticed the gentleman was slightly bald, also that he tended to be particularly paunchy around the middle. He seemed surprised to see me. I realised, afterwards, that he hadn't been expecting to see me. At that moment, all I felt was relief.

I held out my novel, the completion of which had cost me months of laborious work, and explained haltingly that I hoped it might fit in with the requirements of George Newnes' hallowed List.

The pin-striped gentleman looked very much more surprised, and having accepted the package with evident reluctance began to examine it warily, rather as if he thought it might have some unpleasant significance. These days he would probably have suspected a bomb - I had wrapped my precious burden in brown paper and secured it carefully with string, so that by no possible chance could any part of it escape. A minute or so ticked away, while I chattered nervously, then he explained that although their List was fairly extensive it was not often that they took on new authors. . . . By which he probably meant they didn't often take on authors who looked like me. Still only five foot two inches tall, and with a childishly slight figure, I tended to appear at least five years younger than I actually was, an illusion which placed me in the schoolroom category. On this particular occasion I was even wearing my round, velour school hat, teamed with an uninspiring brown tweed coat. In addition I'm sure I looked round-eyed and apprehensive. I knew all this at the time, and in a way I could understand the pin-striped gentleman's attitude, but I *was* a writer - I knew I could write - and my disappointment was acute. More than that, standing in that strange, empty room I felt humiliated. Smaller even than I was. A rejection slip was bad, but at least it meant that somebody, somewhere had glanced at one's work. This was worse, very much worse.

Something of what I was feeling must have begun to show in my face, for the pin-striped gentleman relented a little - perhaps he had daughters of his own - and taking a firmer hold on the package he allowed his tone to alter very slightly. My contribution would, of course, be looked at, it would receive careful consideration. *'We shall, of course, communicate with you in - er - due course. . . .'*

'Thank you!' I gasped. And like a petrified rabbit I bolted out of the room, across the foyer and into the street. Into the world of daylight.

My mother, who had been waiting on the pavement, was delighted to see I had been relieved of my manuscript. Her knowledge of publishing practice being minimal, she supposed this must be a good sign and I hadn't the heart to disillusion her. Nor did I tell her exactly what had just happened. Instead I made a resolute attempt to look confident, and we made our way back along the Strand, heading for the Corner House where we planned to have lunch.

Lyon's Corner Houses, I always thought, were a wonderful invention, in fact, one of the most delectable things about any day spent in London. The food was excellent, the tables beautifully appointed, there were lots of glamorous looking potted palms and - best of all - on every floor a three-piece orchestra was usually to be found playing away energetically. There were wonderful pots of tea, too, the sort of tea that magically restores nerve and optimism. Even to a youthful, dejected author.

During the course of lunch my spirits ascended steadily. Afterwards, as M and I set out on a small shopping spree, they climbed even further and that evening, on the train back to Hastings, I knew that I was happy.

I had a novel being considered by George Newnes, and I was determined not to worry about it any more. I had always believed in the quality of my work, which by and large had received a lot of praise, even if, so far, it hadn't made me very much money. How many novels, I wondered, would Newnes be prepared to take. . . . More to the point, how much would they be prepared to pay for the first one?

I could almost see that cheque dropping through the letter-box. By the time our train chugged quietly into Ashford, I had already started spending it.

Nowadays I have little capacity for believing in anything that isn't virtually a certainty, and it's hard to credit the resilience I possessed in those days. During that far-off time I had the ability to bounce from the depths of despair, straight to the heights of unqualified optimism. That, though, is always one of the advantages attached to being young, and it has a lot to do with lack of experience.

Weeks went by, and then months. Six months passed, and there had been no cheque from George Newnes. There hadn't been a rejection slip, either, and I derived some comfort from that, but still - I knew that six months was too long. Even the *Writers' and Artists' Year Book* took a markedly sober view of six months. With much reluctance I decided to write and enquire, respectfully, after the well-being of my manuscript.

My letter produced a swift and surprising response. The firm, it seemed, had absolutely no knowledge of *Palanquins and Coloured Lanterns*; no record to indicate that it had been received, no note of its author's name. Was I, they wondered, absolutely certain I had delivered my novel to their office? Perhaps I had become confused. Might it not be possible that I had, in actual fact, taken it elsewhere? If, however, I still felt convinced, they hoped I would be good enough to let them have a few details: a description of the person to whom I had entrusted my MS, the date and time, etc. Then they would make every effort to track the typescript down.

That letter was signed: H.A. Pollock, Book Editor.

Far from being dismayed by this, I was immediately intrigued. At least it was better than a rejection slip, and of course they would find the manuscript sooner or later. The fact that they had somewhat carelessly mislaid it might predispose them in its favour, when the time came for it to receive serious consideration. And the letter I had received was extremely polite. There was actually a note of apology running through it.

Who was H.A. Pollock, I wondered? Obviously not the gentleman in pin-striped trousers. Quite apart from the fact that he would have remembered me - *surely* - it wasn't his style, somehow. If he had written the letter it would have been a good deal testier, and certainly it would have lacked that rather attractive note of apology.

I wrote back at once, describing my reception in the room without furniture, and soon afterwards I received a reply. The Book Editor's apologies were now profuse, and he actually seemed to be worried about the situation that had arisen. It seemed he had recognised the setting in which my interview had taken place, but whether or not Pin-stripe Trousers had been interrogated I found it impossible to tell. He said they had no recollection of such a thing happening before, and suggested it might help to clear things up if, in the near future, I could travel to London and discuss the matter personally.

An arrangement was made and I went up to London, this time unaccompanied. Tormented, as usual, by feelings of anxiety and trepidation, I presented myself once again at the building occupied by Newnes. This time, however, I was expected, and after a very brief delay I was directed to the office of Major Hugh Pollock.

'H', then, stood for Hugh. I liked that.

I was shown in by Major Pollock's secretary, a young woman whose name was Margaret Summerton. Miss Summerton had been with her employer for several years, and she succeeded in making me feel almost painfully conscious of my homespun appearance. I was no longer wearing the school hat but I hadn't really become a lot smarter, and there was nothing in the slightest degree impressive about me. Whereas she was tall and elegant, with sleek dark hair, almond-shaped brown eyes, an excellent skin and a cool manner. With deepening embarrassment I realised she was very much surprised by my appearance, and I supposed unhappily that Major Pollock was going to be even more surprised.

From the other side of his desk he stared at me, I remember. I had the impression that he even blinked slightly. Then he stood up, smiled, and held out his hand.

He was a slim man, reasonably tall, with golden brown hair and lightly bronzed skin. Considering the fact that he had already turned forty he was, in fact, extraordinarily handsome, with a firm, humorous mouth and eyelashes that I was sure were at least a third of an inch long, but it was the eyes themselves I noticed first. They were strikingly blue, and for a man's eyes almost beautiful. There was something about them, though. . . a shadow, a touch of sadness, even. His voice, I noticed, was soft and faintly hypnotic. Long after I had left Hugh Pollock's office, I remembered his voice.

As we stood looking at one another, I had the oddest feeling I was re-discovering someone I had once known well. In a curious way, it was an emotional moment - almost, I wanted to say: *'There you are..! Where have you been?'* But of course I didn't.

I am certain now that Hugh and I had met before, in other times and other circumstances. I am not at all sure I agree with Ouspensky's theory, which decrees that we keep on going round in circles, and that everything in life happens more or less exactly as it has happened many times before, but I do think we meet the same people, possibly more than once, and I'm sure Hugh and I had shared a previous life. Naturally I can't say that we recognized one another. It was nothing as clear-cut or as simple as that. But from the moment he started to speak I lost most of my paralysing nervousness, and when a chair was placed for me I was able to accept it and relax.

I don't remember the details of our conversation, but of course we discussed the movements of my typescript, and eventually the pin-striped gentleman was identified as no less exalted a personage than Sir Frank Newnes himself. Sir Frank had been a son of the firm's founder and now, it seemed, he was Chairman of the Board. I'm not sure why, but I don't believe there was any suggestion of approaching Sir Frank then and there. Perhaps he was out of the country or perhaps, in the way of exalted personages, he was 'tied up'. Hugh would not have been in awe of him, because as I was eventually to discover, Hugh was never in awe of anybody. Besides which, as Book Editor he held a fairly important position himself.

As I left the building, though, I was not worrying about *Palanquins and Coloured Lanterns.* I was just thinking how unusual it was to see a man with *real* golden brown hair. I wondered, too, whether Major Pollock was married. And if so, what his wife might be like.

* * * * *

IV

A few days later, I received a letter to say that *Palanquins and Coloured Lanterns* had been found. Apparently it had spent the last few months reposing just a few feet from the spot where I had last seen it - inside the big square safe that occupied a corner of Newnes' waiting room.

Writing to give me this news, Major Pollock apologized on behalf of the firm. Better still - miraculously - he said that having had a chance to inspect my manuscript they had now decided they would like to make me an offer for it. If I agreed they would pay me twenty-five guineas, and *Palanquins* would make its appearance in their Popular Library series, carrying my recently chosen pen-name, Joan Allen.

Perhaps, I thought, they simply wanted to make amends, as I had imagined they just possibly might. But publishers didn't *really* do things like that, and though Major Pollock had a good deal of charm I had not received the impression he was in any way soft.

Up on the cliffs outside Hastings, I walked on air because *Palanquins* had found a publisher. Then having allowed a decent interval for euphoria I started work on an appropriate follow-up, this time a story set in India; and finding myself back in London a week or so later I once again dropped in at George Newnes. Like a dog retrieving a rubber bone I deposited a couple of chapters in front of Hugh Pollock, and he said he would look at them. He smiled - I felt that I amused him, but I didn't mind. On further inspection he seemed even more desperately attractive than I had thought he was. By this time I understood that he was married; but it was to be some little while before I found out exactly who his wife was.

Almost a year went by. *Palanquins* came out and in due time was followed by *Indian Love* - this exotic title was suggested, I think, by a sub-editor. Every few weeks I travelled up to London, and on some pretext or other I usually dropped in at Newnes. For some reason, I realised, Hugh's secretary disapproved of me strongly, and on several occasions she made determined efforts to send me away. At the time I supposed she was simply guarding her boss from unnecessary or inappropriate interruptions. Later on, I came to realise that her motives may have been more complicated.

I knew now that Hugh Pollock was married to Enid Blyton, the successful children's writer. Formerly a governess and school teacher, Enid had started out by making up stories for her pupils, then she had begun to get them printed in magazines. Then, like me, she had found her way to the publishing firm of George Newnes, and - also like me - had run into Hugh Pollock, from which time her career had taken off in a big way. Now they had two little girls, a dog called Patch and a rambling thatched house beside the River Thames.

Hugh did not talk much about his wife, and his younger daughter Imogen was still not much more than a baby, but six-year-old Gillian, it seemed, was beautiful and astonishingly bright. Most normal fathers become powerfully attached to their daughters, but in Hugh's case I felt there was more to it. It was almost as if Gillian were the only being - the only thing in the world - that belonged to him. I sensed there was a part of him that kept well back from everyone else, and increasingly I was intrigued. Hugh had been born and brought up in Ayr, where his father still owned a prosperous book business, but he was proud of the fact that his mother's family came from the Highlands - were descended, in fact, from medieval Lords of the Isles - and in spirit, I quickly realised that he was very much a Highlander. Having joined the Army some months before the outbreak of World War I he had stayed on for ten years, spending time in India and the Middle East before finally coming out and becoming part of the London publishing world. Joining the staff of George Newnes he had quickly moved into an influential position, and clearly he was used to dealing with a variety of important authors (I later learned that around this time he was often at Chartwell, where he had lengthy private talks with Winston Churchill). And, of course, there was his own wife. Hugh had tremendous personal charisma and I soon realised he was immensely popular, with men as well as women. I found him dazzling.

But he was not any part of my life. He was pleasant and courteous and never seemed in a hurry to get rid of me - in the tone of a benevolent uncle, he said things like: '*One day I must take you out to lunch*' . . . . But that, inevitably, was as far as it went. All too quickly our talks would end, then I would run back down the clattering stone staircase and emerge into the noisy Strand. On the train back to Hastings, I would mull over everything he had said.

My Indian piece was completed, sent in and accepted, but the promised lunch did not materialize and I felt rather flat. I took a job that involved looking after four children in the absence of their parents, something which wasn't too bad until the day when all four came down with chickenpox. Having caught the disease many years earlier I ought to have been all right, but I was 'run-down', and soon after my temporary post ended woke up one morning with a blazing pain that cut across both eyes. I had shingles, in a particularly troublesome form, and was to be ill for weeks. The pain was intense, and almost as bad was the fact that I couldn't write or even read. For much of the time I was supposed to wear an eye shade. In those days bed rest was still considered essential, and when I started trying to move again I found I could barely walk, not that I wanted to go out. Physically I was getting better, but mentally I was sliding deeper and deeper into a dark, unfamiliar place, losing control of myself and of the forces inside my head. For such a long time I had been used to the thrill of creating ideas and images, shapes that could be lifted from my mind and transferred on to paper. Now that was gone, and I couldn't cope with the loss. Frustration led to depression, and depression to desperation. I began to experience what would now be called panic attacks, jumping up continually to throw open a window and gasp for air, feeling I was on the point of suffocation.

My mother must have been desperately worried. Her strong, reassuring presence had the power to cure so many ills, but in the face of this illusive dragon she was helpless. The doctor said I needed to see a psycho-therapist; but the NHS had not yet been born and any kind of specialist cost a good deal of money. Once again Aunt Dolly came to the rescue, and before long I was booked in with a Wimpole Street psychiatrist known as J.R. Rees (some years later Mr Rees was to be one of those consultants called in by the Government to check on sad, controversial Rudolf Hesse).

Right at the outset, Mr Rees told me two things about himself. First, he was a great believer in the developing science of hypnotic therapy. And second, he had never lost his temper with a patient. Within a short time he was telling me I would be impossible to hypnotise because - as he phrased it - I would 'fight like the devil'; and before we parted company he had lost his temper more than once. Or so it seemed to me.

His consulting rooms, though, were attractive and luxurious, and I liked them. In fact, so far as I was concerned, this pleasing ambience was fairly therapeutic in itself. While I lay on a couch, thinking my own thoughts, Mr Rees talked, and without much delay he got to what he obviously felt must be the hub of the matter: somewhere, there had to be a man involved. I insisted there was no-one and felt that I was speaking the truth, but Mr Rees was not to be put off easily and it was some considerable time before he gave up. Some friendship, perhaps, that might have turned to an engagement but had petered out. . . ? A spot of unrequited love? It happened to nearly everyone at some time or other. Or perhaps there was some more problematical entanglement. Quite possibly I had fallen in love with someone inappropriate. Such as a married man.

No.

Mr Rees turned to another pet theory, namely the possibility that at some time or other I had been locked into a dark cupboard, hence my claustrophobia. I don't know whether anyone had let him in on the fact that immediately after birth I had come close to being snuffed out with a pillow - I didn't mention it, but I suppose this information, if it had been in his possession, might have given him a few clues. As for the fact that I had never seen my father, I suppose he may have known something about that, but I don't believe it was ever discussed. In the end, however, he did come up with some sensible proposals.

For a period of one year, I was to give up all thought of writing. I should enrol for something such as a secretarial course, then I would have to find myself an interesting job. First, though - and this was the sugar on the pill - I needed to get away for a holiday. If possible I ought to go alone, and the destination really should be of my own choosing.

No doubt I was expected to ask for a week in Brighton, or perhaps a few days among the Yorkshire Dales; but I had other ideas. My obsession with the Far East had switched to a brief flirtation with India, then to a passion for Arabian desert lands. I knew I couldn't contemplate heading for Baghdad or attaching myself to a Bedouin caravan - much as I might have liked to do so - but there was, I thought, one possibility. I wanted, very much, to see Morocco. And it wasn't too far away.

My mother truly was a remarkable woman. Instead of fainting or asking me not to speak again until I was capable of rational thought, she started to make practical enquiries and found that our Vicar - not, by this time, Mr Gordon Duff - knew of a mission hostel in Tangiers. It was run by friends of his, and though founded as a rest-house for missionaries from all over Africa was frequently used as a base by ordinary English visitors. Eventually, it was arranged that I should stay at the mission hostel for a month. Mr and Mrs Gammon - the proprietors - would keep an eye on me, and there would be no shortage of other British people; it would be almost like living at home. I was booked aboard the British India steamship *Mashobra*, and on a wild day in March my mother and Aunt Dolly saw me off from Southampton. I was not nervous and I felt no uneasiness, only anticipation. For the first time in many months, my spirits began to soar.

I went on board accompanied by one large suitcase and enough Luminal tablets to kill off a small military unit. That night I was too tired to take a pill, and when morning came I forgot. I never touched Luminal again.

The *Mashobra* was a small liner, but she was comfortable and well equipped, and just being aboard was the kind of thrill I had been waiting for all my life. The ship's ultimate destination was Calcutta, and she was carrying a cargo of junior Colonial officials, hopeful spinsters and assorted Army personnel. As far as I could see most of the soldiers and Colonial officers were very much married - some had families with them - and this seemed hard on the hopeful spinsters, but then, like the sprinkling of widows amongst them, they were probably expecting to find more interesting fish when they got to the other end.

As for me, I had no real thought of 'meeting anyone'. That wasn't what I was there for. I was simply having a joyful adventure.

On the second day we entered the Bay of Biscay, and with some relief I discovered I was a good sailor. That night I slept like a log, to find when I woke next morning that during the hours of darkness we had passed through a major storm. One woman had been thrown out of her bunk, breaking an arm in the process, but I had known nothing about it. Five days later we reached Tangiers, and as the anchor chains rattled down I felt another wild thrill of excitement. I had got to Africa, and the world of Islam lay in front of me. I hurried up on deck to see whatever there was to be seen. . . . and was a little disappointed.

Tangiers seemed jumbled, untidy and distressingly Twentieth Century. Where, I wondered, were the minarets? Where were the spicy odours that should have been drifting out to sea. . . ? (There was an odour of something, but I didn't think there was much spice about it.) Still, never mind. This was Africa, and I was about to go ashore.

Hardly anyone was leaving the ship at Tangiers, and the tender that carried me over the glittering water was very nearly empty. As I stepped out on to the dockside Africa was all around me, noisy, colourful and noticeably dirty. And for some reason, all at once I was quite alone. Not that it mattered, because I was being met. In just a minute or two someone reassuring was going to emerge from the crowd, take my arm and steer me away in the direction of transport.

Someone did emerge from the crowd and he did grab my arm, only he wasn't quite what I had been expecting. He was a tall Arab in a dusty *burnous*, and if I hadn't known everything was certain to be all right I might have been quite frightened. As his fingers tightened on my arm, he began pulling and pushing me through the noisy, smelly, jostling throng. It definitely wasn't what I had been expecting, but then, from now on everything was likely to be strange.

At last we reached a vehicle that had been parked, haphazardly, beside a roadway. My suitcase was tossed inside and I imagined I was about to follow it, but there was another brown *burnous* leaning against the bonnet, and as a heated discussion began - all this time my arm was being retained in a ferocious grip - I felt it was time to assert myself.

'*Hope House*,' I said, very distinctly. '*I want. . . to go to. . . Hope House.*'

Both men looked at me hard, and their conversation became more animated. It has been pointed out to me, since, that they were almost certainly estimating my likely value on the open market. Fortunately this didn't occur to me at the time, but if something of the sort was going on two factors may have been operating in my favour. First, I was evidently expected to turn up - soon -on the doorstep of a well-known Christian mission house, and my failure to appear might lead to embarrassing investigations. And second, I was a pallid-looking little bundle of skin and bones, probably not worth the equivalent of one camel's leg.

Eventually I was dumped inside the taxi and we moved off. As we rattled and rolled through crowded, twisting streets I did begin to feel flickers of real uneasiness shivering across my skin, and taken together with the stuffy atmosphere inside the closed vehicle they made me distinctly uncomfortable. If there had been a danger point, though, it had passed. Within less than ten minutes the taxi was depositing me inside the iron gates of Hope House, and fumbling awkwardly with my Moroccan francs I handed the driver what I later learned would have been appropriate payment for a double tour of the city. At last, a friendly face appeared. I was welcomed and shown to my room, and in the calm, reassuring atmosphere of the hostel my confidence, never badly dented, began to reassert itself.

Mr Gammon, however, was appalled. Several times, apparently, he had telephoned the docks to check on Mashobra's time of arrival, and had been told she was not due until the following day. The thought that I had arrived alone, and been obliged to find my own way, clearly made his blood run cold. Still, everything had worked out in the end, and tomorrow was another day. In the meantime, I was in Morocco.

Hope House was a Victorian building surrounded by gardens in which giant lilies did perpetual battle with shrubs and waist-high weeds, but there was a lot more to it than that. Sick, depressed and exhausted mission-workers came there from every corner of Africa, then there were people like me, and as far as I could see, within a day or two most of us were feeling better. The Gammons were kind and sensible people, but they had something else as well, some sort of recipe for dealing with damaged humanity. They must also have possessed a well of energy, for in addition to all its other preoccupations Hope House incorporated a small mission school. Most of the pupils were Moroccan girls below the age of twelve. On weekdays they learned to write English words and recite multiplication tables, and on Sunday mornings - controversially, perhaps - they sang hymns in the chapel. I was told that as soon as each girl reached the magic age of twelve her father would arrive, and she would be whisked away to acquire a husband. If she possessed a smattering of British education she would, apparently, fetch a higher price. But the mission would never see her again.

I think about them sometimes - all golden skin and shining eyes and clear voices singing about that Friend for Little Children above the Bright Blue Sky - and I wonder how they passed their lives. Happily enough, I hope.

It didn't take me long to understand the fact that Hope House was a tranquil island floating in the middle of a bubbling melting pot that seethed with colour and corruption. Squeezed between Christian Europe and Muslim North Africa, between the Atlantic and the Mediterranean, Tangiers had for centuries been a meeting-ground for pirates, smugglers and slave traders, and nothing much had so far changed; but at the time of my visit Morocco as a country was just beginning to emerge from some years of French colonial rule, and for various political reasons Tangiers itself had been divided into three sections: French, Spanish and Moroccan. In the French and Spanish zones neat white villas sprouted in rows, and European women went to get their hair shingled in the salons of luxury hotels that existed to pamper rich foreigners. But this was not Africa, I was assured. It was an extension of continental Europe. Never having seen continental Europe I wasn't in a position to check on this statement, but I did know the palm-fringed boulevards and gleaming limousines were not what I had come to see. I had come to see Morocco, and Morocco began on the other side of a straggling, unmarked line that ran across the city - in fact, with the *soukhs*, that maze of narrow, walled alley-ways among which lurked the tiny hidden markets where, once upon a time, copper jugs and slave-girls would have been put up for sale side by side. This being the 1930's there weren't actually any slave-girls on show - at least, I didn't notice any - but otherwise everything was more as less as I had seen it described in books.

When you see them in front of you, though, dirt and suffering are not the stuff of romance. I had spent many hours poring over the works of travel writers, but none of them had said what it would be like to stumble over the rotting frame of a blind, emaciated beggar, or turn to look at a cat whose face has been eaten away. I wandered round the stalls of the traders but didn't, so far as I can remember, purchase any souvenirs. I didn't want to take any of it home.

There was one thing, though, that struck me as impressive and significant, and not just in the context of Arab life. Prominent in every market place was the story-teller. Cross-legged, he sat for hours on end surrounded by an eager, mesmerized crowd. Often I stood to watch. Since I wouldn't have understood a word there wasn't much point in trying to listen, but it was all there, anyway, on the faces of the audience. Love and fear and adventure, tragedy and hope and romance.

I had made myself into some sort of fiction writer because it was what I wanted and needed to do, but I realised now that story-telling was a vocation. You might be brilliant at it or not so good - you might be downright awful - but as long as you could string some kind of narrative together you were helping to fill one of humanity's most fundamental needs. Since the dawn of existence stories and parables have taught us skills, and moral discipline, and the facts of human life. They have also diverted, stimulated and reassured us, and during our low moments the images created have come back to keep us company. I have never forgotten the story-tellers, I see them still. And even more vividly, I see the listeners.

There was something else, too. One day, as I was walking along a track between two very high walls - probably I shouldn't have been alone, on this occasion - a gate in one of the towering walls swung open. A white horse appeared, and on its back was the most spectacular figure I ever saw, before or since. The man could have been some sort of Moroccan prince, if he wasn't, he must have been something similar. Underneath a flowing *djellabah* he was wearing well cut European riding clothes, and as I pressed myself against the opposite wall his gleaming boot brushed my dress. I don't suppose he even noticed me, but as I made my way back to Hope House I hugged to myself the thought that at last I had seen something gloriously exotic. The world really did contain such things, after all. They didn't only exist inside my imagination.

I had come to Morocco partly because I hoped to see the desert, but this had proved difficult, mainly because the handiest scrap of desert was apparently something like five hundred miles further south, but one day I and other inmates of Hope House were taken on a trip to the fringe of the Atlas mountains. I remember a lot of brown rocks and a lowering sky, and also a number of souvenir sellers - most of these, I suspected, had like us been bussed out from Tangiers. Towards the end of April, I sailed for home.

By the time I reached Southampton summer was taking a grip of England, and I was very happy to be back. M was waiting for me on the dockside, and she was almost as happy as I was, not only because I was home safely, but because my problem seemed to have been cured. Six weeks earlier she had waved good-bye to a haunted, mixed up, pill-swallowing wreck, now she welcomed back a healthy young woman with a newly positive outlook on life.

From now on - well, for a time, at least - I was going to stop living in the shadows behind a typewriter.

*   *   *   *   *

32

V

I knew that I needed to adopt a different style of living, also that I had to start earning proper money, so I decided to follow up on the remainder of Mr Rees's recommendations. Left to myself I might have skipped the secretarial course, but common sense and sound advice won, and two or three weeks after arriving back from Morocco I enrolled for a course at Pitman's Secretarial College. Since this was going to mean living in London, I also booked myself in at the YWCA hostel in Fitzroy Square.

The course was fun, at first. I had taught myself to type when I was fourteen years old, but with two or three fingers you don't work up much of a speed, and this had always frustrated me. They say it is usually difficult to unlearn bad habits, but after the first few lessons I didn't have that much trouble. Sometimes we practised to music, and this seemed to help. Shorthand, I thought, was a fantastic invention, and before long I was making excellent progress, but just as I was becoming quite proficient I was told to forget everything I had so far picked up, because there was an even faster, more stream-lined way of doing things, and at this point my patience snapped. My touch-typing was now reasonable and my shorthand, it seemed to me, was adequate. I had also learned quite a lot about office work. In other words, I had done enough.

The Pitman's Principal tended not to agree with me, in fact, my attitude baffled her. Yes, I had done well, but there was some way to go yet, and surely I wanted the school's diploma? I had no wish to offend her - clearly she was concerned for my well-being, which was the more impressive when one remembered the bill had been paid in advance - but no, I did not particularly want their diploma. Or rather, I wasn't going to wait for it. I had enough skills at my disposal, it seemed to me, and I wanted to get on with life. In the end, we parted on good terms. She gave me some advice and a note to say that I had been a good student, and I hurried away to find an employment agency.

And actually, I knew exactly what sort of job I wanted. While lying on the couch in Mr Rees's consulting-room I had noticed things; in particular, I had noticed the fact that smart West End medical premises were actually rather pleasant places, or would be if nothing happened to be the matter with you. I had decided then and there that I wanted a job in some such establishment, and now I headed towards my goal. Even I didn't really think I could become a medical secretary over-night, but I did feel I ought to make an acceptable receptionist. Not surprisingly, perhaps, there didn't seem to be many vacancies of the sort I had in mind, but they did find one or two, and I was sent off to be interviewed by a Wimpole Street dentist. I know he wasn't English - as far as I can remember, he came from Denmark - but this hardly accounted for the fact that after two or three minutes he fell to his knees and made what appeared to be an improper suggestion. I didn't faint, by this time I was made of sterner stuff, but nor did I hang around to enquire about salary details.

This was a set-back, but not the end of the world. A second interview, this time with a Harley Street dentist, turned out to be more promising. Mr Woodford, as I'll call him, had very elegant premises. He also had a pale grey Bentley with a pale grey chauffeur to match, and I remember that his patients included Princess Arthur of Connaught, then a senior member of the Royal Family. He seemed likely to be short-tempered, but on the other hand I didn't think he planned to assault me. Being extremely busy he took me on without much apparent hesitation and I was passed into the care of the Senior Secretary, a super-efficient clerical saint called Miss Denholm. Miss Denholm had been in her job for a considerable number of years, and 'the doctor' was the star around which her life appeared to revolve. Every day a pint of milk was delivered to our office, but we rarely benefited from the cups of tea and coffee this was supposed to provide because the doctor had either requested extra coffee, or had 'felt like a glass of milk, poor dear'.

'She's in love with me, you know,' our employer confided, adding with the weariness of a besieged matinée idol: 'She'll get you out, I'm afraid.'

And she did. Or so he said. Quite possibly he just didn't feel I was up to the job. He did give me a reference, though, and with this in my hand I walked straight into the office of yet another top dentist, this time round the corner in Devonshire Place. After a short, sharp question-and-answer session Mr Steadman appeared to decide I would do, and with a few small reservations I decided the same about him. At least for the time being.

The job certainly wasn't easy. There was a great deal of dictation, for one thing, and though my shorthand held up fairly well the specialist jargon came close to finishing me off. If I ventured to ask for help with spelling I would be told to bloody well look it up, and if a serious mistake did manage to get through, the offending document would be screwed into a ball and hurled back at me. In fact, when not being unnecessarily solicitous - feeling my hands and arms to make sure I was warm enough - my employer had what could only be described as a dodgy temper.

One morning I arrived to find I was expected to sit in on some kind of surgical procedure, an operation involving the removal of two impacted wisdom teeth. It was a bad case and there would be two nurses in attendance, but there seemed absolutely no need for the presence of a secretary. As I passed my employer's nurse in the doorway, she murmured 'I'm so sorry. You shouldn't have to do this'. Whether my boss thought the experience would be good for me, or whether he merely wanted to see me suffer I have absolutely no idea, but I do know I was expected to observe the whole operation. There was a good deal of blood, and altogether it was not a pleasant experience. It crossed my mind, one or twice, that I might pass out, but then I knew nothing would persuade me to give him that much satisfaction.

The day came when I had had enough. There had been a dental conference at Mr Steadman's house in the suburbs - I think it was to select staff for an important new clinic - and throughout a long, hot afternoon I had sat almost motionless, noting everything down in detail. Afterwards I was expected to type my notes out, a job which took me until well past ten o'clock, by which time Mr Steadman was occupied with one or two cronies who seemed to be staying the night. Mrs Steadman came to say I couldn't possibly leave so late in the evening, and if I would like to go with her she would take me to the bedroom that had been made ready for me. She was a charming woman and I felt extremely ungracious, but there was no way I was going to stay in that house. It wasn't that I thought my employer was likely to come trying the door handle in the middle of the night, there wasn't a practical reason, I just had to get out of there. I made up some wild story about needing to be back at the hostel, and Mrs Steadman said that in that case her son would drive me. On the whole she was very kind about it. Perhaps she understood. To my relief the son turned out to be rather taciturn - he may have been in a rotten temper - but he was a good driver. We reached the hostel a little after midnight, and I remember we had to rouse the night porter. A few days later I handed Mr Steadman my notice, and I'll never forget his stupefied face.

'Aren't you happy here. . . ?'

I ought to put it on record that this curious character did have his good side. He could be generous. On rare occasions, he could even be thoughtful. He was also, I was told, an excellent dentist. No doubt he died a long time ago, so perhaps I should just say that I may have misjudged him.

I went back to the employment agency, and it wasn't long before I had obtained another post, this time as receptionist in the Harley Street consulting rooms of a gynaecologist. By this time I was getting more experienced, and the new position was pleasant enough, if not particularly exciting.

In all this time I hadn't thought much about writing, but one day I did ring George Newnes. I asked if I could speak to Major Pollock, and was told he had been seriously ill - with pneumonia - and as a result would not be back for several weeks. I was disappointed, and shocked. But Major Pollock, apparently, was making a good recovery, and I made an effort to put him out of my mind.

I was making friends at the YWCA hostel, and one day I was introduced to a middle-aged journalist who seemed to hold a senior position on the *News of the World*. Told about my literary efforts, he suggested one of my stories might possibly fill a slot in his paper, and as I had a sample or two tucked away in my drawer at the hostel - I couldn't have borne to leave them all at home - I was asked if I would take something into his office. Say, the next evening at six o'clock, when he would be free for a few minutes. At that time the *News of the World* was not quite what it is today, or if it was, I didn't really understand.

When I arrived, just before six o'clock on the following evening, *News of the World* office workers were beginning to leave, flooding away down a long stone staircase, and as I stood in the entrance I was almost engulfed. But there was a doorman on duty, and he directed me to an office on the second floor. As I climbed, up and up, the last few workers scurried past me on their way to freedom, and I began to wonder if I had got something wrong, but sure enough Mr _ was in his office, waiting for me.

He took my manuscript, looked at it and put it away in a drawer of his desk.

'Now,' he said, 'I think you and I can help one another. . . .'

He moved towards the door, and I saw him lock it - but as he came back towards me I slipped past him. I managed to turn the key and darting out on to the landing I fled, racing and stumbling, down the stone staircase. It seemed to go on and on, and I kept thinking he was behind me. He wasn't, of course, he wouldn't have been that stupid. I don't believe I ever thought he was a potential rapist, more what might be called an opportunist, but I was badly shaken, and since I had to share the story with someone I told one of my girl-friends. I think she may have been a bit less naive than I was, and she probably thought I had simply got what was coming to me, but she was supportive.

'Men,' she said sympathetically.

Well, yes. Perhaps M had been right after all.

My confidence had been dented, but I was resilient and after a few days I began to think again about newspapers. The *News of the World* episode had been unfortunate, but then I had been stupid. If I were to make a formal approach to a Fleet Street editor, something positive might result.

I wrote to the Editor of a major daily - at this distance of time I don't remember which one - and received a reply suggesting I should come in with a sample of my work. I was offered an appointment with a sub-editor, and this time it was fixed for mid-morning.

The sub-editor was business-like, if a little detached. He looked at my work carefully, then as it was around eleven o'clock, took me round the corner for a cup of coffee and a chat. About three minutes after ordering, he suggested I might accompany him on a weekend trip to Belgium.

I knew very little about feminism, and it didn't occur to me that either of these men had been demonstrating their contempt for female ability. What I *did* know was that like a silly moth I had fluttered too near the spider's web, and on two occasions the spider had done - or tried to do - what nature intended. It was annoying, but I didn't allow it to bother me too much. I did think, though, that I might not be cut out for journalism. One day my mother came up to London, and as we had lunch together she suggested I might like to go home for a while. What a lovely idea. . . . I packed my job in the very next day.

M was pleased, and so, I think was Uncle George. It was wonderful to relax and be looked after again, and there were other people to see. Reggie was now married to the helpful girl whose family solicitor had known all about China, and they had acquired a chicken farm near the village of Sedlescombe. I didn't think chickens were quite them, somehow - it emerged eventually they had invested in the wrong breed - but it was wonderful to see them, particularly Reggie. Wonderful to be among people I could trust one hundred per cent.

I wanted a job in the Hastings area, and it wasn't long before something suitable turned up. I became a receptionist at one of the town's larger hotels, the Eversfield. The hours and pay were reasonable, the duties manageable, and it was fairly close to home. Nobody saw much of the Proprietor, a single man who lived alone in an apartment on the top floor, but the other staff were pleasant enough and the atmosphere was relaxed, something I had missed for a long time. The guests were friendly and appreciative, and though I was asked out once or twice nobody attempted to seduce me. As for the work, it was mostly supervisory. I checked menus and the setting of dinner-tables, and kept an eye on the chamber-maids' work. I made sure everything was clean and in order and the rooms fully equipped; best of all, I had the job of choosing and arranging some splendid floral decorations. I had never done anything of the kind before, but I took to flower arranging like a duck to water, and soon I began to feel a pride in the place. Every afternoon the chef brought tea and chocolate éclairs to my sitting-room, and possibly I might have settled down.

But the year was 1939. Generally speaking I didn't take that much interest in current affairs - though the recent Abdication had gripped everyone - but even I couldn't help being aware of the threat looming over us. There was a jittery feeling everywhere, and we were all unsettled. A receptionist taken on shortly after my arrival turned out to be a follower of Sir Oswald Moseley's Blackshirt movement; apparently there were quite a number in the district, and they seemed to spend rather a lot of time marching to London. Watching in astonishment as our Blackshirt ironed her 'uniform', I realised she was gripped by a kind of compulsion: the same sort of compulsion that was operating - to very much more dangerous effect - over in Germany.

As spring wore on the Eversfield Hotel welcomed a number of overseas visitors. Several of them were German, and most were charming; but then one day another kind of German appeared. He was tall, thin-faced, blond - rather good-looking - and he behaved with the ice-cold incivility of an SS captain marching into a Paris brothel. He demanded to see several of our bedrooms and the one or two suites that were available, and for some reason it was my job to show him round. In addition to being well furnished and immaculate, every room was filled with fresh flowers, sunlight and the smell of the sea, but apart from one or two adverse criticisms the visitor offered no comment. I'm sure he fantasized about returning at the head of a Gestapo troop. Well, perhaps a Panzer division. We never heard from him again.

Shortly afterwards, around breakfast time on a lovely May morning, somebody went in search of the hotel proprietor and found he was nowhere to be seen. Very early that day, while most of us were still asleep, he had climbed up on to the bright green cliff-top, lifted the double-barrelled shot-gun he had with him, and blasted himself to bits. The papers didn't make very much of it. Hitler had just invaded Poland, and possibly the dark clouds threatening all of us seemed of more pressing significance than one man's lonely torment.

I've often thought about him, though, and wondered whether the threat of a new war had brought back memories too dreadful to live with.

A matter of days after this awful happening, Britain declared war on Germany.

* * * * *

VI

There was a lot of anxiety and confusion about, but there was also euphoria, a desire, now that the inevitable had happened, to get on with things. The Eversfield Hotel had closed down and I was out of a job, but a torrent of war work was emerging and as the Labour Exchange started cracking under pressure new staff were taken on. For a few weeks I joined them, then Orr Place - a Victorian mansion above the town - was taken over by the Army Pay Corps. Conditions were good, and though the work was not inspiring it did make you feel like part of the war effort. Every morning, that summer, I walked to work across the cliff top, and every evening I walked back again, staring at the sea and thinking about the novel I would be writing once life had settled down again.

We all expected the war situation to develop quickly, but as summer drifted into autumn it was almost as if peace had never ended. Men were joining up in their thousands, increasing our work load by the day, but it was beginning to seem as if the whole thing might somehow peter out before a shot had been fired in anger. That year we had a white Christmas, and I remember walking home through the snow, painfully conscious of the fact that another year in my own life was coming to an end, and still I didn't know where I was going.

January, however, brought a change. Orr Place was no longer considered large enough for the work our department was trying to do, so we were expanding, in other words moving to London - those of us who were willing to go. I talked it all over with my mother, and as usual she advised me to do the adventurous thing. So just as the first crocuses were beginning to appear, I found myself back in Fitzroy Square.

This time the hostel felt like a second home, but some things had changed. The girls I had known were mostly gone, and in their place was a different sort. Young women who were in London because of the war, and in a hostel because it was the only way their families could feel easy about such a situation. I made some strong friendships, during the next few months. There was Kitty Waddington from Yorkshire, who was warm-hearted and funny enough to have made a career on the stage, sensible, gentle Marie Moore. . . the Irish sisters who preserved our sanity by singing and playing on the piano in the common-room. And Alice Robbens. Alice was very attractive, with pale hair and skin and a perfect face. Some time earlier she had been very ill with rheumatoid arthritis, and her general health was not good.

I had imagined expansion might mean moving into a good sized Government building and taking on an extra dozen or so girls, probably to be recruited from the London area, but the reality was more startling. For one thing, the good sized building – in Finsbury Park - turned out to be a soaring eighteenth century palace that had once housed the Bank of England. From its marble foyer twin staircases curled towards tier upon tier of galleried landings, and far above everything - about half a mile up, or so it seemed if you were standing just inside the entrance - there was a shining glass dome. As for the dozen or so extra girls, they turned into approximately one thousand Army personnel, drafted in to sort things out and check that we civilians knew what we were doing. I worked on the top floor, in a large room full of people. From the windows we looked out over London, and it was all rather fun. Once you got used to it.

And there was a war, now. German troops had marched into Belgium and our own had gone to head them off, only our men were said to be retreating. As the weeks went by we started getting reports that they had been ordered to fall back on the beaches; but of course that was only going to be temporary. They would rally, get re-organized and push the enemy back. They were being pounded, though, on those beaches, and soon there was talk of an emergency rescue mission. But still it didn't seem real.

Until one morning when Kitty and I got off a bus outside Charing Cross station and there in front of us, coming through the doors, was a straggling column of soldiers. They looked weary and grey-faced. Some were limping, some heavily bandaged, and they were wearing what we were told was 'hospital blue'. As we stood there they just kept coming, on and on, and the odd thing was that they seemed silent, like something glimpsed in a dream. There were nurses and orderlies

41

with them and they too were silent, or that was how it seemed to me. At last Kitty and I turned away, and I remember thinking this must surely be the end. We had been defeated. So what, I wondered aloud, was going to happen now. . . . Could we be invaded?

Well, not until we had been softened up a bit, and so far the Germans seemed to be hanging about beyond the Channel, prowling up and down like dogs checked by an unexpected fence. They meant to soften us up, though.

Somewhere about this time, I got in touch with Newnes. Discovering Hugh Pollock was back again I went to see him, and was startled by what I found.

Hugh was fully recovered, but his illness had left its mark and there was bleakness in his eyes. The humour had not quite gone, but something had damaged the spirit behind it. He seemed pleased to see me, though, and asked if I would have lunch with him.

We went to Rule's, the fashionable restaurant in Maiden Lane, and for me it was wonderful just to sit and talk for an hour or so. Hugh said he wanted to re-join the Army, but Enid was not happy about this idea. (Given the fact that he had already served through all of World War One and followed this up with India, Burma and the Arab Insurrection she may have had a point, but it wasn't wise to try and restrain a man like Hugh.)

Otherwise he hardly mentioned his family, though he did talk a little bit about Gillian, who was now almost nine years old and who had composed a couplet about Hitler: *'I do not love you, Hitler Herr. What a rotten beast you are. . . .'*

He asked me about my work, and I explained that for the time being I wasn't doing any writing. Then he told me he had recently been to visit the author Richmael Crompton, who lived in the exquisitely named Hampshire village of Nether Wallop. Her *Just William* books had always appealed to him, and he took a keen interest in them and in their creator. He took an interest in all his writers. There was no author/publisher relationship between us, not any longer, but it seemed we didn't need one. We were friends.

Our time was up much too soon, and I hurried back to Finsbury Park, all kinds of thoughts going through my head.

Hugh and I met again a week or so later, and then again. We talked about anything and everything, as friends do, and it was magical, for me at any rate. One afternoon we met at Fuller's in Regent Street, where we had tea, and I remember that we didn't say very much. We sat there, as people bustled past outside, and Hugh just kept on looking at me.

We weren't getting anywhere, perhaps, but then I didn't imagine we ever could. I was happy with what I had got. I did sense, though, that something was terribly wrong in the background of Hugh's life.

It was August, and the streets were getting hot and dusty. Offered a week's leave I went home to Sussex and for several days M and I talked, chewing over everything that had happened. We didn't talk about Hugh, though, because I hadn't mentioned him.

Towards the end of the week I returned to London feeling relaxed, and on Friday I went to work as usual. The day dragged a bit, perhaps because I had been away, and I was glad when the clock finally crawled around to half past five. Kitty and I joined the tide flowing down the stairs, eventually crossing the foyer and hurrying into the street. It was warm outside, but at least we were in the open. Then something made me look round. . . . Close beside the door an Army officer was waiting. He was wearing a great-coat and his face was partly obscured by the brim of his forage cap, but there was something about him.

Hugh.

He was wearing the cap badge of the Pioneer Corps – at that early stage he had not yet been restored to his old regiment, the Royal Scots Fusiliers - but I don't suppose I noticed this. I just saw that the weary, over-burdened look - the jaded and depressed look - had gone. His eyes were bright, and he seemed very alert. Standing beside me, Kitty murmured: 'Gosh! He's quite something, isn't he?' Then tactfully she melted away.

Hugh told me he was on his way to Yorkshire, to report for duty at Catterick Camp, and that later that evening he would be boarding a train. In the meantime, he was taking me out to dinner. I was wearing my office clothes and would very much have liked an opportunity to put on something glamorous, but there was no time and it didn't really matter. Hugh was there in front of me, and it was the most wonderful surprise.

He took me to Scott's, which was smart and romantic, and in the powder-room I sorted out my make-up, then as usual we sat for a long time just talking. It was, I thought, like something out of a novel, only it wasn't a novel, it was real. Hugh was there and so was I, and we were going to have dinner together. It was better than anything in a novel.

Usually I drank nothing much stronger than tomato juice, and Hugh had never pressed me to do otherwise, but to-night he suggested there was something I might like. This turned out to be Pimm's Number One, and he was right, I did like it. It was fizzy, for one thing, and it had the most delectable taste. Not really at all alcoholic. After taking a few sips I began to knock it back fairly speedily, at which point Hugh took the glass out of my hand and finished it off himself.

I desperately wanted that evening not to end, but I couldn't hold it back and inevitably it slipped away. I accompanied Hugh in a taxi to St Pancras station and saw him board his train for the north. As the long line of coaches pulled out, in the warm haze of a beautiful August night, flares were falling like fairy lights over the train and over London.

* * * * *

VII

One Saturday morning, a week of so later, I and three other girls went out in search of a snack. It was already early afternoon as we wandered along Oxford Street staring into shop windows, but for several minutes we hung about in front of Maple's, the gigantic furniture store. Eventually we headed off down the Tottenham Court Road, making, as we often did, for our favourite Lyon's Corner House. By the time we got there it was crowded and the din was considerable, but we could hold our own. As far as I can remember we chattered our way through generous helpings of egg and bacon, followed by more than one pot of tea, then we strolled outside again. It was a warm, sun-soaked afternoon, and the azure sky was unclouded. Looking up, one or two of us spotted a flock of silver-coloured birds, drifting high above London.

A long, eerie wail arose, echoing over the city. There had been an air raid warning - a false alarm - immediately after the Declaration of War, and though none of us had been in London to hear it, we knew what we were hearing now. And the things overhead were not birds.

The planes plunged lower, and now they were clearly visible. People were coming out of shops and coffee-houses, pushing their way into the street, and I heard somebody say they were 'ours'. They weren't, though.

One of my friends shrieked that she could see bombs dropping out of the sky, and she may have been right, because almost at once we heard a series of rumbling explosions. No-one was too sure what to do, but we needed to be back in Fitzroy Square. The hostel was something like a mile away, and the sooner we covered that distance the happier every one of us was going to feel. Bombs were falling, the ground was shaking and there was dust in our nostrils. We ran back along Tottenham Court Road, and when we reached the corner of Oxford Street we saw that Maples' store had gone.

Our hostel might well have gone too, for all we knew, but as it turned out the building was undamaged, though structures nearby had collapsed. Shortly after our return the raid ended, and gathered together in our sitting-room we chatted, speculated and listened to the wireless, which told us the facts of what had happened, more or less. For obvious reasons all official broadcasts had to minimize the effects of enemy activity.

We had known for some time that if there should be any kind of attack we would be able to seek refuge in the hostel's basement, and now we were told that in the event of another raid everyone present in our building was to make for this area - in an orderly manner, of course. Also, we were to sleep there every night. A curfew was being imposed, and so long as air raids seemed likely to continue we were to be in every evening by ten o'clock.

There was no panic, and I don't remember that anyone talked about going home. We had always known something like this might be going to happen, and you didn't run away, not when the excitement was just beginning. Besides, there might not be another air attack on London. That illusion was dispelled the following day.

Everyone knows about the London Blitz. The chaos and destruction, the moments of blinding fear, the weird normality of everyday life, the sheer exhilaration of it all. For most of us the day started early, and as gas mains were ruptured on a nightly basis breakfast was not usually an option, so we tended to set out for work without so much as a cup of tea inside us. Usually the tram lines had been damaged too, and though heroic bus drivers kept going wherever and whenever possible, side streets were often blocked completely, so that some of us made a habit of walking to work, picking up transport as and when we could. Every morning, more of the beauty of centuries lay among the rubble, more lives and jobs and businesses had been shattered, converted into the dust that stung our nostrils and lingered, bitter tasting, on our lips.

It was particularly hard to see the comfortable, familiar things go. The corner shop where they had sold sticky buns and where, just the day before, someone had been joking about Hitler; the cafe where they had always, somehow, managed to produce a pot of tea. We giggled, though, as we stepped over the holes in the road, and we were not the only ones. The police and ARP men may not always have been feeling cheerful after a long night of coping with grief and destruction, but they were friendly and helpful. And people sang.

They sang in their homes and in the air raid shelters, sometimes they sang in the streets. At night, when we weren't going out, my friends and I sang around the piano in the hostel common room. Today, at the beginning of what looks like an even more troubled century, people don't sing very much - and it isn't just because singable songs tend not to be written, it's because we have seen the dark side of the moon and we don't want songs any more. In 1940 it was different, even in a battered, tortured city.

Sometimes I fantasised about the devastation that might result if a bomb were ever to smash through the shining glass dome above the building where I worked. Down below the great vaults had been turned into shelters, but there were four or five floors altogether and in order to avoid the possibility of life-threatening chaos a rigid evacuation system had been introduced. The floors were to be emptied one by one - working upwards from the bottom - and nobody was allowed to move until the clang of a bell had signalled the clearing of the level below. Naturally the top floor, where I worked, was last of all, and we had an almost unrivalled view of what often appeared to be the City of London going up in smoke. An officer always waited with us. . . I can remember him leaning on the back of my chair and chatting casually, while outside the windows fire streaked towards the sky, and we waited for the bell that would mean the floor below had emptied. It required a certain amount of discipline to go on sitting there, but nobody attempted to break the rules. Well, only once. Just once, a girl leapt to her feet and ran, through the long room and out of the door. We heard her high heels echoing on the stairs. Nobody tried to stop her, and as far as I know nothing was ever said, but it never happened again.

Once an evening raid had started no-one was supposed to leave the Fitzroy Square hostel, but one or two of us usually managed to slip through the net, and often we made for the nearest picture-house. Cinemas did not close just because a raid was going on, they simply put a message up on the screen: 'Enemy aircraft are now overhead. *Patrons wishing to leave are asked to do so quietly. . . .*'

Sometimes the picture would be halted for a few minutes. Then they would play 'There'll always be an England', and as the words flashed in front of us some people would start to sing. On one occasion a raid began just as Kitty and I were settling into *The Divorce of Lady X*. Already we could hear the assault going on, and out of those seated around us about fifty people began to move. Kitty and I looked at one another. Laurence Olivier was desperately attractive, and so far the film had barely got started. We settled ourselves down again, and saw the whole thing through.

We saw *The Desert Song*, too, five times. I might not have been all that keen on the reality of Morocco, but John Bowles in a *burnous* was something else altogether.

By this time Alice Robbens had got herself accepted as a WAAF. Her health should have made this impossible, but it was the realization of a dream and I have never forgotten how happy she looked in the sleek uniform she had been longing to wear. As for those of us who remained, some time during October the Pay Corps decided to give some of us a week's holiday. Marie, Kitty and I were all among the lucky ones, and Marie decided at once that she was going home to the Midlands for a few days. Kitty and I went with her to King's Cross station, and when her train had steamed out we sat on the platform, watching the other trains and the hurrying grey crowds, and a wave of desolation crept over us. Simultaneously, we decided what to do. We each collected a few things from the hostel, and later that afternoon we set out in opposite directions. Kitty started out for Yorkshire, while I made for Charing Cross and a train that would take me to Hastings.

It was high time I checked on my mother. In addition to being in the front line herself - almost every night the bombers passed over Hastings - she had been worried out of her mind about me. She wasn't on the telephone, and I was not a good correspondent. Heaven knows what she had been going through. I nearly sent a telegram to warn her I was coming, but realised this was scarcely a good idea. That autumn, in the streets and villages of England, nothing was dreaded so much as the telegraph boy.

I reached Hastings a little after eleven o'clock that night. Neither buses nor taxis were available, so I walked through the blacked out town and on to the cliff top. As it happened there wasn't a raid that evening, and when I got to our front door everything was still peaceful.

Uncle George had gone to bed, and M was just about to climb the stairs. I don't know what she thought when I knocked on the door, but she opened up without hesitation, and I'll never forget the look upon her face when she saw me standing there.

* * * * *

VIII

We were getting close to Christmas, the first real Christmas of World War 11. I would be going home, and was occupied with buying presents. Then one morning I received a letter from Hugh.

Catterick Camp had dealt with him rather quickly and for the last three months he had been in Surrey, where he had been made Commandant of a new War Office school for Home Guard officers - at least, that was the establishment's official designation, though in practice it was also used for weapons demonstrations, and possibly for other things as well. Short of being sent to the front line on active service, nothing could have delighted Hugh more. He had always talked a lot about the vital importance of internal defence.

Having been invited to choose between two or three large Surrey houses, he had settled eventually on Denbies, Lord Ashcombe's gothic mansion not far from the town of Dorking, and now the school was in operation. Military staffing was complete, but he had yet to take on a couple of civilian secretaries. If I thought I might be interested, I should present myself in Dorking no later than the following evening. Just in case I felt like saying yes, my release from Finsbury Park had been arranged already.

I could hardly believe what was happening. Hugh had not disappeared, and it was possible for me to see him. Soon, if I wanted to, I could be in a position to see him every day. I was confused, but didn't hesitate. I don't know what I told my friends, or how I got my things together, I only know that the following afternoon I was at Paddington Station, ready to board a train for Dorking. It was a dark, overcast day, and as we pulled out of London the sky seemed to be threatening snow.

There was no snow, but by the time we drew into Dorking it was a dark, dreary December night. Following directions enclosed in

Hugh's letter, I found a taxi and headed for the White Horse in the High Street.

The White Horse is a coaching inn, and its jumbled facade has been part of Dorking High Street for several hundred years (Charles Dickens, staying there early in the nineteenth century, was so struck by the building that it found its way into *Pickwick Papers)*. But that evening I wasn't really thinking about my immediate surroundings. Suddenly I was nervous. Not only because I was taking on a different kind of job, in a place I hadn't visited before, but because I was facing unexplored emotional territory.

Nevertheless I slept soundly enough that night, under the roof of the White Horse, and in the morning an Army driver arrived to collect me. We drove away along the High Street, and a short distance outside the town turned right into a narrow lane that wound steeply uphill between brown December hedgerows. The road levelled out and we came to a pair of gates, beyond which a drive went on and on, passing between acres of bare woodland and tangled undergrowth, until finally the trees thinned at the edge of a park and there in front of us was a sprawling Victorian house.

At that time Victorian architecture was still unpopular. Usually I found it boring, but this was different. A hundred years earlier Lord Ashcombe's family - the Cubitts - had made themselves a fortune in the field of construction. Called upon to create an Isle of Wight holiday home for the Queen herself they had come up with Osborne House, and perhaps in celebration of this success had purchased themselves an estate near Dorking and proceeded to build what amounted to a replica of their regal triumph. Despite its size, though, and its self-conscious nineteenth century grandeur, Denbies was a family house - a place for winter fires and lazy summer garden-parties, a place where turbulent human emotions could be absorbed and converted into timeless peace. This morning there were jeeps parked by the entrance, and near the edges of the park khaki figures milled round a line of Nissen huts, but once you got inside it became clear that this was still very much a large country house. Some paintings and items of furniture had been taken away, but most of the atmosphere remained.

Hugh was very busy and my first encounter with him was extremely brief. But I had seen him, and that was enough.

Apart from me, and a dozen or so ATS girls, there were just two female staff at Denbies. Another secretary, who had arrived before me, and a QA nursing sister called Bridget Casey. Sister Casey, from County Down, was ideal for the job, combining disciplined competence and a fairly sharp tongue with just a suggestion of Irish charm. She and I and the other secretary, a girl called Lilian, were to share a table in the Officers' Mess, while the secretary and I were also to share a bedroom, a huge, sunny room with a bow window that overlooked the park. Some of the room's original furnishings still remained, and though various items had been removed for safe keeping, Hugh's adjutant had been charged with the task of making good any serious deficiencies.

It felt strange, being at Denbies. Everything in my life was changing - for one thing, I was away from London. Quite a lot of bombs had already fallen on Dorking and as a military installation Denbies itself was likely to be vulnerable, but after the daily pressures of the London Blitz it felt profoundly, reassuringly secure.

And I was going to work for Hugh. I was going to be in his company for several hours in every day. I knew now that I was in love with him, and I believed he felt the same about me. I didn't think, though, that we were tumbling into a full-blown affair. Not yet, anyway. In an odd way, it was because our relationship was too special. As for his wife. . . whatever her skills as a children's writer, I felt she had hurt him in some way that went too deep for words. Though he loved, always would love Gillian and Imogen, she was no longer part of his life.

*   *   *   *   *

IX

It wasn't particularly easy, working for Hugh. For one thing he was an exceptionally quick thinker and had a tendency to want vital correspondence dashed off at a moment's notice, sometimes late at night or early in the morning. He also had a blazing temper, but I noticed that his temper was almost never unjust, and also that the outbursts of fury didn't last for long. On most occasions an appeal to his sense of humour would calm things down miraculously. And he never lost his temper with me.

Denbies had been set up to provide Home Guard representatives from around the country with training in military tactics and resistance techniques. Each course was supposed to last one week, and to be attended by approximately eighty men. Hugh had been allowed to choose his own staff and he had assembled a good team, but a major problem was looming. The War Office wanted him to take on a group of Communist guerrillas.

Left over, as it were, from the Spanish Civil War, the Communists had for a short time been permitted to operate a school of their own at nearby Osterley Park. It was felt they had a real contribution to make - the War Office thought so and Hugh was in agreement - but under their control Osterley Park had got out of control and there was talk of closing the place down. One idea being put forward now was that Hugh should absorb the guerrillas on to his Denbies staff, the business of arranging matters being left to him. Before I had been in Dorking a week, I found myself accompanying him on a visit to Osterley Park.

There had been some idea that he might need the assistance of a secretary, but when we reached our destination I was not allowed to go inside. It was a grey, bitter December day, and as I waited outside in Hugh's camouflaged car - parked beside a towering brick wall - I decided Osterley must be one of the ugliest houses in England. It was a false impression, but then I only saw one side of the building and I never went there again.

After an hour or more, Hugh came out. It was obvious his temper had been tried, but there had been some progress. The Communists had agreed that some of their number should join the school at Denbies, furthermore in this new situation they would 'co-operate', more or less, with military authorities. Ten individuals had been singled out: four Britons and six Spaniards, the latter group being chosen for their skill and experience in the area of underground tactics. Hugh, an instinctive psychologist, had somehow induced these people to become part of a system they apparently despised. Among other things, he had evidently offered the four Britons a chance to become fully commissioned Army Lieutenants. I'm not sure he had been given authority to offer the Commissions, but it soon became clear that he had managed to square this with the War Office, who must have been only too glad to have such an awkward business settled.

Osterley Park closed down, and the ten guerrillas arrived at Denbies. They really were useful, and Hugh recognised this, but he disliked their behaviour and attitudes and also distrusted their basic motivation - though happy enough to fight against Hitler's fascists, it sometimes seemed uncertain what their reaction might be if called upon to deal with any other kind of national enemy. Being - so far as I can remember - reluctant to mix with the regular staff, they slept and ate in Nissen huts.

That December it seemed an odd time to be talking about celebration and hope, but the churches filled up, we sang familiar carols, and many of us prepared to go home for Christmas. Most of the Denbies staff were breaking up for a few days, and despite his other preoccupations Hugh insisted on driving me all the way down to Hastings.

I wouldn't let him stop outside my mother's front door, though. I hadn't yet explained him to her, and I wasn't sure when - or how - I was going to do so.

I know now that Hugh's own Christmas was punctuated by savage rows. He had been told that his wife's bridge party guests regularly included a number of unattached men; and there were other stories. By this time he had little feeling left so far as Enid was concerned, but he was trying to preserve the outward appearance of his marriage.

Because of the children, and also because of his Scots Presbyterian upbringing, he was attempting to struggle on.

Anyway, as soon as we got back to Dorking the year's first intake arrived, and he was up to his eyes in work. The men came from every part of Britain, sent by their own districts to absorb skills that could be passed on when they got back home again. They all slept and ate in the Nissen huts - those hideous metallic tubes that scarred the park - and though part of every day was usually spent inside the main house, attending lectures on everything from psychology and camouflage techniques to the care of ammunition, they also spent a lot of time learning to crawl unobtrusively through ditches, leap over walls and cope with lethal weaponry.

For a long time now TV viewers have loved to laugh at the men of 'Dad's Army', but most of us also regard the programme and its subject matter with affectionate respect, for everybody knows these slightly clownish figures symbolize and represent something that really was a vast, real-life army - seven thousand half-trained civilians who were ready to die for the land that surrounded them. At Denbies we saw only the officers, and most of these were older men who had once been part of World War One - among them several Captain Mainwarings and at least one Jonesey - but there were those who had never known anything but civilian life, and there was no screening for any but the most obvious kind of health difficulty. This was how it had to be, though. If ever the Home Guard went into action it would be operating as a primitive guerrilla force - as the core of a nation entering upon its last ditch battle for survival.

Over the next few weeks life was complicated and confusing, different from anything I had been used to. And though I wasn't really aware of the fact, there were moments when it was too much for me to handle. I couldn't look forward, I didn't want to look back and the present wasn't a time for making sense of anything - quite literally, there *wasn't* time. The job I was being paid to do was demanding, and not infrequently it involved very long hours. In the evenings, after dinner, I'd often be hauled from my quiet corner of the Mess and required to spend the next two or three hours typing. While Hugh paced up and down in his office - formerly Lord Ashcombe's gun-room - letters and memos and reports poured from him in much the way that data tumbles from a present day computer. And while sometimes the work was genuinely urgent, sometimes it was simply that he could not relax until the thoughts surging through his mind had been committed to paper. There was the progress of individual trainees to be recorded, and also the success or otherwise of instruction techniques. And, there were things I didn't understand. Things, looking back, that I still don't understand.

Lilian and I were required to make detailed notes, and partly for this reason I was expected to turn up, regularly, for the Friday weapon training sessions that took place at nearby Brockham Pits. Two and a half months' experience of the Blitz, not to mention Mr Steadman's dental surgery, had gone quite a way towards toughening me up. But Brockham Pits were distinctly worrying. Once the pin has been pulled out of a hand grenade there is a certain urgency about getting rid of the thing, and if you don't bear this in mind you tend to be in trouble, but every so often one of the trainees would freeze, either hanging on to the object or allowing it to drop almost at his own feet, and on these occasions someone had to intervene. More than once I saw Hugh do so himself, retrieving the lethal missile and tossing it away as carelessly as if it were a stray tennis ball. He knew how to handle such situations. He also knew how to warn and correct a man without either humiliating him or destroying his confidence.

He spent a lot of time with the trainees, coaching, supervising and encouraging. He was a brilliant Commandant and they loved him, as for that matter did the Regular soldiers serving at Denbies. With the officers, though, it was sometimes a different matter. He expected a lot from them, and they quite frequently felt the impact of his temper - or his arrogance, as some of them called it. Hugh didn't care what they thought.

According to everything I heard from time to time, bombs were still raining down on London, and on Plymouth, on Coventry, on Birmingham and Tyneside. America was helping in all sorts of ways, or so we were told, but reasonably enough Congress still hesitated before tumbling over the edge into war, while across the Channel Western Europe was filling up with a tide of Nazism. The RAF and the Royal Navy had been doing an amazing job, but with every day that passed it was beginning to seem more of a miracle that we were still free - still safe. I thought a lot about my friends at the hostel, but communications were not easy. I knew that several were not in London any more, and I did hear news of Alice Robbens. Following several arduous weeks as a WAAF she had evidently suffered a return of the rheumatoid arthritis that had plagued her earlier. Removed to hospital in a fairly desperate condition, she had died a few months later. I still see Alice, radiant in her new uniform, and can only be thankful that she was able to achieve something of what she wanted from life.

January rushed into a grim, forbidding February. One morning I awoke feeling unwell, and with crisp professionalism Bridget Casey suggested I should stay where I was until the following day. Two days later, as my temperature soared, they sent for a doctor from Dorking. His name was Brice-Smith, and he was a coolly reassuring, old-fashioned family physician. He prescribed the wonder drug known as M&B, and was sure that this ought to do the trick.

It didn't. Or at least, not for several days. In the meantime I didn't know much about what was happening, except for the fact that I felt strangely terrible, and people were looking after me. Bridget, I think, came to see me often but Lilian seemed to be always there, changing my sheets and my pyjamas, shaking up my pillows, coaxing me to swallow the powdery white tablets that were supposed to make me better. Once, I thought, Hugh appeared beside my bed.

After what seemed like a very long time, but was probably ten days, the temperature came down and I started to feel better. I was fairly limp and didn't particularly want to move or talk, but as time passed I felt rather relaxed, more so than I had done for a long time. Bridget and Lilian were still fussing round me, and a cheerful orderly plied me with anything he thought might tempt my appetite. Hugh had given me a kitten - it was the sort of thing he did - and I had named it Ribbentrop, after the former German Ambassador. While I lay and stared at the February sky Ribby purred at the foot of my bed, and during the evening he crouched close to my bedside lamp. In Dorking Library Lilian found me something new by my favourite Jeffrey Farnol, and slowly I found the energy to read. Dr Brice-Smith said I could never have become so ill if my stamina and resistance had not been worn away, and learning that I had been in London thought it was probably to do with the Blitz. A number of people were suffering in the same way. Now I would just have to try and build myself up again - take things gradually for a bit, if that turned out to be possible.

Having once turned the corner, though, I got better very quickly, and soon I was back at work. A certain amount of whispering was going on by this time, but I wasn't going to let the gossip get me down. My own thoughts and conscience were one thing, but I didn't really care that much what other people thought. Hugh, of course, was rather different. When his Adjutant - an old friend - remarked that 'Ida ought to marry some decent young curate', he became so enraged that he accused us of holding hands in the cinema and picking flowers together in the woods .This was so hilariously funny that I laughed aloud.

But he was beginning to be rather more considerate. Once a week he drove up to London for briefings and discussions in Whitehall, and as the spring wore on he started taking me with him. Having dropped me off among the shops he would go on to the War Office, then later we would meet for lunch at the Waldorf Hotel, driving back to Dorking through the quiet of afternoon. We laughed a lot during these excursions and Hugh was usually relaxed, which was good for him as well as for me. Sometimes, too, he took me to dinner at the Burford Bridge Hotel, a sprawling, white-walled coaching inn that had stood for centuries in the shadow of romantic Box Hill. Lord Nelson - a connection of the Crowes and one of my heroes - was reputed to have stayed there with Emma Hamilton, and I loved to think that Hugh and I were in some way treading in their footsteps.

Denbies was turning into a complex responsibility, though, and quite apart from anything else the 'guerrillas' were a thorn in Hugh's side. Dedicated to showing off their politics at every opportunity, they displayed a tiresome contempt for convention. Common sense and a typically British willingness to live and let live tended to avert the most serious problems, but for Hugh it was a difficult situation, not least because the guerrillas were chronically reluctant to see themselves as being under orders from anyone. Tom Wintringham - one of the group's leaders and later to become well known as a Member of Parliament - chose to adopt an unshaven look, very much as if he had only just emerged from some lost fold of the Pyrenees, while the group's explosives expert, Major Vernon, ambled around in an eccentric daze, his pockets bulging with detonators and bits of string.

But the guerrillas issue was only one among several sources of friction between Hugh and his superiors. The War Office undoubtedly thought a lot of him, for his energy, his determination and his talent for making things happen, not to mention the charm that enabled him to get on with just about anybody, but as an Army officer Hugh suffered from one serious disability. He did not much like being told what to do. Not when, as very often happened, he thought he could see a better way.

As summer approached, though, everything was running smoothly, at least on the surface. Every week large numbers of Home Guard officers were sent back to their units armed with an impressive range of skills and an entirely new understanding of what it was all about; and every few days representatives of the Top Brass arrived, to be entertained by Hugh and to find out what was going on. Sometimes I wondered why quite so many important people did come to Denbies, particularly as a lot of their visits seemed linked to weapons demonstrations in which the trainees played no part whatsoever. I watched the lines of gleaming staff cars as they paused at the door to off-load men in swirling great-coats, and I noted the endless discussions that went on behind closed doors - given that Hugh invariably spent several hours a week chewing things over in London, what on earth did they find to talk about? I didn't give it very much thought, back in 1941, but since that time I have wondered, occasionally, whether there could have been something else going on at Denbies. Hugh would never have said a word, not to me or to any other unauthorized soul. Not then, or at any other time. Maybe Denbies was just a training place for officers of the Home Guard. And yet . . . I think of those summer evenings, and the imposing figures who paused as they left to chat quietly on the steps. The endless staff cars, creeping away down the drive. And just sometimes I wonder.

Lord and Lady Ashcombe, who still occupied a corner of the house, may have suspected, even known, more than I did. They had an excellent relationship with Hugh, who had gone to some trouble to ensure they did not suffer too much inconvenience from the commandeering of their property (in his opinion they had suffered enough already. During the first Great War they had lost six sons). When the house was taken over some furniture and *objets d'art* had been removed for safety, but the Ashcombes were always co-operative, and if something such as an extra table or bed was needed they were always happy to supply it. Hugh and Lord Ashcombe tended to sort such things out between themselves, and on one occasion, as they were walking round one of the attic store-rooms, Hugh noticed a painting propped with its face to the wall. Turning the picture round, he saw it was the portrait of a good-looking, youngish woman in Edwardian dress.

'This is a fine painting,' he pointed out. 'What's it doing up here?'

Lord Ashcombe stared at the portrait. 'That,' he said, 'is Mrs Keppel. We don't talk about her.'

Mrs Keppel - notoriously the mistress of King Edward V11 - had been Lord Ashcombe's great-aunt.

That summer Hugh discovered that Enid was having a serious affair. While on holiday in Devon she had met a man called Kenneth Darrell-Waters, a surgeon, and their relationship seems to have developed quite rapidly. Enid even took a flat in London so that they could meet there in secret. I never knew exactly when or how Hugh found out, but when he rang home one day Gillian answered the telephone, and when he asked if her mother was there a housekeeper heard her say:

'Oh, no! She's gone to London, to see Uncle Kenneth. . . *you* know!'

When Hugh did go home he now slept in a guest bedroom, and I believe the couple rarely spoke. They were heading fast towards dissolution, but there were still the children to think about - little Imogen, who was not yet six years old, and the much loved Gillian, soon to be celebrating her tenth birthday. Hugh always had a fund of stories about Gillian - her special fondness for rabbits, which he was sure she had caught from him, her intelligence and her happy, positive outlook on life. On the whole he was under a lot of pressure, but he coped well. And his military superiors were impressed by his performance at Denbies, even if there were occasional eccentricities.

On one occasion a very senior General was expected to arrive for a pre-arranged lunch and inspection tour. His scheduled arrival time was, I think, twelve o'clock, and as he stepped from his car the Commandant would normally have been on hand to greet him personally, but there had been a series of discrepancies affecting the Regular soldiers' pay, and on this particular morning Hugh had decided it was his duty to check the cash personally. He was about a third of the way through this task when his Adjutant came in to say the General had just that moment arrived.

'Tell him,' said Hugh, 'I'll be with him in a few minutes.'

Ten minutes later the Adjutant came back. The General, he said, was showing signs of impatience.

'Give him a sherry,' Hugh recommended, checking a bundle of five pound notes.

'He's had one, sir.'

'Give him another one.'

Fifteen minutes went by, and the Adjutant - for whom I felt some sympathy - re-appeared. The General was now red in the face, and was expressing himself with force. The Adjutant's account did not get too specific, but it wasn't difficult to guess at the visitor's tone.

Something like half an hour later Hugh finished counting. Securing the final bundle of notes with a rubber band, he placed everything back in the safe, locked it securely and strolled away to deal with the General. I remember that the Adjutant and I sort of drifted along behind, drawn irresistibly by the prospect of a *denouement*. Hugh opened the door of the room in which visitors were received, and we heard him speak.

'Good-morning, sir! I do apologise. . . . You've been looked after, I hope?'

The door closed and we waited for the rumble of raised voices. In a moment, surely, that door would open again and the General would come striding out, having lingered just long enough to give Hugh a sizeable piece of his mind. But nothing happened. A couple of hours later, I saw the two of them standing on the terrace. The General was laughing as if at something pretty amusing, and I heard his voice.

'My dear chap. . . .'

Hugh's charm - or rather, his easy determination to do more or less as the fancy took him - had won the day again. Sooner or later, though, some kind of a crunch was likely to come, and we didn't have to wait all that much longer.

It was August, again. The weather was warm and dusty, the woods dark and heavy with leaf. War or no war, the schoolchildren were on holiday. It seemed increasingly incongruous to hear the rattle of gunfire coming from beyond the trees, the rumble of explosives shaking the ground, but during these clear summer days the range at Brockham Pits was in more continuous demand than ever. For the time being Hugh had overall responsibility for the Pits, but units outside his control could and sometimes did obtain War Office permission to train there, and somewhere around this time a small Canadian group was permitted to use the site for testing explosives. The Canadians may have imagined that someone would be coming along to tidy up after them; the War Office probably didn't think at all, but then they did have a good deal on their minds. Some days after the Canadian visit a ten-year-old boy wandered into the Pits area - perhaps he was playing soldiers, or maybe he was just curious about the giant rock-filled hollow. He trod on an unexploded missile, and he ought to have been killed. By some miracle he wasn't, but one of his legs was blasted off, and in a desperate condition he was removed to hospital. There Hugh visited him, and I believe he also saw the parents. When he got back to Denbies he didn't say very much, but I noticed he was rather pale underneath his light golden tan. He asked me to take a letter, and pacing up and down beside me he dictated it. It was addressed to the War Office, and was for the attention of someone important.

That letter was a white-hot explosion of fury, and if addressed to some raw subaltern who had just smashed every rule and disgraced his regiment it might not have been considered out of place. But it wasn't intended for a subaltern, it was intended for someone very high up in the hierarchy of the British Army.

A few days later a letter arrived from Lord Bridgeman, who had special responsibility for South-Eastern Command. He and Hugh had always maintained a good relationship and he had always been willing to help push things through; perhaps because of this his letter seemed to express more of regret than personal outrage, but at the same time he did not hesitate to be blunt. He said that great things had been planned for Hugh - an important new assignment in the offing, promotion to higher rank, almost certainly an eventual knighthood. But now every bit of this was under threat.... to say the least.

He had been very foolish, Lord Bridgeman said. He should never have written such a letter.

If anything, Hugh seemed elated. He had acted out of principle, and was gratified the effect had been so dramatic, in fact, he was on a kind of high. Since the early 1930's he had been in favour of pursuing a war against Hitler with every weapon that came to hand, but just because there was a 'war on' he saw no reason to place the innocent, civilian or military, in unnecessary danger. He had felt very much the same when he was a young officer in Gallipolli, and later on behind the Western Front. When the future of a ten-year-old Surrey schoolboy was involved, he felt it all the more passionately. If he had been in control, on the day in question, everything possible would have been done to ensure that such an accident couldn't happen.

The fuss appeared to quieten down, and life at Denbies went on more or less as usual. Every other week there was a fresh intake of trainees, and apart from anything else Hugh had very little time to spare for worrying about his own future. The Nazis were now in Russia, and on a rather less sensational note my cat Ribbentrop, who had recently turned into Frau Ribbentrop, was found to be expecting a family. She was feeling the heat and I worried about her, but she seemed happy enough, so long as she could continue to doze beside my bed.

And Hugh had his diversions. Ever since coming to Denbies he had been working to get a Scottish piper on to the staff, and now his Pipe-Sergeant's unearthly wailing could be heard every evening during dinner. It was a performance much appreciated by Hugh, and I think also by his Adjutant, who was very likely the only other Scotsman present. The rest of us were - to say the very least - ambivalent. At one point, greatly daring, I referred to the 'squeakling pipes'; fortunately Hugh thought this was amusing, but I was never allowed to forget it.

Autumn came and a golden hush descended on the fields around Dorking, though of course it was still a hush broken by snatches of machine gun fire. More batches of Home Guard leaders came, stayed for their eight days and left again, carrying with them the things they had learned. Then as autumn turned into winter, Hugh received bad news from Scotland. After enduring several years of ill health, his mother had died. At the time he said very little - for various reasons he didn't even succeed in getting home for her funeral - but somewhere within his complex being there must have been a new layer of hidden anguish. I knew that he had adored his mother, but also that there had been little closeness between them. The former Jessica McBride had been a talented singer and pianist, before her marriage she had even made concert appearances, and Hugh cherished memories of lying in bed and listening while his mother sang and played in the drawing-room below. According to him she had a beautiful voice and was a remarkable pianist. But sadly his relationship with her had been tarnished when, soon after the birth of his younger brother Fred, he had succumbed to diphtheria. Banished - for the baby's sake - to the top of the house for two or three weeks, he seems to have seen only the maid who looked after him, and this left him jealous and insecure, particularly where his mother was concerned. In his twenties, he seized with eagerness upon something he noticed when he came home on leave towards the end of the First World War. . . waiting alone in the drawing-room of his parents' house, he spotted a piece of sheet music propped up on the piano. It was a song that had recently become popular: 'God send him back to me. . .' His brother had been invalided out some time before, so she must have been thinking about *him*. Mustn't she? Perhaps she did love him, after all.

I have seen pictures of Jessica Pollock, perched on a rock and laughing, her hair blowing round her face. I know that her husband adored her too, and I don't believe she can have been a cold-blooded woman.

The year was drifting towards its end. I think that for everybody there is one brief spell during which life takes on a special kind of intensity, and this was my time. Each season in its turn had been more vivid than anything I could remember, and winter, when it came, was cold and brilliant. Not that the winter of 1941 seemed likely to be a pleasant experience. Food and other shortages were worsening by the day, life in every respect was getting harder, and the long, black evenings were certain to offer greatly improved chances for killers coming out of the sky. Then rumbles from a distant explosion brought us a new kind of hope.

The island of Hawaii had been harbouring a significant portion of the US Navy, and on the morning of December 7th ninety-four warships were at anchor there. Within the space of half an hour four had been severely damaged and two lost forever, two hundred aircraft had been destroyed and thousands of American men and women lay dead. Many more had been seriously injured. It was a cruel and terrible tragedy, for the United States as a whole and for the families and friends of all those courageous Service people, but for us in Western Europe it brought just the hint of a possibility that our torment might one day come to an end. Hearing the news in his Downing Street bunker, Winston Churchill, himself half American, may have been shocked, but that initial reaction will have been followed by more than a bubble of elation. Together with Britain, and perhaps France, America was a natural successor to the guardianship of Christian civilization. Some Americans - perhaps not surprisingly - had been reluctant to assume the responsibilities associated with such a burden, but now the die was cast. We in Britain had been surviving on a mixture of stubbornness and blind faith. Now, things were beginning to happen at last.

Once again Christmas was an island of calm, and it was always wonderful to see my mother. As for Hugh, I tried not to think about him. To me, Christmas had never had a lot to do with romance, or even parties. It was a time for curling up in some warm, safe corner with a stack of new books and a fat box of chocolates, and M's reassuring presence, not very far away. I don't suppose I ever knew just how that Christmas went for Hugh.

The New Year began with a spell of mild, dank weather, but as January drew to a close the air sharpened and on Friday, February 6th, we woke to the sight of snow clouds brooding over the Surrey hills.

*　*　*　*　*

X

By breakfast time the lawns around Denbies were turning white, but it was Friday, and snow or no snow Friday meant Brockham Pits, though mercifully I was not expected to join the party in such conditions. Comfortable in our cosy office, Lilian and I spent the morning working through a pile of correspondence, while snowflakes flattened themselves against the windows and slowly, gently, the park disappeared under a counterpane of white. Round about lunchtime, a telegram arrived for Hugh. Normally it was my job to check everything that came in, and it was not until I had slit the cable open that I realised it was from his brother in Scotland. It may be that I have forgotten something, but so far as I can recall the message was very simple:

'*Father died this morning.*

Fred'.

His heart already weakened, William Pollock had obviously found it impossible to survive more than a few months without his wife. Poor Hugh. Soon he would be coming in, cold and irritable, and I would have to tell him he had now lost both his parents.

Considering the weather, we assumed the Brockham Pits convoy would probably be back a bit earlier than usual, but it wasn't, it was late. Presumably Hugh was seizing the opportunity to coach his men in the finer points of winter weather strategy. It was four o'clock, and dusk was almost on us when I saw the first of the returning vehicles as it rounded a bend in the drive. It was moving through a curtain of snowflakes but despite the conditions was approaching quite fast, so I grabbed a coat and hurried out on to the steps.

One by one, the cars and jeeps came bumping past me to make their way round the side of the house. Normally Hugh got out just about where I was standing, while Hollis, his Cockney driver, took the

65

car on to its garage, but so far his car did not appear to be in sight. I stood, peering into the dusk, and then I saw the car coming. It was almost at the end of the convoy, and only when it drew level did I realise Hugh was not inside. Furthermore, Hollis was not going to stop. I huddled my coat around me and ran down the steps. The big black staff car went past, but there was one more vehicle in the line, and it was driven by a Sergeant-Major who had been at Denbies from the beginning. He saw me and braked, skidding a bit. As he wound the window down I looked in at him.

'*Where's the Colonel?*' I asked.

'Haven't you heard. . . ? They've got him in the hospital.' He drew a hand across his forehead. 'I never saw. . . . There was so much *blood*.'

I had never collapsed publicly, not for emotional reasons, and I didn't do so then. I'm not quite sure what I did, or said, but I remember getting back into the house and finding Sister Casey there, with one or two of the officers who had just returned. As far as I can remember, they said that it hadn't been anyone's fault. Some kind of explosive had been demonstrated, and things had gone wrong. A fragment of shrapnel had entered Hugh's throat, and he had been rushed off to hospital in Dorking. They didn't really know any more than that. Or so they said.

Nora telephoned the hospital and was told that Colonel Pollock was, at that moment, under-going surgery. They were endeavouring to remove a piece of shrapnel which had lodged at the side of his throat. Looking at me, Nora remarked that her job being what it was, she really ought to be there. As Hugh's secretary, she added carefully, perhaps I should be there as well. Somebody pointed out that the roads were getting worse by the minute, but Hollis was ready and anxious to drive us, and the town was only three miles away. Just as darkness came down, we set out in the teeth of a thickening blizzard.

The recently returned convoy had covered much of the route we needed to follow and its tracks were still visible, but a fresh storm was coming fast and the flakes were freezing as they fell. Outside Denbies' gates a winding lane tumbled away steeply between high, snow-covered banks, and on two or three occasions the big staff car lost its grip of the road. As we drifted drunkenly towards the bank, Hollis remarked that at the present rate of progress we would all be ending up in much the same position as Hugh.

'Little white beds,' he said cheerfully. 'All in a row.'

I remember that I laughed, in my freezing corner of the back seat. I was grateful for Hollis, that night.

Eventually we found our way into a snowbound, silent Dorking, and a few minutes later reached the blacked out cottage hospital. Nora went to find out what she could, and soon afterwards came back to tell us Hugh was still on the operating table. There was nothing we could do but wait.

The waiting-room was reasonably comfortable and there we sat, on straight-backed chairs, while the hands of a large clock ticked the evening, then the night away. It was frightening - numbing - but I could hardly show what I felt, even though both my companions must have guessed. We had several cups of tea, and the irrepressible Hollis kept us going until, about three o'clock in the morning, a doctor came to tell us Colonel Pollock was now out of surgery. The operation had been extremely delicate - if the shrapnel had penetrated further, or had entered at a slightly different angle, Hugh would not have survived - but the metal had now been removed and he ought to be all right, though there was, always, a slight risk of infection. In the meantime, we could see him for a minute or two. By tacit agreement, we all went in. Hollis had been anxious too, and there was no question of leaving him outside the door.

Hugh was still unconscious, but we were allowed, briefly, to stand and stare at him. Above the bandages swathing his throat his face looked gaunt and ghastly white, almost unrecognizable. But he was going to be all right.

I think it took us something like a couple of hours to struggle back through the blanketing snow, and by the time we reached Denbies even Hollis had fallen silent. Safe in my own room again I didn't want to think, not about anything. I simply tumbled into bed and fell asleep immediately.

When I woke up, it occurred to me that somebody would have to tell Hugh's wife, Enid Blyton. Probably his Adjutant should have done it, or Nora Casey, but nobody seemed anxious to take the job on, so I did it myself. Perhaps I wanted to hear her voice, to talk for a few minutes to the woman who shared Hugh's name, his children and - officially, at least - his life. Perhaps I wanted to see what it was that had attracted him, once. The word 'once' was central. At that moment Hugh and I still had nothing much more than a romantic friendship, but rightly or wrongly I never had any feeling that I possessed a rival.

I told Enid what had happened, and asked if I should make arrangements for her to be met at Dorking station. As far as I can recall, she replied that I would probably think her very odd, but she simply couldn't stand hospitals. Consequently, she would not be travelling to visit her husband. Perhaps, though, I would do something for her. Could I telephone her every evening? Just to let her know how things were going on? Not before nine o'clock, though, if I didn't mind. She sounded calm and fully in control of herself. By this time, of course, she probably knew that her husband had become interested in another woman. She may even have known exactly who that other woman was - according to Barbara Stoney[*], some time during 1941 an anonymous telephone caller had advised her not to 'let Ida crow over you' - but I detected no animosity in her voice. No emotion of any kind.

The snow stopped, and a couple of days later I visited Hugh again. He claimed to be 'fine', but he didn't look it and he was desperately weak. His father's death had shocked him, too, and he very much minded not being able to attend the funeral in Ayrshire. It had been thought he would be out of hospital quite quickly, but some form of infection had erupted and now he was being told, very firmly, that he would not be going anywhere just yet.

His temper exacerbated by fever, he snapped at all of us, and when he had been in hospital for a fortnight, and still the infection had not quite cleared, he made a sudden decision to discharge himself. The hospital had no power to hold him against his will, and announcing that he was going to Scotland, to 'see his father's grave', he got out of bed one morning, dressed himself and sent for Hollis. A short time later he arrived back at Denbies, wearing the blood-stained great-coat in which he had been admitted to hospital.

When he walked through the door he looked painfully ill. Though most people were afraid to comment I said exactly what I thought, but it had little or no effect. In a couple of days, he said, he would be leaving for Scotland, by train. So would I please check on estimated departure times?

That afternoon he made an effort to do something about the papers that were waiting for his personal attention, but this attempt had to be

---

[*] Enid Blyton's biographer

abandoned. That evening, his wound burst open again. Nora was on leave for a few days, and it was scarcely a job for the Adjutant or for Hollis. Without stopping to think about it I removed the sodden bandages, cleaned the wound thoroughly, disinfected it and bound it up again. The next day Hugh seemed a little better, and the day after that he left for Scotland as planned.

He was to stay with his married brother, who occupied a house in the centre of Ayr. When he got there the atmosphere must have been sombre, but he had always got on well with his brother's two sons, if not with their father, and though the elder was now serving with RAF Bomber Command the younger boy, Ronnie, was still just on the edge of joining up. Pleased to see his uncle, he seems to have suggested a fishing expedition, or perhaps the idea came from Hugh. There is a photograph that shows the two of them sitting together in a rowing-boat, on a loch. Hugh is wearing uniform - at that time serving military personnel rarely changed into civilian clothes, even on leave - and perhaps because Ronnie is looking away Hugh's face reveals very plainly the fact that he is feeling ill.

But there was one lighter moment. In addition to his two sons Fred had a much younger daughter, a golden-haired five-year-old called Sylvia. Sylvia must have been a treasure in that grey household, but spoiled she was not. She knew that children were supposed to be heard as little as possible, and as she sat at the breakfast table, facing this gaunt-faced man who was supposed to be her uncle, she got on with her porridge and kept herself to herself. Until at last she ventured to steal a look at Uncle Hugh and found, to her astonishment, that he was making 'rabbit' faces at her. Solemnly she stared back at him. But she never forgot.

It was a relief to see Hugh back from Scotland, but his wound had not yet healed and quite clearly he wasn't out of the woods. There had been a chance he might resume control of Denbies, but within days he was on the edge of collapse and the War Office directed him, very firmly, to take a further three months' sick leave. Then another directive came through.

Hugh's term at Denbies was at an end. As soon as he was fit again, he would be notified of his next posting.

I think I was devastated, but I'm not at all sure what Hugh felt. He had real admiration and affection for the Home Guard, and on the whole he had enjoyed his time at Denbies. Certainly he had relished the challenges it represented, complex as they may have been. But he knew that many things were changing. So long as hostilities

69

continued the Home Guard would go on being important - even with America involved there was always the chance that Hitler might seek to create a diversion by seizing part of Britain - but our fighters had smashed the Luftwaffe, and now that US troops were actually quartered on British soil the possibility of invasion had receded dramatically. Hugh had overseen the training of several thousand Home Guard officers, and given the circumstances he had done enough in that direction. I think he was excited by the prospect of a new posting, and that, I suppose, was natural. The bitter pill, from his point of view, was that he had still got to complete his sick leave, and for this purpose could hardly avoid going home to Beaconsfield. He and Enid were married, and they had two daughters. There was no reasonable alternative, but it was excruciatingly difficult for him.

For me it was awful too, but in a very different way. According to Hugh, it would be best for me to stay on at Denbies. It was a good job, I knew the ropes, and the environment was relatively secure. And of course we would continue to meet - in London, probably.

It couldn't possibly be the same, though. Why did things always have to change?

As soon as Hugh left Denbies, the place began to alter almost beyond recognition. No doubt the new Commandant was a competent officer, but I could see that he was merely doing a job. His way of running things could not have been more different, and everybody seemed to feel it. There was no fire any more, no inspiration, and a dreariness settled on the place. In a letter to Hugh, Lord Ashcombe said:

'. . . *We have got on so well in our somewhat unusual relations that I feel that any change, whatever it may be, cannot be for the better. . . .*' And a Kentish Home Guard officer wrote: *'All of us here regard this as grievous news for the Home Guard in general, and for ourselves in particular'.*

But spring flew by, and suddenly it was May. Hugh's period of convalescence was over, and he was restored to normal health (apart from a hearing problem which had started during the First War and been greatly worsened by Denbies weapons demonstrations). I had decided to leave Denbies and go home to Hastings for a week or two, then just before I left Hugh rang to say he had now been given orders regarding his new posting. It was not top secret, and if I would meet him in London, the following Monday morning, he would discuss it with me.

It was good to be back in Hastings again. More so, even, than it usually was, probably because I knew I had got to a crossroads and this time it wasn't something I could negotiate by instinct. Through most of my life I had moved like a migrating bird or a salmon cruising towards the sea. Now that system didn't seem to be working any more, and I needed to think.

During a recent trip to London I had purchased one of the latest wireless sets to take home as a present, and while Uncle George spent much of that weekend twiddling knobs M and I talked, about everything and nothing. Early on Sunday evening I stood at an ironing-board, pressing the suit I planned to wear in London the following day, then for a while sat reading a popular historical novel, *The Amateur Gentleman* by Georgette Heyer. There was still a touch of sharpness in the air, and because of this a small fire had been lit in the sitting-room across the hall - these days Uncle George was not as spartan as he had been. He liked a little comfort, now and then - but it had been a clear, summery afternoon and when I glanced through the window I could see people walking by to attend evensong at the nearby parish church.

I was probably thinking a lot about Hugh, but I was also more than usually conscious of the fact that home was a reassuring refuge. Somewhere in the distance I heard the dull, familiar throb of bombers, probably heading towards London.

And then the world blew apart.

A roaring, rattling explosion rocked the ground underneath my feet, and everything folded in on top of me. My ear-drums seemed to splinter, and something hard and smooth fell across my back, forcing me face downwards on to the floor.

I don't know how long I stayed there. Not very long, probably, but quite long enough. For one thing I was being choked by dust, and also I was being crushed by the object lying across my back. I moved, and found that my bones seemed to be more or less intact. Somehow I struggled out from underneath the hard object, which turned out to have been the kitchen door.

The walls had gone, and the roof, and just about all the things that had made up our kitchen. Our house. There was nothing but rubble.

I looked up, and through a dense haze of foul-smelling brown dust I could just about make out the gentle, fading blue of the evening sky.

* * * * *

71

XI

We were removed to the Royal East Sussex Hospital, two or three miles away. Other bombs had fallen in the Hastings area that evening, and the staff were extremely busy but doing their best to take adequate care of everyone. I felt very odd. One half of my head seemed to have been blown away, my hair was standing up as if I had suffered an electric shock, and I don't think I was absolutely sure where I was. I can remember being examined and then given several injections, a procedure to which I would normally have objected violently. After this I was put to bed, for some reason or other, in a little room of my own. I was knocked out for something like ten hours, and when I woke I still felt odd. But the cobwebs had lifted from my mind.

I had been bombed, and was in hospital. My mother was there too, and Uncle George, but I had been told they were both going to be all right. Then something else hit me with the force of a lightning strike. It was Monday morning, and I had an appointment to meet Hugh in London.

When a nurse came in I told her I was fine, and would have to be leaving soon. I needed to be in London, I told her, by half past twelve. She placed a thermometer in my mouth and told me I must wait until the doctor came round. 'Then we'll see.'

When she had gone, I got out of bed and took the thermometer out of my mouth. Opening a window I started to wave the thing about, hoping against hope this would have the desired effect of cancelling out any feverish indications. I had to get out of there. I had to go and meet Hugh.

My hair was still standing on end and my thinking processes were wrapped up in cotton wool, but I forced myself to do what I felt was necessary. My own clothes, torn and full of dust, were unwearable, but I could see M's emergency suitcase had been placed in my room, and with the determination of the temporarily unhinged I opened the case. There was a black dress, and a coat. Rather elegant, actually, but definitely the sort of thing better suited to a woman considerably older than I was. Never mind. I scrambled into the clothes and hurried out.

Because the hospital was extremely busy I managed to reach a telephone without being asked any questions, and knowing Hugh was at the Waldorf Hotel I dialled that number. My fingers were trembling, all the more so because I needed to catch him before he thought about going out anywhere. The phone rang in his room, and he answered. As soon as I heard his voice I felt better and everything started tumbling out, but he interrupted me.

'I can be down there in two or three hours.'

'No. . . . No! I'm coming to London.'

'You mustn't do that. Stay where you are, and I'll be with you by lunchtime.'

'But I can't stay here.'

Panic and desperation were making me almost incoherent. When I replaced the receiver, a minute or two later, I wasn't absolutely sure how we had left things, but I knew I wasn't going to hang about in that hospital.

There was nothing to be collected from my room. I would have loved to see my mother, but had been told she was still sleeping and had better not be disturbed. Anyway, I would be back, later on.

The hospital entrance was crowded with uniforms and strained faces, but no-one was paying any attention to me and that was just as well, because if anyone had tried to stop me I might have struggled pretty hard.

I felt wobbly, outside in the cool morning air, but as I set off down the long hill that ran towards the station – I couldn't waste time waiting for a bus – things did get better. One side of my head appeared to have severed relations with the other side, but I supposed that was something you got used to. I must have been quite a striking sight, in my dignified black silk dress, but no-one seemed to stare.

I didn't have long to wait, and as I boarded the train and settled down I felt, for the first time in fourteen or fifteen hours, something like a sense of security. I was on my way to meet Hugh, and that meant that somehow or other everything was going to be all right. This euphoria persisted until we were rather more than halfway to London, then a thought occurred to me and I crossed back into reality.

What if Hugh had not really believed I meant what I said? Suppose he was at this moment heading towards Sussex, travelling down while I was making my way up. . . ?

At any time this sort of possibility would have thrown me into a panic. At that moment it was like a threatening gargoyle, rearing itself up and grinning at me. At Charing Cross I queued for a taxi. By this time I felt cold and shaky and close to the end of my tether. It was only a short distance, from Charing Cross to the Waldorf Hotel, but that afternoon the journey seemed to last for hours.

I paid the taxi off, walked through the revolving doors and crossed to the reception desk. By this time I was probably a pathetic spectacle, and the receptionist smiled at me.

'Miss Crowe. . . ? Colonel Pollock isn't here, he had urgent business in Sussex. He did leave a message, though. If you will take a taxi to Claridges Hotel, he will be in touch with you there.'

I felt sick with relief. In a way my worst fears had been realised, but it didn't matter, because Hugh had thought it all out and had made some kind of arrangement. I couldn't think beyond that. By this time I could barely think at all, but that was all right because without being asked to do so the Waldorf receptionist was calling a taxi for me.

Ten minutes later I arrived outside Claridges, and made the discovery that Hugh had booked me in.

*   *   *   *   *

XII

Guilt and anxiety tugged at me. While I rested at Claridges Hotel, my mother was still striving to recover from her ordeal inside a shabby, war-battered Sussex hospital.

But I was tired and muzzy, and Claridges was wrapping me in a warm cocoon. It wasn't just the luxurious decor, or the courteous service, or even the feeling that Adolf Hitler would never be allowed to cross this particular threshold. More than anything, it was the kindness exhibited by Claridges staff. They must, all of them, have seen plenty of people who had been 'bombed out', and most had probably looked worse than I did, yet they behaved as if I were unique. No doubt they usually did their best to be helpful, but their kindness to me went beyond the call of duty, even for the staff of an internationally famous hotel. It's true there was a lot of kindness about in those days. About half a century was to go by before ordinary human warmth would begin to flicker and fade in the chilly light of the Caring Society.

Sitting on the edge of my bed I telephoned the Royal East Sussex Hospital, and a nurse who didn't seem to have heard about my unauthorized departure told me my mother was still resting comfortably. She might need to stay in for a few days, mainly so that she could recover from the inevitable shock. But for a sixty-nine-year-old woman whose heart had already been damaged by rheumatic fever, she was doing very well.

I left a message for M, and lay down on the bed. Several hours later, I woke to the shrilling of the telephone beside me, and when I grabbed the receiver I found it was Hugh.

He said that he had just got back from Sussex. He sounded faintly anxious, which was not like him, but the whimsical note crept back as he told me he had been certain I would make for London, but had thought it best to cover every eventuality. He had been to visit my mother, checking that she was all right and had everything she needed, then he had driven over to view the site of our old house. It was, he stressed, no more than that. There was nothing left.

It was something I had needed to know.

Despite an ARP warden's efforts to stop him Hugh had searched through the ruins, and had come upon two items which he knew belonged to me. A gold bracelet, found gleaming faintly through several layers of dust, and - astonishingly - the suit I had been ironing minutes before the bomb dropped upon us. Whatever the explanation for this, Hugh said it seemed to be undamaged, though it could do with a clean. He would bring it to me the following day; the staff at Claridges would soon get it tidied up. He hoped I understood that he had booked me into Claridges for a fortnight, and that there was absolutely nothing for me to worry about, so far as that was concerned. As for the future, well, we'd have to talk about that. Anyway, we would be meeting the following day.

'I'll be with you in time for lunch,' he promised. 'I've got one or two things to tell you.'

After he had hung up, I started pacing up and down my luxurious bedroom. I felt mildly elated, as I always did after talking to Hugh, but I also felt a twinge of fear. I knew what he was going to tell me, what he would have told me already, if I had not been hit by a bomb. His new posting had come through, and already I had a horrible feeling about it. He might be sent almost anywhere - overseas, even. And my chances of going with him, this time, were lower than zero.

*   *   *   *   *

XIII

By the time I saw Hugh he had already handed my suit to hotel staff and it was in the process of being cleaned. I was still wearing my mother's dress, but if Hugh thought I looked odd he didn't betray the fact. Instead he asked whether - bearing in mind my hasty departure from hospital - I intended to get myself checked by a doctor.

'No.' I had seen enough of doctors, and the mere thought alarmed me. Anyway, I was all right now.

As we sat together in the cocktail bar, Hugh took my bracelet from his pocket and handed it over. He had cleaned it up a bit, but I knew it had come from underneath the rubble and just touching it made me feel odd, especially when he told me that our house had not been the only building in that immediate area to suffer a direct hit. The Vicarage had also been destroyed, and the Vicar's five-year-old daughter had not yet been found. This tragedy has always haunted me.

We sat talking quietly about his meeting with M, and about the ruined house, and for the first time I began to take in just how much we had lost. There had been all those things my mother cherished, mainly pictures and bits of porcelain inherited from my grandfather, some of them valuable, all of them irreplaceable. Then there had been the tall cupboard crammed to capacity with manuscripts, all the work I had ever done, in fact. With the exception of a dozen or so published items, everything I had written was now lost.

We had all survived, though, M and Uncle George and I, and that was a kind of miracle. As for the rest, there was no way of getting anything back, and none of it was that important, not by comparison with our lives. From that day to this, I have never really set much store by tangible possessions.

We moved into the dining-room and embarked upon a pleasant lunch. I was dimly aware of people around us - be-jewelled dowagers lunching with uniformed grandsons, smart young women, some of them also in uniform, whispering to one another over the hors d'eouvre. Though I hadn't much appetite I was feeling better, and when we got as far as the main course, and still Hugh hadn't mentioned his own immediate prospects, I began to feel almost as if the moment might never be going to arrive. That I was safe. And then it came.

Hugh said ruefully that he had known it wasn't going to be North Africa or anything of that sort, if only because of his age, but he had hoped to be given a job at the centre of things. It had never entered his head that he might be sent to the United States.

I was dumbfounded. *America. . . .*

He started to talk about Britain's steadily increasing indebtedness to the US. Quite apart from the fact that American troops and equipment now made up a huge proportion of the Allied war effort, every day more and more of Uncle Sam's gifts and loans were being unloaded in British ports, and apart from lending our ground for use as a jumping-off point there were only one or two areas in which we could attempt to reciprocate - one of these being our ability to supply certain kinds of advice and expertise.

Somewhere about the middle of the previous year, two Americans from Massachusetts had come over to visit Denbies. At that time the US had felt no particular, pressing need to worry about internal defence, but there had always been a possibility of danger and an enterprising band of Massachusetts citizens had decided it was always better to be prepared. Now America was no long living in its own separate, secure universe, it was at war with both Germany and Japan and was said to fear a land invasion, possibly via Canada. American interest in home defence was therefore expanding, and they were asking for our advice. More specifically, they were asking for Hugh. At the moment, the plan was that he should tour north-eastern states of the USA, where arrangements would be made for him to visit National Guard units and training establishments. He expected to be away for four or five months.

I was having difficulty in thinking straight, but one or two questions rose to the surface.

'How are you going to get there?' I asked.

That - in his opinion - was one of the best bits. He would be sailing aboard the magnificent liner Queen Mary. She had been converted into a troop-ship, but nonetheless it would be an interesting experience. In the course of his extensive travels Hugh had sampled the amenities of several great liners, but never the Queen Mary. He hadn't been to America, either, so it really would be something of an adventure.

I was beginning to feel sick. Troop-ships got torpedoed, it happened all the time. Crossing the Atlantic, practically everything got torpedoed. For the second time in thirty-six hours, whole sections of my life were disintegrating.

It was like my grandfather's china, and the cupboard stuffed with manuscripts. The tide of life swept over you, taking things away, and there was nothing you could do.

The dessert trolley arrived, and Hugh changed the subject. Now, he said, there was something else we needed to talk about. After returning from Sussex, the day before, he had gone straight home to Beaconsfield and had become involved in a blazing row with Enid.

'I told her I wanted a divorce,' he said. As I stared at him, he added that his wife had agreed. 'The whole process will take around a year,' Hugh went on. 'But when it's all settled, we shall be able to get married.'

*   *   *   *   *

XIV

A day or so later I travelled down to Hastings, and was relieved to find M was making progress. She had been shaken up very badly and was upset about the loss of so many possessions, but I soon realised she was not upset about the Hastings house. That old life was over. From her point of view it had never been a particularly happy life; it may have been more difficult than I had ever understood. Now it was as if she had woken up, and found a locked door standing wide. Whatever challenges might turn out to be waiting in the future, she wasn't going to walk back through that door.

Uneasily, I told her about Hugh. I had no real idea what her reaction might be, and I was afraid. But she had met Hugh now, and she liked him. She accepted that - to put it no more strongly - Enid had been an odd, unsatisfactory wife, and that for some considerable while she had clearly been enjoying diversions of her own. These were strange times, too, filled with things that were a lot more shocking than divorce. Probably she also noted the fact that Hugh was the first man in whom I had ever shown a serious interest. She accepted the situation, and I went back to London feeling as if a burden had been lifted from me.

Hugh sailed for America on the fourteenth day of June. For security reasons I couldn't be told the Queen Mary's precise embarkation time, or any other details of the voyage. I knew other things, though. I knew that during the last year or so thousands of men, women and children had lost their lives while attempting to cross the Atlantic. And as I wasn't even 'next of kin' it might be weeks before anyone told me a thing.

A day or two later M was released from hospital, and I went down to collect her. My cousin Emmie had invited us both to stay with her for an indefinite period, and if we accepted I should be able to find another worthwhile job. Emmie lived in the City of London, where she and her husband shared a wonderful apartment high above the Hong Kong and Shanghai Bank, and M loved the idea of being in London again. We knew we might feel a bit vulnerable, particularly when there was a raid, but we had just escaped being blasted out of existence and that had been in Sussex, so what was the point of worrying? We asked one another what we really wanted, and London won.

Uncle George was another matter. He would not be going to London, he would be joining his two unmarried sisters in their house outside Hastings. It really was a parting of the ways. M had to be my main concern - and she was right to break free - but I always find it hard to think about Uncle George. In a way, that Sunday evening nightmare gave my mother the chance to take her life back. For Uncle George it was the end of almost everything.

In the black coat and dress, now restored to her, M seemed alarmingly frail, but once we were in a taxi and on our way to the station she looked more like her old self. We had just missed the early afternoon train to London, but another came along quite quickly and we settled into our seats with relief. The train left on time, and we chugged our way towards Eastbourne through the stillness of an early summer afternoon. It all looked so peaceful, and familiar. The Channel with its barbed wire barricades on one side, the long green backbone of the South Downs keeping us company on the other. We would come back, of course, if only to visit Aunt Dolly. But I wondered if either of us would ever come back to live.

We were getting near to Eastbourne when all at once something swooped out of the sky, plunging towards our train. It was an aircraft, one of ours - no, it wasn't. It was German. There was a rattle of gunfire, and we heard the sound of breaking glass. Someone dashed along the corridor, past the entrance to our carriage, but otherwise there was no sign of reaction from any of our fellow passengers. The plane swooped away again, circled and came back.

I looked at my mother. In her younger days she had been given to bursts of hysteria, but she hadn't panicked when a bomb destroyed her home, and she showed no sign of doing so now. Not in front of the Luftwaffe.

The first plane was joined by another, and another. They seemed to be cruising up and down our train, peppering us with gunfire, and all the time our driver, who should have been awarded some kind of medal - perhaps he was, I never knew - kept steadily on, towing his string of battered coaches, racing towards Eastbourne through the gentle summer landscape. As we rattled into the town I think we probably felt like the occupants of a stage-coach just mauled by the Cheyenne, but a further shock was in store.

In front of us, drawn up beside the left hand platform, was the train we might have caught if we had reached Hastings station a few minutes earlier. It had been running a short distance ahead of us, and as we pulled alongside we could see it was now riddled, from end to end, with bullet holes. Every window had been shattered and clearly a number of people had been injured - as we watched, some were being lifted on to stretchers. I helped my mother out on to the platform, and slowly we made our way towards the place where the London train was waiting.

After a few days of Emmie's care M began to look very much better, and within a fortnight she really seemed herself again. Within the same period of time, I had found myself a job. Someone had suggested I should try the Law Society, where they were rumoured to be in need of typists; it wasn't the sort of work I had been used to, but I didn't really want anything too demanding and the pay was said to be good. I made my way to Chancery Lane, and was snapped up as soon as I put my head round the door. It didn't take me long to work out why.

We were placed, ten or fifteen of us, in a large room adjacent to the Law Courts. For the most part our work involved typing out official Court documents, and because of the documents' size our typewriters were mostly of vast proportions. Everything had to be done at speed, often with a be-wigged barrister peering over your shoulder, and there were to be no mistakes - none. No rubbings out. Any error meant the whole thing would have to be re-typed, and if you started getting through too much of that heavy parchment-like paper, that was probably the end of you.

I liked it, though. I liked the tension, and the nearness of the great courtrooms. I even liked the heading that had to be typed at the top of every document: *'In the High Court of Justice, Admiralty and Divorce . . . .'*

And by the time I was settled in at the Law Society, a cable had arrived to say that Hugh was safely in America. From that time onwards I received a letter about once every ten days, and I found that Hugh was a remarkable correspondent. Not only was he expert at stringing words together, he was also a natural diarist, perceptive and amusing. Because of wartime restrictions he was never able to say much about military matters or even specific places, but this didn't cramp his style. If the occasion had demanded it, Hugh would have had the ability to be entertaining on the subject of woolly socks.

Not surprisingly Emmie was intrigued by Hugh, particularly as we were now - apparently - going to get married, and I'm sure she and M had chats on the subject. Of course, it would have been better if the situation had not involved an impending divorce. Divorce was no longer regarded as an unmentionable aberration, but it was still frowned upon. On the other hand, Hugh was a significant personality, and he was well placed. In fact, he was a catch. Beside which, he had made a very good impression on my mother. I think, too, they all felt it was time something 'happened' where I was concerned; time I became linked to someone with the ability to control my will-o-the-wisp approach to life.

When a week or two had gone by M and I began to think seriously about finding an apartment of our own, but Emmie and her husband refused to allow it. We all got on well, and I think Emmie in particular enjoyed having us around. During much of her life she had suffered badly from asthma, and when war first broke out she had panicked and run away to the country. Renting herself a cottage in Sussex, she had told her husband to come and visit her at weekends. Until the bombs started falling on Bishopsgate, when she promptly returned and joined the WRVS. Now she was on duty regularly, dispensing tea and practical sympathy wherever the devastation was at its worst.

Once again we were more or less in the thick of things, but somehow it didn't seem too bad, and when raids came we simply took refuge in the bank's own underground shelter. I think we felt extra secure down there, but then, it was some shelter. The bank stood on the site of Crosby Hall, a medieval palace that had once belonged to King Richard III, and though this fifteenth century treasure had been removed, stone by stone, to a new site on the Thames Embankment - where I believe it remains to this day - its ancient cellars, unavoidably, had been left where they were. King Richard's wine store had been turned into strong rooms and record repositories and it was here, among shelves stacked high with the bank's filing system, that we sheltered from air raids. Superstitious *and* claustrophobic, I should have been in permanent fear either of being bricked up alive or of running into Richard III, but perhaps because of everything that had happened my panic mechanisms seem to have been suppressed (this suppression was not to prove permanent).

The summer wore on, and one day in the post I received papers citing me as co-respondent in Hugh's divorce. Enid's affair with Kenneth Darrell Waters had almost certainly been going on a good deal longer than my relationship with Hugh, but as a children's writer Enid had special reasons for needing to be protected from scandal. I knew that Hugh was well aware of this, and that he wanted to protect her - therefore, he had allowed her to initiate divorce proceedings. He might have arranged to be 'caught' with a woman hired for the occasion, thereby protecting the reputation of his future wife, but when that sort of charade was played out everyone concerned usually knew all the facts anyway, and it simply wasn't Hugh's style. At the time I did, I think, feel a small niggle of resentment. But at least the divorce was going to be amicable, and that meant Hugh would enjoy more or less unlimited access to Gillian and Imogen.

On November 5th Hugh returned from the US. He looked thin and exhausted, but the assignment had been a success. He had fallen in love with America, and the feeling appeared to have been mutual. There was a strong likelihood, he told me, that he would very soon be going back.

But in the meantime he was home on leave, and for a few weeks it was marvellous. We dined at Rule's and the Waldorf, and spent a lot of time at the theatre, where we saw Ivor Novello's *Dancing Years* no fewer than four times (we never actually saw Novello himself, and it was not until years later that I realised this was because the star was serving a prison sentence for having apparently purchased Black Market petrol. In wartime this was a serious offence, but considering the morale-boosting quality of Novello's work his punishment does seem to have been a bit harsh). We also attended a performance of *Dear Miss Phoebe*, a romantic musical based on Barrie's *Quality Street*, and shortly afterwards Hugh gave me a copy of the book. It was the first present he had given me. Apparently, I reminded him of Phoebe (he also said I bore a striking physical resemblance to the actress Jessie Matthews, but looking in the mirror I could detect no basis for this).

For a few weeks Hugh was on duty at the War Office, but we had always known he was going back to the US, and on March 28th he once again set off in convoy across the Atlantic. It was dreadful, but I did realise that it could have been so very much worse. At least, when he got to the other side, he would be more or less secure.

And my job at the Law Society was working out well. So far I hadn't made too many mistakes, nor, apparently, had I been too slow. It was repetitive work, but I did enjoy the atmosphere and might have hung on indefinitely, if a young female solicitor had not asked me to copy some notes for her. The following day she asked me to do some more, then I was summoned to her office and invited to take the place of her secretary, who was about to leave. It was a better job, with a higher salary attached to it, and I would have been mad to turn it down. Anyway, I liked my new employer. It turned out she was involved in looking after the private legal problems of servicemen and women, and just recently she had been up to her eyes in something I found astonishing. Unnoticed by most of the country, Parliament had voted through a measure which allowed anyone currently in the armed services to obtain what amounted to a 'quickie' divorce. Each applicant was asked to produce a statement, written or verbal, and to pay over the sum of five pounds. Provided no credible defence appeared to be forthcoming, the marriage was usually terminated - as far as I could see - within weeks. This was odd and rather disturbing, but the war had already spawned thousands of spur-of-the-moment unions, and in a world where ancient certainties were crumbling fast many of these marriages had probably been doomed from the start.

The petitioners often came to my employer's office, and on such occasions I was expected to take notes. I had seen rather a lot of life by this time, but even so I was startled by some of the things I heard. In almost every case the petitioner was male and drawn from the lower ranks - officers, generally speaking, would have sought private advice - and usually his statement concerned some occasion when he had arrived home to find his wife embroiled in what might be termed a compromising situation. The bitterness, and the language used, left a sour taste in my mouth.

I did the job, though, and my new boss seemed to feel we worked well together. I suppose we did. But I don't believe I ever confided in her, or asked her advice about my own situation. It wasn't the sort of thing I could have done. In any case, my own life didn't seem real.

By the beginning of 1943 millions of people across the world had been killed, tortured or driven from their homes by the nightmare emanating from Berlin. Every day thousands more were added to the toll, and with these sort of echoes haunting the atmosphere it seems difficult to understand how any decent human being, living under the same sun, could have managed to enjoy a cheerful second. But life doesn't work like that. If it did, the human race would probably have given up a long time ago.

In London things could often be grim, particularly for those who had suffered bomb damage, but most of us still managed to get some pleasure out of life. M and I wandered round the shops, gossiped about celebrities and consumed endless Corner House snacks, just as we might have done in peacetime. Sometimes I met one of my old girl-friends, and once or twice Reggie came to London (a previously undetected heart problem had rendered my cousin unacceptable for military service, but he regularly did a stint on fire watch). Once, we got together with Aunt Dolly. And of course there were always Hugh's letters – varied, funny and romantic. The next time we met it would be 'after the divorce'.

After the Divorce seemed like some strange, far-off place - an unexplored country where everything was going to be different. When we reached that place something hugely important was going to happen – some strange, significant rite of passage – and life would never, ever be the same again.

The trouble was, I had never been able to deal with anything that was too far away in the future, and I really wasn't sure how I felt about it all. I did know one thing, though. I knew that I wanted a situation where Hugh and I would somehow be together, where M would not be far away, and where we would all be safe.

Finally, towards the end of August, Hugh's solicitor wrote to let me know that the divorce had now been pronounced Absolute. Hugh Alexander Pollock was a free man, and for that matter Enid Mary was a free woman. On the sixth day of October, she was married to Kenneth Darrell Waters.

Looking back, it seems a bit odd that none of this reached the newspapers. These days the divorce of a prominent writer would certainly succeed in stirring up a bit of media attention. But this was wartime, and while the entire nation was living under stress editors did not want to print stories that might have a negative impact. Noddy and the Famous Five were yet to be invented, but millions of children already took Enid Blyton to bed with them, and while they explored her mysterious caves, played in her poppy-filled meadows and caught up with her small-time crooks, they remained in a world where evil was generally fragile and good almost always secure. Already, Enid Blyton had become part of the fabric people clung to. Who wanted to be told that her personal world was a broken down sham?

And it wasn't only newspaper sensitivity. Enid and those around her were well aware of the need to preserve her image, and with Hugh's willing co-operation they pursued this aim industriously. Perhaps because Hugh had helped to build the Blyton legend he never ceased to be protective towards it; and so Enid slipped soundlessly from one marriage to another. As far as her public were aware, there had been no change in her domestic arrangements. Right up to the day of her re-marriage, children reading *Sunny Stories* were regularly shown a picture that included 'Gillian's Daddy' – away in the Army, like so many Daddies, but still a powerful presence in the life of his family.

In reality, though, Hugh was free, and as this began to sink in I did feel a sort of deep satisfaction, even if it was going to be some time before anything happened for us. Since Hugh was scheduled to be in America for months yet, there was hardly going to be a hasty wedding.

And then I received a cable from Hugh. He had obtained special leave, and would be coming home at once. As soon as he arrived, we would be married.

*   *   *   *   *

XV

Hugh and I were married on October 26th, in the City of London's Guildhall Register Office. A month or so earlier our ceremony might have taken place in one of the building's more splendid chambers, but a well aimed bomb had ruled that out and instead we were directed to a makeshift room nearby - here the only concession to elegance was a hastily imported set of gilt legged chairs. As for the marriage ritual, it seemed bewilderingly brief and made little impression on me. Since that day I have witnessed various register office ceremonies and they have all seemed to last twice as long, but this was *my* wedding and therefore bound to be odd. My ring was made of platinum, which was fashionable at the time, and Hugh told me he had had some words engraved on the inside. He didn't tell me what they were, though, and since the ring has never been off my finger - a superstition handed down by my mother - I have never found out.

Hugh was in uniform and I wore a rather smart navy blue suit, with a small hat. My mother, of course, was there, and Emmie with her husband, but to the best of my recollection there was no-one else. Hugh had not even provided himself with a Best Man. I should have liked Reggie to be present - not to mention Aunt Dolly - but in October 1943 people didn't often travel the length of two counties just to see a relative tie the knot.

Besides, it didn't feel like a wedding, and I didn't feel like a bride. For me there had never been anyone but Hugh - not one other man on whom I had wasted a moment's serious thought. But Hugh had once belonged to someone else, and in the eyes of the church, presumably, he still did. Which was why we were being united in a small, plain room beside a bombed out building. Hugh seemed abstracted too, and I wondered if similar ideas could possibly be going through his head. He had been brought up in Scotland, in a deeply religious household, and if either of his parents had survived to see our wedding day they might have been less than ecstatic. Hugh may have entertained such thoughts, or they may have crossed his mind. But, though I didn't know it then, they weren't the main reason for his abstraction.

Hugh's divorce had gone through, his former wife had re-married and he was about to do the same. By this time, arrangements concerning access to Gillian and Imogen should have been, as it were, fully operational. But they weren't, and furthermore they weren't going to be. Enid was starting to make it abundantly clear that she had no intention of letting her former husband see either of his daughters. Not then, not in a few months' time. Not ever, if she could help it.

Afterwards we went back to the Waldorf for lunch and the atmosphere lightened, I think. But I'm not sure of anything because I have no real memories of that day. I never did have. All I know is that Hugh and I were all right, at least after everybody had gone. A few days later he went back to the US, and I returned to my job.

Everything was almost as it had been before. I wore a plain band on the third finger of my left hand, and I had turned into something people called 'Mrs Pollock', but nothing had really changed. I had rounded a sharp bend in the road, but the view stretching in front of me was still a jumbled blur.

* * * * *

XVI

When I first started feeling unwell I tried not to take any notice. I said nothing and I carried on working, but instead of getting better things grew rather worse. An idea started forming in my mind, and real fear took hold of me. At last I went to the doctor, and my fears were confirmed.

I was going to have a baby.

Some time before, when I was very young, it had occurred to me that one day I might have a child. I had supposed it would be a girl - I couldn't imagine having a son - and of course she would be unusual. Beautiful *and* intelligent. At the time this prospect had seemed quite attractive, but then it had all been a long way off in the future and there had always been the chance it might never happen. During the last four years I had hardly given such matters a thought; my life simply hadn't been heading in that sort of direction. Eventually, it had become something that wasn't going to happen.

It was happening, though, and I was panic-stricken because I felt that this was something I couldn't do, not now. Some strange creature was going to take over my body, growing and developing inside me, destroying my health and taking away my freedom, and I could not get away from it. I was trapped, and my only escape was going to be through the repellent nightmare known as childbirth. Claustrophobia swept over me in waves.

My mother, of course, was delighted, and so was Emmie. Then I telephoned Hugh, and as usual he coped very well. I knew he was pleased, but at the same time he understood my feelings, and calmed me down. The first thing I had to do, he pointed out, was see a reliable gynaecologist. I must go, he stressed, to the best available, and remember that cost was totally irrelevant.

Within a few days I had been referred to Harley Street, to a consultant whose name was Geoffrey Bourne, and almost immediately I knew I had come to the best possible place. Geoffrey Bourne had a pleasant, reassuring manner. He examined me, and listened while I told him how I felt. After that he took a photograph from his desk and asked me to look at it. Apparently it was a picture of his own sixteen-year-old daughter.

'When your daughter, or your son, is sixteen years old. . . ' He smiled at me. *'You will look back on this day, and the way you are feeling now, and you won't be able to believe it.'*

He confirmed I was approximately six-and-a-half weeks pregnant, and as far as he could tell the baby was all right, but he was a little concerned about my general health. In the long term, he was sure, I would be fine, but just for now he would like me to spend a short spell in hospital, perhaps two or three weeks. I would be going in for rest and observation. Apparently he knew where he would like to send me, but there was a good deal of expense involved, so perhaps I would like to discuss that aspect with my husband.

Hugh gave the go-ahead immediately, and a day or so later I was admitted to St Mary's Hospital, Paddington. In fact, to the Lyndoe Wing. By the 1980's this was to become the most fashionable maternity ward in London - Princes William and Harry were both born there - and even in the middle of World War II it was already a remarkable place to be. The atmosphere was relaxing, the nursing care amazing. I went in armed with a pile of novels, and when I wasn't reading I simply slept. My mother and Emmie both came to see me quite frequently, but in between their visits I didn't want to see anyone. I just rested….and rested.

When I was feeling a bit better, Geoffrey Bourne had suggested, I could try strolling along to the nursery and having a look around. I'd soon start to feel different about babies. On this one detail, though, he was wrong. I did visit the nursery and I did take several looks at its occupants, but the more I looked the worse they seemed. They didn't even seem *young*. Most of the time their red, wrinkled faces were twisted by what appeared to be unexplained fury, and when this became too wearing they settled into a baleful stare. No doubt their families adored them and they all grew into utterly charming adults, but - awful as it sounds - I thought they were repellent.

I was getting used to the idea, though. I also felt very much better, and at the end of three weeks Mr Bourne said my physical condition had been transformed. There had been 'murmurs all over my heart', and I gathered he had not been sure I would make it through the pregnancy. Now, I was a different woman.

And Hugh had arrived home. As usual his leave would not be lasting long, but before disappearing again he wanted to make all the necessary arrangements. Emmie had been marvellous, to me and to my mother, but with a baby on the way we couldn't stay on in her apartment. It was time we went back to the country. Hugh and I both liked the idea of Dorking, and with his customary energy he almost immediately located a house on the outskirts of Dorking town. Called Whitegates, it was to be let for a period of nine months or so, with an option to continue. It wasn't old, or particularly interesting, but it was bright, roomy, well furnished and well equipped - in fact, just about everything I wanted at that particular moment. In addition, the local GP turned out to be none other than Dr Brice-Smith, who had looked after us all at Denbies.

Evidently working well as a team, Hugh and M organised the move. Afterwards he stayed on for a few days, then he went back to America. We had talked about names, and in the end had agreed upon Ian Alexander for a boy, Barbara Ann for a girl.

It was more than usually horrible when Hugh left, but M and I were thrilled with our new home, and I was feeling better than I had felt for a long time. I still didn't want to make a study of babies, but by this time it had struck me that they came with one out-standing advantage. They needed to have things bought for them - clothes, particularly. Hugh was making me a very satisfactory allowance, and as he was also paying all regular bills I had every incentive to indulge in a little shopping. My child might be making its way into a sad, confusing world, but if I had anything to do with things, it would own more matinee coats than any other baby this side of the Atlantic. It was due to be delivered round about the beginning of August, and when the time came I was to enter a privately managed maternity clinic known as Mount Alvernia. Run by Roman-Catholic nuns, Mount Alvernia was comfortably placed on the outskirts of Guildford, just four or five miles from where we were living, and this was re-assuring. Now and again I was seized by little spasms of uneasiness, but on the whole I was calm. The early summer weather was pleasant and very warm, and I was feeling well.

Until about the middle of July, when an unthinking grocer's boy placed a heavily loaded box in my arms. Immediately I felt a sort of discomfort, but it faded and I didn't give it much thought until that evening, when I climbed on a stool to adjust the blackout curtains, and a stabbing, frightening pain shot through my lower back. The pain came and went over the next few days, but it didn't get any better and soon I could hardly bear to lie down or even sit. M told me briskly that symptoms of this sort were common, particularly during the later stages of pregnancy, and I accepted she was probably right. But I did wish this particular symptom could have held off just a bit longer.

At the weekend, Emmie came to see us. By this time I was only comfortable when I was standing at the ironing-board, and it was a relief just being able to talk about it. Emmie didn't say much, but she made an excuse to go out shopping and on her way she called in on Dr Brice-Smith. An hour later he came to see me, and by that evening I was installed inside Mount Alvernia. I had been examined, and told that the baby had somehow or other turned itself upside down. It was an unfortunate development, but the doctors would do their best to put things right.

My mother was terribly upset. She believed it was her fault, that she should have realised - but she couldn't possibly have known.

They started trying to turn the baby, but they couldn't manage it, so instead they decided to speed up delivery. And then the pain began. In the end they gave me something - I don't know what - and after that I didn't know very much about anything. I came round at some stage, but all I could see was what appeared to be an ocean of blood, so I went back to sleep again.

The next time I surfaced, I was back in bed and everything seemed to be clean and orderly. The pale beginnings of a glorious dawn were just visible outside the window, and I was alone in the room.

One of the white-robed Sisters appeared, bending over me, and she was smiling.

'You've got a little girl,' she said.

Another nun brought my baby to me, and as she held out the tiny, six-and-a-half pound bundle I could hardly believe my eyes. Her skin was clear and smooth, and she had quite a lot of curly brown hair. She didn't even look bad-tempered, just tranquilly asleep.

Well, I thought, that's different.

* * * * *

XVII

Mount Alvernia was an oasis. The white-robed Sisters were kind, and they were fun. *'So that's the cause of all the trouble'*, one remarked as she studied a photograph of Hugh. As the heat wave wore on some were rumoured to be sun-bathing on the Convent's large, flat roof, but there wasn't much information on this. Since I was very tired and the baby had developed jaundice - nobody told me, at the time, that this could have been serious - we were kept in for about a fortnight, which was fine as far as I was concerned, though not so good for my poor mother, who visited me every day, toiling up a steep hill from the nearest bus stop. Following an arrangement made before Hugh's departure she had organized a delivery of flowers in his name, and of course she had sent the all-important cable. *'Rosemary Ann arrived safely. . . .'* I had changed my mind about 'Barbara'.

At last we went home, and Rosemary Ann made her first public appearance in Dorking High Street. Like all babies she attracted attention, and like most mothers I was proud of her. I had spent much of my life avoiding reality. Even my own wedding hadn't meant much, though there had been reasons for that, but this *was* reality and I was happy, though not, of course, all the time. There were moments when fear took possession of me, and there seemed a lot to be afraid of. Germs, for instance. Because of various problems I hadn't been able to breast feed for long but the bottle had seemed a reasonable alternative - until I started to worry about the millions of microbes that just might be slipping through. I became paranoid, making feeds only to throw them away and start again, until finally my mother intervened and forced me to see reason. She was a tower of strength, and I can't imagine what I would have done without her, not that we didn't argue. Rosemary Ann was almost certainly the only grandchild she was ever going to get, and she intended to occupy a central role. There were days when I wasn't even allowed to push the beautiful, bouncy pram we had somehow managed to acquire. But M knew exactly how to manage a small baby, and that was a lot more than I did. Besides which, it was high time she started to get some pleasure out of life.

Hugh came home in September, and perhaps fortunately showed no sign whatsoever of wanting to push a pram. He did contribute one thing, though. He made it abundantly plain he couldn't stand the name Rosemary. For one thing, as the child grew she was certain to be called either Rose or Mary, neither of which appealed to him. It might be too late to name her Barbara, officially, but he wasn't going to let a little thing like that stand in his way. As far as he was concerned, she would always be known as 'Babs'.

Actually 'Rosemary' had begun to seem rather a mouthful, especially when attached to a small baby. My mother thought so too, and she rather liked the sound of Babs. Before very long the baby's official names had been all but forgotten and I had begun using a variant of my own. I had started to call her 'Ba'. I didn't really know why, but later I discovered this was a name once applied - by her family - to the poetess Elizabeth Barrett Browning. Since that time, I have never really liked the name Rosemary.

None of this mattered, though, because everything else was rather wonderful. If I had been cross-examined I would have been forced to admit that I still didn't feel married, but at the same time I did feel we were a real family - my mother and I, and Hugh and Babs. And once the war was over there would be Hugh's other daughters too, at least for part of the time.

The war, Hugh thought, could not last all that much longer. Soon, perhaps very soon, there was certain to be an Allied invasion of the Continent, after which Hitler's days would be numbered. If some major mistake were to be made there might still be wastage of lives and time, but the end of World War II had got to be close. Hugh envied, enormously, those who were going to be involved in that final assault. But other options were still being put in front of him. Soon there would be new priorities for everyone to worry about, and from the Government's point of view one of these was likely to be India. Turbulence was spreading through the sub-continent, and there was a question mark over its future. It was a situation that called for skilful handling at every level, and perhaps because he possessed the right mixture of abilities Hugh was now offered an appointment in New Delhi. I realised he was tempted - apart from anything else, he had served there twenty years earlier. In those days, though, the whole thing had been a great adventure. Now he was older and recently re-married, with a small child. I don't believe I put any kind of pressure on him. I didn't mean to do so, and I don't remember saying 'you can't go', or anything of that sort. But India was a terribly long way off, and the idea was a shock. Even when the war was over, Ba and I were hardly likely to be joining him on the other side of the world.

Anyway, the United States wanted Hugh back - again - and as the choice was left to him, in the end he picked America. He liked and valued the American people and he had made a lot of friends, notably Wendell Endicott, the Massachusetts delegate who had first asked our War Office to send him over. His trans-Atlantic acquaintances were certainly generous, and as Christmas approached a substantial package reached us from New England. Knowing what things were like in Britain, they had sent stockings and other items for me, and two exquisite gifts apparently intended for a little girl of six or seven years old. (They seemed to be rather vague about the precise details of Hugh's family circle, but in the circumstances most men – at that time, anyway - would probably have blurred the edges a bit). One of the gifts was a large doll, the other was an apricot-coloured velvet coat. It would be years before either could be of any use to Ba, so at my suggestion we immediately sent both over to Green Hedges. The doll, I believe, was given to Gillian - though at twelve she was getting a bit too old for dolls - but the coat, Enid said in a brief acknowledgement, was too small for either child. Accordingly, she had decided to sell it.

The Nazi war machine may have been heading towards its demise, but it wasn't finished yet and as the wintry days grew shorter there was an increase in bombing raids, at least around our area of Surrey. These attacks weren't usually severe enough to justify taking a three-month-old baby out of the house and into an air-raid shelter - particularly not in the middle of the night - but they were bad enough for some of us to crouch underneath an up-turned sofa. 'Some of us', in this context, being me, my mother and the baby. Hugh invariably slumbered peacefully throughout. Once he had gone to bed, he had no intention whatsoever of disturbing himself for the German Air Force.

Christmas came and passed, and Hugh went back to America. Through a wet, dreary January the bombing raids went on, and then one evening there was a bad one, and I panicked. I just wanted to get away, to run away into deep, untouched countryside, until I got to a place where the bombs wouldn't find us so easily.

I looked through the advertisement columns of the *Lady* magazine, and there it was. *'Rooms to let in Shropshire farmhouse. Two bedrooms and a sitting-room. . . home cooking. . . every service provided. Beautiful countryside'*.

Eagerly I showed this to M, who was sick of the bombing too, perhaps even more so than I was. We telephoned the number displayed and got in touch with a Mr and Mrs Cohen, who told us their farm was known as Whitcott Stile. It was outside the village of Bishop's Castle, which - the map told us - was strikingly close to the Welsh Border. It sounded wonderful, and without any hesitation I booked us in for a period of three months. The only problem was going to be the journey. Because of Ba we would have to take a reasonable amount of baggage, and the western edge of Shropshire was not just down the road. Neither of us was feeling particularly energetic, and with a baby to worry about as well as the baggage it was going to be quite a struggle. Then once again Emmie came to the rescue. She would travel up with us, stay for a night or two, and travel back again.

When we set out it was raining, an awful February day, and things got worse as we travelled northwards. Cocooned in several protective layers and with little more than her nose showing to the world, Ba seemed almost indifferent. The rest of us were soon too exhausted to care. By the time we reached Bishop's Castle a gale was blowing, but the little country station seemed peaceful, and it didn't take long to find a taxi. Within minutes, we were being wrapped about by the reassuring warmth of Whitcott Stile.

The Cohens were cheerful, friendly and obviously anxious to do everything they possibly could for us. Childless themselves, they had been looking forward to having a baby in the house, and they weren't the only ones. There was an Italian prisoner-of-war working on the farm, and as we drove up he was on hand to help with our luggage; in reality he had obviously been longing for a glimpse of *la bambina*. Perhaps he had children of his own - I don't remember, now - or perhaps he just thought that having a small child around would somehow make ordinary, familiar things seem that bit closer. He asked if he could hold our well upholstered bundle just for a moment, and rather uneasily I handed her over, whereupon she screamed as if he had stuck pins into her. It's a pity he couldn't have known that at a later stage the bundle was to become rather fond of Italy.

We were dizzy with tiredness, but when we woke the following morning it was wonderfully obvious that we had landed on our feet. Whitcott Stile was comfortable, the food was excellent and Mr Cohen was an interesting man who loved to talk, especially to M. He had been awarded the OBE, apparently for something that involved telephone engineering, and thirty or forty years earlier had been sent to install telephone equipment in the bedroom of King Edward VII. (Assured the room was empty he had been getting on with his work when a deep, guttural voice had addressed him from behind the bed curtains - this had turned out to be the King. His Majesty had been extremely pleasant, even charming, but according to Mr Cohen had spoken with a decidedly German accent.)

The rain stopped, and spring came on quickly. Setting out to explore we discovered long, twisting lanes crowded with primroses, soaring beech woods and fields full of wriggling lambs. And one day, pushing on just to see what was round the next bend, we found something else. Something that has been printed on my mind ever since. In front of us the fields sloped away towards a valley, and on the other side there was a sprawling hunk of downland, the Long Mynd. Beyond, the hills of Brecon lay spread out like a rumpled counterpane. Everything was coloured in the greys and greens of spring, and the air in our faces smelt of clean downland and opening flowers. And I knew, at that moment, that I'd never forget.

The village of Bishop's Castle was just about half a mile from Whitcott Stile and we often went there, prowling about the picturesque streets and sometimes slipping in for a cup of coffee before making our way home for lunch. It puzzled me, at first, that in this magic place there seemed to be hardly any food shortages. It wasn't that the war had not touched the Border Country; like everybody else, people here had sons and daughters, husbands and fathers and brothers serving in the armed forces and in other dangerous occupations. They listened to the wireless and read the papers and worried, while on their land the old and the very young, the land girls and the POWs toiled to produce food for the War Effort. But always there was enough for local people, and it seemed to me that this was right.

Now and again we took a bus into Shrewsbury, but with a baby this could be awkward. The Cohens repeatedly offered to take charge of Ba for an hour or so, but I was reluctant to leave her - so far, after all, she hadn't often been out of my sight. Eventually, however, I agreed and one sunny spring morning she was handed over. We went off to Shrewsbury, and when we returned two or three hours later she was sitting in the middle of the kitchen floor. Happy and very dirty, she was surrounded by the contents of the cutlery drawer, and she also had to hand a few other items that had caught her attention. Everybody said she had had a marvellous time.

June came, and we heard that it had happened at last, the thing we had all been waiting for. Allied Armies had stepped ashore on the beaches of France, and with every day that passed more towns and villages were getting their liberty back. It seemed almost unbelievable; but at the same time we knew the end could not be in sight yet. There was a long way to go, and there would be heavy losses. If you had someone in the front line, this was probably the worst moment of all.

It was another hot summer, and perhaps because we were out of doors so much I began to feel fit again. M was better, too, and though Ba was too fair-skinned to stand much direct sunlight, she was beginning to look less fragile than she had done. She loved the animals. . . the sheep who came to be shorn outside our windows, the cows with their calves. Even the huge bull who was occasionally brought from some distant pasture to engage in rituals of a sort best left to the imagination.

Bees hovered round the hedges, and the ripening corn wore a deep, burnished glow, like the shimmer of twenty-four carat gold. It wasn't fair. Only a few hundred miles away in France the crops were being trampled and stained with blood, and we were surrounded by all this glory.

We made friends too, that summer. There was the tramp - eccentric - who lived near the edge of a wood, occupying a house he had built from empty petrol drums. Whenever he heard us approaching with the pram he would come rushing out for a glimpse of our Little Princess, and once we even accepted an invitation to inspect his home, which turned out to be crammed with labour saving devices, mostly constructed from bits of string and clanking iron pulleys. He wore a rusty top hat - always tugged off for our benefit - and spoke like a Shakespearean actor. Perhaps he was a Shakespearean actor.

Then there was the easy-going postman who ambled around on a battered bicycle. The day came when our morning delivery didn't arrive, and several hours later he was discovered, a little distance from the road, crouching beside a stream. He was dropping his letters into the water, and as they drifted away he could be heard murmuring to them. *'There. . . you find your own way.'* He must have suffered some sort of trauma. Possibly he had lost someone in the war. We never knew what happened next.

When harvest time came everyone worked from before dawn until late in the evening. Our lanes filled up with loaded, slow-moving wagons, and there seemed to be people toiling behind every hedge. This went on for weeks, then all at once it was over. Everything was in, and silence settled over the acres of stubble. Gates stood wide open, like the doors of rooms that have just been emptied, and on our morning walks we were met by thin strands of mist. It was autumn.

And one evening I got a telegram to say Hugh was back in London. When we spoke on the telephone he sounded tired, but it seemed he would be in Shropshire within a couple of days. Which was marvellous, and not only for all the obvious reasons. Hugh would stay for a week or two, probably, and I would show him all our places, the things we had found. He might even meet the petrol drum man. Then of course he would have to go away again, and we would stay on for a while.

When Hugh arrived he was obviously exhausted, and he was painfully thin. He was irritable, too. No, in a blazing temper would be closer to it. Still, I couldn't wait to see the look on his face when Ba appeared in front of him. She was walking now, and she was incredibly beautiful, or so we thought - M and I and the Cohens, and the Italian prisoner-of-war, and the people of Bishop's Castle.

Hugh glanced at her, then he looked away.

I couldn't believe it. I drew attention to her hair, and her eyelashes, and the specially chosen dress she was wearing. He said something - I've no idea what - and a little while later suggested it must be past her bedtime.

I realised he had two daughters already. I also realised he had not seen either of them for a very long time and I thought that was absolutely dreadful. But it didn't mean – mustn't mean - his youngest child had no right to a place in his life. Perhaps because she rarely expected much from men, my mother was more philosophical. She pointed out that he was tired, and probably had a lot on his mind. Anyway, men were like that.

After supper, the Cohens came in. They had been looking forward to meeting Hugh and I had been looking forward to showing him off. The conversation dragged on for a while, but it was awkward. Pale and tight lipped, Hugh made it plain he could hardly wait to get rid of them. This was natural enough, probably, but I could see they were hurt and I was upset on their behalf. And Hugh did not normally go around hurting people for no reason at all.

Worse was to come, though. With the arrival of morning, my happy vision of staying on in Shropshire evaporated like the mist streaming up from the valley. To begin with, Hugh was not going back to America. The war could not have more than a few more months to run, and this had definitely been his final mission. From now on he was going to be in London, and I would no longer be permitted to hang about in Shropshire. He had been making enquiries about a London apartment, and thought he might have found what he wanted. He planned to go back, the next day, and start making arrangements - we would be joining him, he hoped, before the end of the following week. He accepted that my mother would be coming to live with us, and for me that was just about the only glimmer of comfort.

Of course, it should not have been like this. I should have been ecstatic, like all those other women whose men were beginning to think about coming home, but the truth was, I knew something was wrong. Wrong with Hugh. I couldn't work out exactly what it was, but it chilled me and at that moment I didn't really want the everyday experience of marriage. I had no thoughts about breaking things up, I loved Hugh and anyway we had a child, but just for the moment I wanted to go on living my own life - which meant Ba and my mother and the Cohens, and all the wonders of Shropshire. It would have been different if I had known what was going on, if Hugh had told me more, but he wasn't that kind of man and it was to be months before I began to understand.

If I had understood, that day in Shropshire, I might have been able to offer support, would certainly have felt differently. As it was, I only knew Hugh was in an impossible mood. My mother continued to point out that he could hardly be expected to hang around on the Welsh Border, and as for his being in an awkward temper, well, he had been under strain, and I would have to make allowances. She was well aware of the fact that her own marriage had been a disaster, and she didn't want mine to go the same way.

I did make allowances. There was no quarrel, and very sadly I told the Cohens we had to leave. They were upset as I had known they would be, and they were worried for us. What about bombing raids..? Everyone knew they hadn't stopped, and the Cohens begged me to consider leaving Ba with them. '*Let the baby stay where she's safe.*'

But of course I couldn't do that.

Hugh went back to London and we prepared to follow him, then two or three days later I received a call announcing that plans had changed. While making his way round to the War Office Hugh had been struck by a flying splinter from an unexpected bomb, and though he had not been hurt the incident had brought it home to him that London wasn't yet safe. He had since been in contact with an estate agent and had discovered a small furnished house in Buckinghamshire, very close to Eton - good from my point of view, because my cousin and Aunt Dolly lived nearby. Hugh was going to take the house for a period of something like eight months. After that, he reckoned, London ought to be all right.

The day before our departure, a box was delivered to Whitcott Stile. One or two of the local shops had got together and made us a farewell present of groceries and provisions. We were going back to the world of ration books, and we must - they said - have a little something to take away with us. Saying good-bye was awful, almost unbearable. Never in my life had I encountered such kindness or so much warmth, and I was going to leave it all behind.

Arrival in Buckinghamshire wasn't much fun, either. For nine months we had been free from food shortages, blackout curtains and bomb damage, and now here they were again. But Reggie was there too, and his wife and Aunt Dolly. It was wonderful to see them, *and* they took an interest in Ba. The little house was pleasant, too, and spring seemed to come early in 1945. On March 24th - my mother's birthday - we had tea in the garden.

Early in May, the war in Europe came to an end. Despite everything that had happened, I don't remember much about VE celebrations, except for the fact that our 'help' vanished for three days and nights, eventually turning up, battered and bleary-eyed, to announce that she had been with a group of Australian soldiers. I gave her some presents I had bought for her family, and told her not to come back because I didn't want her near my baby. It was an instinctive reaction. *'Ecstatic crowds. . . .'* the newspapers said, but I don't think I could quite take it in. The Blitz, Denbies, the Hastings bomb – Hugh's divorce and our marriage, Ba's arrival in the world - everything seemed to have come out of the war. It had been with us for so long that I could hardly begin to imagine life going on without it.

*　*　*　*　*

XVIII

Our new address was to be 84 Beaufort Mansions, Chelsea. Sited midway between the King's Road and the Embankment, it was a roomy, comfortable apartment, and I liked it. Being back in London wasn't so bad, either. A lot of the city had been destroyed, but I had known about all of that before Ba was born. There were buildings that would never be put together again, just as there were lives that were never going to be repaired, but at least it was all over, and everyone's wounds could be licked in peace.

Not that there weren't reminders of horror. Across the road from our apartment there was a Roman-Catholic convent, and every day we saw the black-robed nuns slipping in and out. They seemed calm and good-humoured and quite often they had a smile for Ba. Sometimes, through an opening in the wall, we spotted one or other of them pacing up and down, armed with a breviary. The place seemed drenched in peace. It no longer possessed a chapel, though. The gaunt, broken remains of its chapel loomed over the southern end of the building, empty and open to the sky. One evening during 1940 - I think - it had been on the receiving end of a direct hit. More than a hundred people had been inside the building and few, if any, had escaped. Plans to extricate their remains had been abandoned, at least for the time being, and in 1945 we were told they were there still there, buried under countless tons of rubble.

Hugh had inherited some furniture from his parents, and with the help of a few new acquisitions the apartment was soon made very habitable. I hadn't got much to complain about, and I didn't - complain, that is. My mother liked being in Chelsea, and I knew that just at the moment it was certainly the most convenient place for Hugh.

And at last I understood something of what Hugh had been going through. It had started when he returned from his last overseas assignment, just before our reunion in Shropshire. Knowing the war was in its final stages he had begun thinking about what he might do when the Army was behind him, and not surprisingly had contacted his former boss, Herbert Tingay, who was Managing Director of George Newnes Ltd. In 1940, Hugh had been one of Newnes' most notable assets - not only had he dealt effectively with authors such as Churchill and Edgar Wallace, he had also been a successful editor of the prestigious Strand magazine. On leaving, he had been assured that a responsible position would be more or less held for him, but in the summer of 1944 he had received a devastating shock. Because of his divorce, and for no other reason, Newnes had decided to turn its back on him. There was no longer going to be any place for him within the firm. Enid, apparently, had made it plain that she would not tolerate a situation in which her former husband was allowed to reclaim his old post - if he did return, she would terminate her relationship with the company. Her work was protected by contractual arrangements which had been very carefully set up - mainly by Hugh - and basically she had her publishers exactly where she wanted them. Most of the contracts covered no more than a handful of books, so any publisher could be got rid of without difficulty. And as Herbert Tingay apparently remarked to Hugh: *'In the end, Enid is more important to us than you are'*.

Hugh tried another firm, then another and another, then he didn't want to try any more. Of those he approached, some were already publishing Enid Blyton, some others nourished ambitions in that direction, and there was a third category. It soon became clear that the Blyton 'camp' had started to set in motion a serious smear campaign. Hugh Pollock, the story went, was an adulterous alcoholic who had shamelessly betrayed, then cold-bloodedly abandoned his brilliant and long-suffering wife. The damage was very widespread, and its impact went deep. It was a time when - rightly, in my opinion - any 'innocent' victim of divorce could be sure of attracting sympathy, and Enid was turning into that innocent victim. Of course Hugh had friends, but many of these were away in the armed Services, and most of the London publishing world lined up against him, with few prepared to tell or even recognise the truth. As much as thirty years later, a newspaper critic was to come up with the bizarre suggestion that Hugh - a valuable officer - had been sent to America, at the height of a desperate war, for no better reason than that Enid had begged the War Office to 'get rid' of her former husband.

Just two honourable figures were eventually to emerge. Eric Major, former Chairman of Hodder and Stoughton, who told the Sunday Express (1975) that 'Hugh Pollock made Enid Blyton, but she gave him the hell of a time', and George Greenfield, Enid's last literary agent, who met Hugh just once but liked him, and in a short biography of his former client was to be meticulous with the truth. In the summer of 1944, though, no-one came forward, and Hugh had no taste for continuing to batter himself against what amounted to a solid wall.

Just before his final departure from the USA, an American report to our War Office had observed that Colonel Pollock had 'done a superb piece of work'. The report went on: *'He has covered thousands of miles by air, train and motor. . . . he leaves this country commanding the highest respect and confidence. He has. . . from his general attitude just naturally played the role of a good will emissary. Relations between your good country and ours have automatically been strengthened as a result of Colonel Pollock's splendid and natural presentations. We are all very grateful to you. . .'*

The FSC Tactical School, Connecticut, presented him with a gift which bore the following inscription: *'To one of the Finest Officers we know in any Army'.* Perhaps not surprisingly, soon after his return he learned he was to be awarded the American Legion of Merit.

And now that he was back home the Army did have another assignment for him. This had nothing to do with active service or even with inspirational training programmes, but it was, on the whole, his kind of thing. Plans were being made for an official history of World War II, a detailed, factual account which was to be written and produced under Government auspices. As the conflict was so far advanced work was to start almost immediately, and those in charge were looking for people with the right mix of literary and military experience. Hugh was among the first to be singled out.

He was told he would be working under the roof of the Cabinet Office and would be allowed, more or less, to choose the people who were to assist him. He was to be placed in charge of a section dealing with the Normandy Invasion, but would probably go on to other things - it was a job, apparently, that might last some considerable time, almost certainly well beyond the ending of hostilities. Putting aside any other ideas about his own future career, Hugh bent his mind to the work in front of him. Aspects of the new job certainly appealed to him. But he must have felt bitter about the options that were now beyond his reach.

And there was something else. Hugh had once again approached Enid about the possibility of seeing Gillian and Imogen, and once again had been refused. So long as their mother had any say in the matter, there was evidently to be no contact of any kind. He had consulted a barrister friend about the possibility of taking legal action, and the friend had assured him there ought to be very little difficulty. No Court was going to refuse him reasonable access to his two older daughters. Under pressure, however, the friend had agreed that there *might* be repercussions. If Gillian or Imogen were to re-establish any sort of relationship with their father Enid might find some way of getting back at him - even, possibly, at them. She was by now a very rich woman and there was always the chance that she might, for instance, seek to cut the girls out of her Will. Some men might have thought, 'So what. . . ?' Hugh had already established a Trust which would cover his daughters' education. Both, almost certainly, would one day find husbands, and in the meantime it must have seemed unlikely that he would ever be too hard up to offer some support. Anyway, if such a Will did materialize it could very probably be set aside. And I don't think Hugh really believed Enid was capable of treating her own children in quite that kind of way. For the time being, though, he decided not to push things. I urged him not to let the situation go on, to demand access - at least to establish a link with Gillian, who was now fourteen years old - but at some point he had arranged a meeting with Imogen's nanny and from her he seems to have received the impression that both girls were 'all right'. No doubt the nanny was trying to set his mind at rest; I don't suppose she meant to suggest that either would be better off without her father, but Hugh felt he had had his answer, that he knew what to do. Gillian and Imogen were safe and well and happy without him, and for the time being at any rate he wasn't going to risk ruffling the surface of their lives. It was a tragic decision, for Hugh himself and for both girls. The hurt was to warp the rest of my husband's life, for Gillian and for Imogen it was in some ways to be disastrous. On a May morning in 1942, Gillian had walked with her father to Beaconsfield station, holding his hand all the way. She had known he was going to America and she might not see him for a while, but although she had overheard a few rows - quite a few, probably - she seems to have had no idea her parents were on the edge of breaking up. As the train steamed out, she noticed that Hugh waved until a bend in the track carried him out of sight, and that wasn't like him. Suddenly feeling she would never see him again, Gillian ran home in tears. She was not quite eleven years old. Later, she was to say that it wasn't *so* bad when her father failed to return, because 'lots of other people's daddies weren't coming home'. She did well at school, was helpful to her mother and did her best to get on with her new stepfather, and with her life. But the scars were there. As for little Imogen, just six-and-a-half when her parents separated, she probably suffered more than anybody. Born too late to remember the happier bits of her parents' marriage, knowing only that she had an irritable, abstracted father and a cold abstracted mother - she was five years old before she fully realised Enid *was* her mother - she turned for reassurance to the Green Hedges staff. She hadn't loved her father but she had wanted to, and she had wanted him to be on her side. One day, she thought in her dreams, he might turn into a real father, someone who would fight her battles for her. But then he left, and the dream was squashed. In *'A Childhood at Green Hedges'*, she says:

'I cried. . . not because I had loved my father, but for opportunities lost and second chances wiped out; much as one may after a death. I cried in fear of the future. . . .'

I made it absolutely plain that I thought Hugh should ignore Enid, and all the rumours about what she might or might not be prepared to do, and get in touch with both daughters. I didn't think their mother was likely to contemplate cutting them out of anything, and looking back now, I'm quite sure I was right. I also think I know why Enid behaved as she did. At the age of thirteen she had seen her own father leave his family for another woman. They had been very close and from her point of view the break was devastating, but eventually she managed to catch up with him, only to find that he had another daughter, worse, that he no longer wanted *her*. She had been supplanted. This shock seems to have marred the whole of Enid's life, and it may be that - consciously or unconsciously - she wanted to protect her own daughters from suffering the same trauma. I tried, repeatedly, to make Hugh change his mind. But he didn't believe the girls needed him, and he wasn't going to place them in the middle of a battle ground, just so that he could have the satisfaction of being in contact.

In the meantime, one morning a letter arrived from Enid. It wasn't addressed to Hugh, though, it was meant for me. I can't remember exactly how the letter began, but I know she expressed a hope that Hugh would not 'ruin my life as he had ruined hers'. If there was a formal purpose to the letter, it centred on a piece of information she had to impart. She didn't suppose Hugh had mentioned the fact that she, Enid, had not been his first wife. There had been someone else. In Scotland, when he was still very young. That marriage had also ended in divorce, but it had produced a son. The boy's name was Alistair, and he was now grown-up. He had also been in contact with *Green Hedges*, asking for his father's address.

I could hardly believe what I was reading. I stared at the letter, then I said something to my mother and we took it into the kitchen. Away from Ba and our daily help, we stared at it together.

M, of course, was less surprised than I was. Men had a way of hiding little details such as this, and at the time of his marriage to Enid Hugh had been nearly thirty-six years old. Considering his looks and popularity it followed there must have been quite a number of women, so why not another wife?

When Hugh came home that night I showed him the letter. And I asked if the story were true.

'Yes,' he replied, 'it's true.'

By this time I was not so much angry as puzzled and bewildered. 'Why didn't you tell me?' I asked.

'I didn't think it was important.'

Eventually he told me the story, or most of it. He and Marion Atkinson had been married when he was twenty-four years old and she was nineteen. She had belonged to a wealthy family, and his parents had liked her - not just because of the money, I gathered. They had wanted the marriage, and he had wanted to make up for the various ways in which he had already disappointed them, most especially over the family business on which he had turned his back. He had been attracted to her, too, at that stage. The marriage had gone ahead, a son had been born, then the First World War had arrived and by the time it was over Marion had run away with another man, taking her young son with her. Hugh had made maintenance arrangements and then persuaded his mother, who lived not far away, to keep an eye on Alistair. After that, he had come down to London and gone into publishing. Not wishing to distress his deeply religious parents - his father was an Elder of the Presbyterian Church - he hadn't thought about divorce, but as Enid was eventually to reveal through her diaries, she had set out to get him and when it emerged he was married already her uncle had helped to organise a divorce.

'But surely,' I said, 'you must have seen Alistair, sometimes.'

Not for more than twenty years

I tore Enid's letter up and put it on the fire, but shortly after this Hugh heard from his son. The boy's letter was touching, or so I thought, though actually, of course, he wasn't a boy any more, he was somewhere around thirty years old and planning to get married. He wanted his father to be at the wedding. Or at least, he wanted them to meet - somewhere, somehow. One line from his letter has always stuck in my memory. *'I'm so proud of you, Father. . . .'*

'You must go to his wedding,' I said to Hugh.

He hadn't got the time.

'Make some arrangement, then. You can't refuse to meet him.'

'Leave me alone. I'll think about it.'

Probably he did think about it, but to the best of my knowledge that was as far as he got. Looking back I can see that he may have been worrying about the financial aspect. Young men about to get married have a tendency to need money and plenty of it, and this was especially true at a time when wives - unless they happened to be heiresses - were not expected to contribute all that much. But as always with Hugh there was something else, something I didn't discover until many years later, when the information was handed to me by a television researcher. Marion's first son, it emerged, had been born in 1914 and christened Alexander, but two years later the little boy had died while his father was away at the Front. According to Alexander's death certificate just two persons were present at the time - young Mrs Pollock, and her father-in-law. Across the decades it's possible to feel the pathos of the scene this conjures up. Marion's suffering must have been appalling, and I don't suppose Hugh ever recovered from the anguish he felt. Edward Alistair – born one year after his brother - obviously failed to save the marriage.

I don't know, for certain, whether Hugh ever contacted his son. All I know is that Alistair got married, acquired a family, bought himself a farm in Aberdeenshire and in his fifties died tragically of cancer.

Gradually I began adjusting to Chelsea, and to real married life. Sometimes M and I caught a bus and went off to look at the West End shops. More often, especially when the weather was good, we went to Kensington Gardens, which were near at hand and better for Ba. The rationing system looked like going on indefinitely, but normality was creeping back and suddenly most of us were in a position to start thinking about the future, to stop marking time. And one day I woke to find that an old, long suppressed craving had been re-ignited inside me. I wanted to write again.

There was more to it, actually, than just the revival of a creative urge. I needed to make money. I knew Hugh's income must be reasonably substantial, but like a lot of men at that time he never discussed his salary's precise dimensions. Anyway, the divorce had been expensive, and he probably needed to be careful. To cover housekeeping and personal expenses I received an allowance of seven pounds a week, but living in London it wasn't enough and any application for extra funds led to maddeningly predictable exchanges. *'I really ought to buy another skirt. . . .'* *'I thought you got one of those last year.'* My mother, who had recently received five hundred pounds' worth of bomb damage compensation, was immensely, endlessly generous to me, but I didn't want that to go on, I wanted to look after her for a change. And what better way of getting extra money than by finding my way back into print?

Besides, though I was happy enough with Hugh, and I loved having Ba, there seemed to be a cage around me. By stringing words together, creating people and situations, I might somehow break out of that cage. I had done it before, and it had worked.

The Hastings bomb had destroyed almost all of my unpublished work, but one item had escaped because it had been lying about in the offices of John Murray. *Rustle of Silk. . . .* Murray had been fairly enthusiastic, but had explained that because of wartime restrictions they were unable to publish. In the end it had been returned it to me, and when I looked for it there it was, safe and clean and tidy inside its folder. I read it through, made one or two alterations and sent it back to John Murray's office. A fortnight later it was returned, accompanied by a short, courteous note. They still liked *Rustle of Silk*, but unfortunately their requirements had altered since the war. With great regret, therefore, they were returning my manuscript. This was disappointing and it also hurt, probably only another author would understand how much. I talked the situation over with Hugh, and he suggested I should go to another publisher. I didn't think he really wanted me to start writing again, and looking back, now, I suppose I can understand why; but he didn't oppose what I was doing, and I knew his advice was likely to be sound. I didn't want to keep pushing *Rustle of Silk*, though. I wanted to focus on something new. I had been reading about Mary, Queen of Scots - a particularly gripping biography that had wormed its way under my skin - and all at once I knew what I was going to do next. I was going to write a novel based on aspects of the Scottish Queen's life, and it was going to be a *tour de force*. Already I felt as if I had been drawn into her world. And what better way to make one's name than with a powerful historical novel?

I started work, and was taken over immediately. I seemed to feel Mary's frustration and terror prickling under my skin. I saw with my own eyes the grey walls, and the mist, and the shadowy friends who surrounded her. If my mother had not been there, of course, I might not have been able to do so much. Ba was growing fast by this time, and toddlers are time consuming. But M *was* there, and also we had a wonderful Cockney daily, a lady called Mrs Lang. I began spending long hours at the softly lit writing-table in our sitting-room, oblivious to the world around me, startled every evening by the sudden recollection that I had a husband coming home. Of course I broke off sometimes to help with the cooking or put Ba to bed, but generally speaking I wasn't in touch with reality, except when I stepped outside our flat.

At Hugh's suggestion I found myself an agent, Jasmine Chatterton. Miss Chatterton asked me to go and see her, and when I did she made some very helpful suggestions. She was encouraging, and I felt I was getting somewhere - I knew that I was. The work was going well, too. Hugh didn't take all that much notice, but M did and I could tell she was impressed by what she read.

Then the headaches began. I had been concentrating hard and supposed I needed to ease up a bit, but easing up - when I tried it reluctantly - didn't seem to make a lot of difference. Lying down in a darkened room didn't help either, nor did aspirin. There was an iron band tightening round my temples, and almost every day something winched it in a little bit further. In the end, I went to see a doctor. He examined me, talked a bit and finally ran some tests, after which he announced that I was probably entering the menopause, ten or fifteen years too soon. This, he thought, might easily have been brought on by my experiences during the war. Quite a number of women in their thirties were coming up against the same phenomenon; all one could say was that it was just another undesirable consequence of World War II.

It didn't really strike me as being all that undesirable. I didn't actually care about the menopause, I just wanted the headaches to stop. And I didn't want to be ill.

The doctor's advice was sensible enough. Eat a reasonable diet, get plenty of rest and exercise, try not to worry. As for the literary work, perhaps I ought to give that a miss, just for the time being. I did cut my working hours, but I couldn't give up on Mary, not yet. It was all going so well, and I had to carry on.

Slowly and steadily the headaches got worse, but there was just one thing that helped. If I could only get out and into Kensington Gardens, they tended to fade away. Morning after morning M and I made sandwiches and set out for the Gardens, taking Ba with us. By this time, fortunately, it was summer, and the weather was warm. Sitting in the dappled shade by the Long Walk, with M deep in a book and Ba playing on the grass, I let my mind drift and slowly, very slowly the iron band invariably began to unbuckle itself.

I had recently bought Ba several pairs of primrose-coloured socks, and for years afterwards I kept a pair of those socks. Now almost four years old, she had big blue-grey eyes and wavy hair that tumbled halfway down her back, and she was starting to turn heads. *'Now that's the kinda gal I like,'* said a GI to his companion, as they came to a standstill in front of us, *'can I give her a piece of gum, ma'am?'* (If I remember rightly she responded with a frosty look, but then she never showed any favour to her admirers).

It was a huge relief just knowing there was something that could check the headaches, but at home they rarely lifted for more than half an hour at a time and they were still getting worse. Gradually I began to lose my taste for the Queen of Scots. The story was going well, but it was almost as if my troubled subject had begun casting some of her burdens on to me. I struggled for a while, but in the end I couldn't go on.

Not that there weren't other possible causes. My husband was doing a demanding job, co-ordinating the work of a rather mixed team, and when he got home he was not always in a happy temper. Worse, I knew quite well that the temper wasn't only connected with stresses at work. I knew he found it infuriating if Ba still happened to be up when he got home in the evening - this was something that struck me as almost insanely unreasonable. Worse still, he had begun to resent my mother.

Of course I understood that Ba probably reminded him, too much, of Gillian and Imogen. What I didn't realise was that there may also have been a special reason for the other problem, that it may have been something more than mother-in-law phobia. During the latter part of Hugh's previous marriage, life at Green Hedges had begun to be dominated by a woman called Dorothy Richards, and this development had infuriated him. Taken on to cope with the birth of Imogen, Dorothy had stayed to look after the baby and in the process had become Enid's devoted friend and confidante, retaining this position until eased out by her employer's second husband. Even when Hugh and Enid embarked on a cruise - arranged for the dual purpose of speeding his recovery from pneumonia and saving their fractured marriage - Dorothy seems to have gone along too. She certainly had some good qualities - Imogen, neglected by mother, father and stepfather alike, loved and depended on her. She seems to have had very little time for men.

Already affected by childhood problems, by a failed earlier marriage and by the nightmare of the Western Front, Hugh had viewed Dorothy as a disaster. Now, he had my mother to contend with. As it happened they rather liked one another, and he had special affection for her cooking, particularly the sizzling curries she produced just for him. But she was an influence on me, a sometimes intrusive influence, and we were all living under the same roof. Increasingly he set out to provoke her, stirring up endless arguments, causing her pale skin to flush with resentment. Politically they were both life-long Tories, but Hugh managed to find endless differences between them and M gave as good as she got. There was never - I don't think - anything overtly personal about these disputes, they were more like ritual combat, but that didn't make them less distressing.

I blazed away at Hugh and I lectured my mother, but when the blood was up, as it were, they didn't notice me. I was furious with Hugh for being so antagonistic, but sometimes I was just a bit fed up with both of them. Why did she always have to react, when it was perfectly obvious he would keep quiet if only she would? She was easily goaded and he knew it, so he went on teasing - if you could call it that - and she went on reacting. I was in the middle, trying to keep them apart, and in the process was being used for target practice.

As always in this kind of situation weekends and holidays were the worst times, and our second Christmas in Chelsea was especially fraught. To cheer things up I decided to make a bowl of punch, and not having much idea how to set about it threw in just about everything I could get my hands on. The punch was described as having an interesting flavour - I didn't try any, myself - and it certainly proved popular. Hugh and M each consumed several glasses, and miraculously became rather mellow. Next day, they were both unwell. I was horrified, but at least we had got through a dangerous period without bloodshed.

And Hugh did relax, sometimes. He had a much loved gramophone on which he played a lot of jazz, Gilbert and Sullivan and traditional Scottish music, and he did not always ignore Ba. On Sunday afternoons he sometimes played draughts with her - good mental training, he said - and more than once she was taken to Buckingham Palace to see the Changing of the Guard (this scared her, particularly when she was picked up and passed over the heads of the crowd, but she would never have complained to Hugh, though in fact he might have understood).

During the winter my headaches got worse, perhaps because the Gardens were out of bounds, and by the time spring arrived I was desperate. I no longer had any work to blame, and it seemed increasingly unlikely that I was yet menopausal. I went back to my doctor, who decided I should be referred to a consultant, and having gone into everything the consultant became convinced my system was being poisoned. Around this time teeth were particularly fashionable suspects, and it was decided that half of mine should be removed. All at once.

As usual on these occasions Hugh was very considerate, and I was admitted to an expensive nursing-home, where under general anaesthetic they took out all but one of my upper teeth. I have been told this proceeding was not merely dangerous but probably unnecessary. I came through it, though, and it did give me a feeling that something was being done. The necessary replacements took some time and the headaches didn't evaporate, but once I was more or less sorted out Hugh booked a furnished cottage in the Sussex countryside, and together with M and Ba I was packed off for a three week holiday.

The cottage had a thatched roof, eyebrow windows and a garden crammed with roses. It was early June when we arrived there, and the summer was warm. One of our nearest neighbours was a young Scottish engineer - I think he had been put in charge of some construction project - and his small son, a carroty-haired four-year-old called Dick, struck up a friendship with Ba. Every morning Dick arrived at breakfast time. *'S'Baabs comin'oot. . . ?'* And for the rest of the day they played among the roses and the yew hedges, happy and mysteriously in harmony, like children in some Victorian story-book. During the afternoons M and I read and relaxed, and at weekends Hugh joined us from London, which was nice. I'd have missed him dreadfully, if he hadn't been able to come at all.

There were squirrels who played nut football in the loft, and a sugar-munching pony in the paddock next to the garden. And when our three weeks were almost up, the last of my headaches slipped quietly away. This development may have been linked to my brand new dental arrangements, or perhaps it had more to do with the sunshine of a Sussex garden. Perhaps it was a bit of both. Whatever the reason, I was cured.

I can still see that cottage, with its pretty sitting-room and little emerald lawns, and if I try I can hear the sound of a childish voice drifting through open windows.

'Coming, Dick. . . .'

Though as far as I could tell, she was usually the one in charge.

On the day of our departure it poured with rain - for the very first time - but for once I wasn't depressed. I was feeling so much better, for one thing, and although I had loved the cottage I was looking forward to going home. And I had the germ of an idea in my head.

*   *   *   *   *

Ida Pollock

Durrants Hotel

Hotel Viktoria

Ida's book jackets – Ida's novels have been produced under
10 different names

Painting by Ida Pollock of the Sussex coast

XIX

Perhaps inspired by Sussex, Hugh had decided it was time we acquired a pet. Ba ought not to be growing up without animals, and though a dog would be too much in London, a cat ought to fit in quite nicely. Ideally, a Siamese. He had owned several in the past, and couldn't imagine a more desirable pet.

Over this, M was in sympathy with him. A cat-owner for most of her own life she would have been more than happy with a glossy black tom like the one who had dominated our home in Hastings, but on the whole she was intrigued by the idea of entertaining some exotic foreigner. Hugh knew of a breeder in the Channel Islands, and when this person was contacted it emerged that she had two kittens available, one male and one female. Both would be ready within a few weeks. We plumped for the female, who had already been given the name Tschinki San Toi. According to Hugh she would be less outrageous, and with a Siamese this was evidently important. Besides, we might want to have kittens.

As befitted a VIP Tschinki San Toi was flown to London, and Hugh took the afternoon off to go and meet her. That is to say, he met a travelling basket the size of a Fortnum and Mason's hamper, brought it home by taxi and set it down in the middle of the carpet. As he lifted the lid, a splash of cream and chocolate popped up, tumbled over the edge and disappeared behind the heavy Victorian sideboard that had come from Hugh's old home in Scotland. The sideboard was immoveable, and so for that matter was the kitten, in fact, it was an *impasse* that seemed likely to last for some time. In Hugh's opinion she should be left alone until she felt like coming out, which would be soon after she started to get seriously hungry; but I wasn't so sure. Asked to choose between us and starvation, it seemed to me that Tschinki San Toi might well prefer the latter.

We tried reassuring noises, and saucers of milk. Ba was eager to coax her out, and I thought at first she might succeed. She wasn't a clumsy child or particularly noisy, and being smaller than the rest of us might seem less alarming. But still the kitten stayed behind the sideboard. In the end, my mother solved the problem. She had long experience of getting round awkward felines, and eventually she persuaded Tschinki that coming out might, after all, be the best option available.

And now that we were able to see her, she really was a beautiful thing. Most kittens are delectable, but this one could have knocked any competition hollow. We decided to call her Sally, Tschinki San Toi being for formal occasions, and she decided to eat her supper. After that we introduced her to her bed, to her litter-tray and finally to the rather boring communal gardens behind Beaufort Mansions. After which we brought her in, and she disappeared again.

Finding that she wasn't behind the sideboard, we searched every nook and cranny, from the space beneath the sofa in the sitting-room to the back of the Ideal boiler. We even looked inside the oven. But she wasn't anywhere.

I went to check on Ba, who with great reluctance had gone to bed half an hour earlier, and there I found Sally, curled up on Ba's bed, on top of the eiderdown. They were both fast asleep.

All things considered, Sally settled in quickly. My mother was her anchor, the centre of her universe, but she socialized quite nicely with all of us, and Ba - who tended to call her 'Sally-the-cat' - quickly learned to treat her as a Seal Point Siamese of ancient lineage expects to be treated. On the whole, she adapted with considerable *sangfroid* to the life of a city cat.

It seemed to me she would be better off in the country, though. We all would. Which took me back to the idea I had been chewing over when I first arrived home from Sussex. I had no desire to start writing again, not for some considerable time, anyway. The headaches had been terrifying and I had a feeling that any return to literary work might bring them back, even if I stayed away from the Queen of Scots. I still needed to make a bit of extra money, but my new idea would do just that, *and* enable us all to live a little distance outside London. Not too great a distance, because Hugh wouldn't want to give up the Cabinet Office, but he had commuted before - from Bourne End and from Beaconsfield - and my idea would make it well worth doing the same thing again.

I talked my plans over with M, then took my courage in both hands and put the whole thing to Hugh. Why didn't we buy a house in the country? Just far enough out to be clear of suburbia. There were thousands of likely properties about, and prices were at an all time low - in any case, the house could be made to pay for itself. If we wanted to, we could turn part of it into a tea-room. Just at first I hadn't been too clear about the details, but I had got all that sorted out now. After getting back from my holiday, I had even started learning how to make pastry. Up till then I had left such sophisticated techniques to my mother, but she had decided it was time I got started and rather to my surprise I had found I was good at it. I had also baked one or two cakes, and they hadn't turned out so badly, either.

Up to a certain point Hugh had kept one eye fixed firmly on the Daily Telegraph, but my tea-room caught his attention. *Why a tea-room*?

Because it was something I felt I could do, and it was something I wanted. Because it would make money.

Rather to my surprise, he didn't try to discourage me. He merely said that I had better get in touch with some agents and find out what was available. So the next morning I got going, and by lunchtime I had assembled a haul of about ten properties, all of which, rather like an eager Labrador, I dumped in front of Hugh. He glanced through them and we sorted out the most likely, then he said I had better go and look at one or two. He didn't have the time, but if I narrowed the list down a bit further, he might come along.

Over the next few weeks I travelled all over South-Eastern England. Leaving Ba at home with my mother, I made my way into Kent and Sussex and Buckinghamshire and Essex, on the way taking in Berkshire and Surrey, Hertfordshire and Middlesex. I saw some wonderful houses and some unbelievable bargains, and every evening I brought my reports and deposited them in front of Hugh. There was the Tudor house, near Lewes in Sussex, that was said to have formed part of Anne of Cleves' divorce settlement. Then there was the modern residence with a garden that backed on to Ascot race-course. Both of these were available at giveaway prices, and they were only the tip of the iceberg. Every evening, though, Hugh thought up fresh excuses. It was too far from London, or it was too close in. It had too many rooms, or it was too small and poky. If everything else failed, he would simply say the price was too high.

'It isn't,' I'd protest 'It's unbelievably cheap.'

'Rubbish! Anyway, they expect to be beaten down.'

'We can't ask them to take any less. . . .'

'Well, it's out of the question.'

I began to lose heart. Hugh had been humouring me, that was all. He had no intention of buying anything, or of leaving London. I might as well give up.

And then I found a small Georgian country house called The Rookery. It was near the village of Westcott, surrounded by rolling countryside and just three miles from Dorking. It had been built for a well-known eighteenth century mathematician, but by the 1930's had fallen into disrepair. After the war, it had been acquired by something called the Eyre Development Company, and as a result had been splendidly renovated. At the same time it had been divided into three sections, two maisonettes and one very large first floor apartment. The walls and ceilings were gleaming white, the floorboards had been professionally polished and there were newly equipped kitchens and bathrooms. On the other side of a long south terrace, lawns dipped towards the woodlands that clustered round the foot of Box Hill.

All three sections were to be let on lease, and two had been let already. A young doctor and his family had one of the maisonettes, and the large apartment was now occupied by a middle-aged 'tobacco heiress' - this lady, it seemed, had moved in with her unmarried daughter and their manservant. The best section of all, though, the second maisonette, was still available. There wouldn't be any possibility of running a tea room on the premises, but I might easily find something nearby.

Partly because of its proximity to Dorking, partly because it didn't appear to represent vast financial outlay, Hugh went with me to inspect The Rookery. It was February, and as we stood in what would be our sitting-room - formerly the main drawing-room - a fragile winter sun gleamed on the floorboards, turning them to sheets of gold. I knew that I wanted The Rookery more than I had wanted anything for a long time. And miraculously Hugh agreed we should take it, on a fourteen year lease.

We surrendered our tenancy of the Chelsea flat, then it was just a matter of packing up and arranging for a removal van. We had been in London for two and a half years and in some ways the move was going to be a wrench, but it wouldn't be an unpleasant one. M was very fond of the West End shops - as I was, if it came to that - but they weren't going to be beyond reach, and on the whole she seemed to be as thrilled as I was. If she hadn't been, I don't think I would have wanted to go.

It was late March when we arrived to settle in Westcott, and primroses were clustering along the drive. That morning Hugh had seen our furniture out of the flat before going off to spend a few hours in his office. With Ba, now four and a half years old, M and I travelled by train to Dorking, and by the time Hugh re-joined us late in the afternoon our furniture van had arrived and everything was more or less in place. We were in, and London was behind us.

I had done it, at last.

The next few weeks passed like an ecstatic dream. This was the first time since our marriage that Hugh and I had found a real home, and I was happier than I had believed possible. Dorking, with its pleasant memories, was just a short bus ride away. And as spring grew around us, *The Rookery*'s park filled up with budding daffodils. Sally became a country cat, roaming the fields and gardens and hunting through the woods; and soon she was also in the family way. United with a suitably aristocratic mate, she was set to produce what would undoubtedly be a very valuable litter of kittens.

Then something terrible happened, and I found myself standing on the edge of an abyss so horrifying that even today, more than half a century later, I can't bear to dwell upon the details.

One day my mother had a heart attack, and seven days later she was dead. She was only seventy-four and should have been with us for years to come, but at the age of sixteen she had suffered a bout of rheumatic fever, which had apparently damaged her heart. The shock and strain of being bombed, obviously, would have been likely to cause further damage. I had known for some time that there was a problem, but had never believed it was so serious. Now I was devastated. More than ever, during the last few years, M had become the pivot round which my life revolved, and I could not see a way forward. My relationship with Hugh had become comfortable but rather cool and detached. Ba, even, had been so close to her grandmother that sometimes it had felt as if she wasn't really my child. I hadn't minded that, but now I had lost my only anchor, and I think my mind rocked.

It was Hugh who saved me. As always in a crisis, he knew what to say and what to do. He understood, he checked the tide of horror and took control. Aunt Dolly, too, stayed on for weeks after the funeral, helping to fill the gulf of loneliness. As for Ba, after shedding a few tears she merely became quiet and reserved, creating no problems and showing no signs of resentment or distress. M had left her a valuable necklace and bracelet, and her own Bible, hoping - as she told me - that this very small five-year-old would always remember 'my grandmother'. It was a wish that was to be fulfilled.

Sally mourned for more than a fortnight, wailing as she paced from room to room, then she gave birth to her kittens: Pittapat Pooh Bah, Pittapat Yum Yum and Pittapat Pitti-Sing, known to their friends as Bill, Michelle and Nina. When they were a few weeks old Hugh entered the Pittapats in the Cat Club's annual show, where they gratified him by winning third prize for the whole of England - it was generally agreed they might have gone to second or even first place if they had not unlocked their own cage and sprinted round the arena, defying pursuit for well over an hour. At home they climbed to the top of the dining room curtains, hid there and when you were least expecting it leapt on to your head; if shut in a room they stood on one another's shoulders and leaned against the crack of the door, waiting for the moment of release. Once, having prepared fillets of plaice for supper, I went to collect the dish on which they had been arranged, only to find Sally tossing its contents down to her offspring, one fillet per kitten. It was lovely to have them all. But soon the kittens would be going to carefully selected homes, and anyway it was difficult to look at them without thinking how much pleasure they would have given my mother. I had Aunt Dolly, and a wonderfully understanding cleaning lady called Margaret Polden. I had Ba, and I had Hugh. There were moments of deep depression, though, and as summer went on they got worse.

In August Ba developed a chill that turned to bronchitis, then to something which Dr Brice-Smith - once again our GP - identified as asthma. Up till now she had been a healthy child, despite the fact that she looked like a china doll, and it seemed strange she should become so unwell in high summer. We wondered if the loss of her grandmother had upset her more then we realised. Dr Brice-Smith suggested a holiday. A break - two or three weeks, preferably - would be beneficial, for Ba and for me. Hugh had a week's leave coming up, and we could go to the seaside, perhaps. But if we went to the coast Hugh would not be able to stay for longer than a week, and at that moment I did not want to be away from home without him. Besides, the weather was cool and rainy, and I was half afraid the sea air might be bad for Ba's chest. In the end we booked a month at the Burford

Bridge Hotel, the place where Hugh and I had dined so many times during our year at Denbies. It was full of happy memories, and even when Hugh's brief holiday was over he would still be able to stay with us.

The Burford Bridge was what I needed. It was peaceful and at the same time diverting, above all, it wasn't home. There was rather a lot of rain while we were there, but even so we managed to do some walking. Several times we climbed the lower slopes of Box Hill - where Jane Austen's Emma picnicked with the Knightleys - and once we walked to Mickleham, where the newly married Fanny Burney watched her French emigre husband struggle to create a vegetable garden.

One day, I would begin writing again.

* * * * *

XX

A month went by, and it was time to go home. I would have liked to stay away longer, but at some point I had to pick up the pieces and now I was ready for that. Ba's chestiness seemed to have disappeared, and it was time we found a school for her. Time we all got back to Westcott. I could carry on, now.

I telephoned Margaret Polden, and when we arrived home she was waiting to meet us. The kitchen was gleaming, and Margaret had the kettle on. There was something, though. . . something wasn't right. And there was a funny sort of smell in the air.

Inside my mother's bedroom the carpet was covered with thin, greyish fluff, and there was that smell. Because I couldn't bear the sight of it, the room had been shut up for weeks before we went away. Margaret had been in to clean, but she had thought we ought to see the fluff, so she hadn't disturbed anything. There was something else, too. In the middle of our pretty dining-room there was a large and spreading puddle.

It was odd - frightening, I thought - but Hugh called in a surveyor, and we soon had some answers. It seemed that in the course of restoring and converting the old building a well had been bricked up, right underneath our dining-room floor. After the heavy rain of the last month, the well had over-flowed and damp had spread upwards through the walls. Furthermore, without vast expenditure and a certain amount of re-construction, there was apparently nothing to be done.

We went back to the Burford Bridge, and Hugh got in touch with his solicitor. We had no alternative but to try and free ourselves from the lease; but then came another bombshell. We had not thought of employing a surveyor before taking the property, and for this reason, Hugh was told, we might find ourselves without redress. Our wing of

The Rookery might be regarded as uninhabitable - especially in view of the fact that our five-year-old daughter had developed chest problems after living there through barely six months of spring and summer - but that did not mean it would necessarily be possible to obtain an order directing the landlords to tear up our lease. We had not sought to find out whether or not there were structural problems, consequently we could well be obliged to put up with them. According to Hugh's solicitor a judge might disagree with this view, and if so we might yet secure our freedom, even some kind of compensation. On the other hand, if the judge should fail to sleep well the night before the hearing, or if he had reasons of his own for disliking obstreperous tenants, we might just as easily end up paying heavy court costs on top of fourteen years' rent for a place we were unable to occupy.

Hugh instructed his solicitors to go ahead with a law-suit against the Eyre Development Company. There was a chance, and he had made up his mind to take it. Anyway, with the outcome so uncertain the EDC might just decide to go for a quick out-of-Court settlement.

Sally was sent to board with an old friend of Hugh's, a dedicated cat person (by this time her kittens were settled in their separate homes). For the time being our furniture was put into store, and it was decided that for a few weeks we should stay on at the Burford Bridge Hotel. Ba had recently started learning to read and write, and this wasn't her only diversion - every evening, after Hugh and I had gone down to dinner, she entertained the chambermaids with an account of our daily activities. The woods around Box Hill turned crimson and gold, and as the nights drew in cheerful fires were lit. I was living in a pleasant world. But it was also an expensive world, and although the lawyers said this could all add to any damages we might eventually receive, we did need to find a way of living more cheaply, so as November began we moved to the old White Hart at Lewes in Sussex. The White Hart was an 18th century coaching inn, cosy and Dickensian, and we were comfortable there. The elderly proprietor, who had been commended for helping to keep Lewes going during the war, made sure we were looked after and constantly thought up little treats for Ba, on one occasion taking us both below stairs to see a collection of new-born chicks - these were eventually located in the kitchen, where they were ambling round a batch of freshly baked apple pies, but this was before the days of Health and Safety. Perhaps not surprisingly, around the same time I developed a mild stomach upset, and during one of her evening chats Ba informed a maid called Rose that 'Mummy says it's the food in this hotel'. It may have been an odd life for Ba, but she played happily enough with her toys and games, and for an hour or so every day she concentrated on lessons. There seemed to be no further sign of that disturbing chestiness.

I was getting worried about Hugh, though. Now that we were in Sussex he had a lengthy journey to undertake every day, and he also had a lot on his mind, not least the possibility that in twelve or thirteen years' time he might still have an expensive, uninhabitable dwelling hanging round his neck. His daughter Gillian had now turned seventeen, and there had been no contact between them for six and a half years. He didn't know what either of his older daughters looked like or how their voices sounded, what they thought of the world or what they wanted from it. He did know that on the orders of his former wife their surname had now been changed from Pollock to Darrell-Waters.[*]

I have no real idea how much or how little Hugh thought about his son. It was never easy to tell what he was thinking, and though our relationship felt right, there was to some extent a gulf between us, a gulf of age and particularly of experience. Very often he was irritable and abstracted; also he was drinking too much, and I felt this might be partly my fault. If only I hadn't been so desperate to get out of London, if I hadn't discovered The Rookery, things might have been different. But it was too late to worry about that. Hugh was in touch with one or two old friends, and he got on rather well with someone who occasionally stayed at the White Hart, a magistrate called Charles Innes who regularly presided in the County court-room across the street. Mr Innes had a severe, taciturn manner and he didn't appear to like children much, but he and Hugh sometimes chatted throughout the evening.

This way of life, I realised, could not go on forever. It was likely to be a good many months before our case arrived in Court, and the possibility of a settlement seemed to be receding. It wasn't the moment to think about hunting for another permanent home, but we could not go on living in hotels. We had to locate some kind of temporary dwelling. Apart from anything else, we needed to get Sally back. Once Christmas was over, I would start looking around for a furnished cottage that we might be able to rent.

---

[*] At some point both girls appear to have been adopted by their stepfather

Christmas was a haze of parties and carol singing and roaring fires, and Hugh joined in with everything. Ba, always shy when surrounded by large crowds of people, was less enthusiastic, and when the time came for the Proprietor to hand out presents she flatly refused to accept hers. Until someone thought to ask whether she would take the package if someone else gave it to her.

She nodded at once. 'Mr Innes,' she whispered.

After Christmas Hugh seemed slightly more himself, and just as the first crocuses started to appear we found a house to live in. It was a small Georgian terrace house, and it was tucked away near the river that flows round the edges of Lewes. It was immaculately furnished - the owner's name was Mrs Perfect - and it made me think of *Quality Street*, the musical version of which Hugh and I had seen together. Hugh liked the house as much as I did, and within a matter of days we had signed a three month tenancy agreement. Days after that we moved in, and by the weekend Sally was back with us. She had turned into a magnificent, over-bearing Siamese matriarch, but within a very short time it was as if she had never been away.

And it was fun, having a home again. Until Monday morning, when Hugh set off for the Cabinet Office and for the first time I realised that - except for Ba - I was going to be alone. Almost since my mother's death I had lived in an atmosphere of companionable bustle, and I had become dependent on that.

It wasn't too bad, though, because the Quality Street house came with an established help, an Irish lady known as Bridget. Bridget turned out to be cheerful and companionable, if somewhat overwhelmed by Hugh's military rank, which in her mind changed several times during the day - when she arrived before breakfast he was the Colonel, by mid-morning he had turned into the Captain or the Brigadier, and there were some days when he switched Services and became the Admiral or the Squadron-Leader. This appealed to Hugh's sense of humour, and in fact he did seem more relaxed. I knew he was still under strain, also that he was drinking too much, but it didn't often show and things were, I thought, improving. Apart from anything else he was showing more interest in Ba, taking her for walks and talking to her, and that was a really encouraging development. It was also good for Ba. Her health was still not one hundred per cent, and the local doctor felt it would do no harm to delay the start of her school career for a little bit longer, particularly as she would almost certainly have to be moved on again in a few months' time.

Then one day Hugh caught a chill. The spring weather was cold and dank and as the problem moved to his chest our GP prescribed M&B, the new infection-beating drug. He agreed to spend a few days in bed, but after about forty-eight hours seemed quite a lot better. When I took his breakfast up I was told he would soon be getting dressed and coming downstairs, but before I left the room he asked me to take a look at the large antique mirror that faced the bed - to tell him if I could see anything unusual reflected in it. I looked, and saw what I might have expected to see - rose-sprigged wall-paper, a small mahogany dressing-table and one of the square Georgian windows that looked on to the street.

Hugh was seeing something else, though. A pretty room with long windows that opened on to a sunlit garden. In the room there was a young woman, and according to Hugh her dress had long, sweeping skirts. She was bending over a small child and there was a man standing beside them; he was dressed in some kind of colourful coat and he was laughing. The child ran into the garden and the man went to fetch it back, then one or two other figures appeared. I looked, but still saw nothing but a corner of the familiar bedroom.

Whatever this vision or fantasy was, Hugh seemed quite relaxed about it. As far as he was concerned these things were appearing in the old mirror, and though it might seem like a bizarre phenomenon, somewhere there had to be an explanation. I didn't know what to think, but I had always enjoyed a mystery and this was a good one. If Hugh had still been feverish it might have been worrying, but quite obviously he was more or less recovered. This had to be some kind of psychic development, and I was excited about it. After the first few minutes, though, Hugh didn't seem quite so enthusiastic. He took the mirror down and turned it to face the wall. The following morning, when Bridget took his breakfast up, he warned her to keep well away from the giant who was brandishing an axe on our staircase.

I telephoned the doctor, and he came at once. He spent twenty minutes or so alone with Hugh, then downstairs in the little front sitting-room he told me my husband had delirium tremens. DT's. If he had known there was a risk such a thing might develop, he could have taken steps to try and prevent it. Hugh's recent illness would have meant sudden isolation from alcohol, something which could occasionally lead to DT's - only, of course, when a patient had previously been drinking fairly heavily. I must try not to worry, though. A few days of rest and continued abstinence might well see an end to the problem. We would just have to wait and see. In the meantime the important thing was not to argue with him. If he said there was an axe-man on the stairs, there was an axe-man on the stairs.

With heroic Irish cheerfulness, Bridget refused to be alarmed. Carrying regular cups of tea up the stairs, she assured my husband she was staying well away from the axe-man. And as the day went on Hugh did seem a lot more normal. I was pleased to notice that his appetite was starting to come back - even if he didn't, now, seem inclined to get up and dress. That night, when I climbed into bed beside him, he was already sound asleep.

An hour or so later, I woke to find him pacing up and down in his dressing-gown. He had been downstairs, he said, and the axe-man was still there. He needed a weapon. . . . *Where the hell were his Burmese knives?*

I sat up in bed. Mercifully the knives had been put into store together with our other belongings, but for the moment details like that had been wiped from Hugh's mind. I realised he might think I was hiding them, keeping them from him deliberately, and I knew the situation could be about to get dodgy. Slipping out of bed, I said I would go downstairs and hunt for the knives. I'd just make sure the axe-man didn't notice me.

'You get back into bed,' I said. 'You mustn't get cold. I won't be long.'

Downstairs I crept into the sitting-room, where the telephone was. I needed advice and a familiar voice, so I rang Nora Casey, the nursing Sister who had been with us at Denbies. She had kept in touch and on one or two occasions had come to visit us. She knew Hugh and understood him, and she might tell me what to do. Nora was asleep when the telephone rang beside her bed, but like most nurses and doctors she had the ability to wake up quickly.

'So you're downstairs, in your sitting-room,' she said briskly. 'Now lock the door and telephone your doctor. Tell him he's got to get there, as soon as he possibly can.'

With a flash of horror I remembered Ba, asleep in her room just across the landing from ours. But Nora said I must not go back upstairs.

'He won't touch her, but if you go back up there you might provoke something. Just lock that door and phone your doctor. Then call me back.'

Within minutes, the doctor arrived in his dressing-gown. He thought it might be better if he saw Hugh alone, so I went to check on Ba and then returned to the sitting-room. When the doctor came down again, he told me he needed to use the phone.

Hugh, he said, would have to be taken away. Now, to-night. There was a place, not far away, where he could be given appropriate treatment. It might take a few weeks, but eventually everything ought to be all right. The difficulty was, he was refusing to sign a consent form and we were going to need a magistrate. I didn't understand, at first, then I was horribly shocked. They couldn't take him away by force, not just because he was seeing things.

The doctor said it was the only thing to do, and the best for everybody concerned. Anyway, it was his decision - his responsibility - not mine, and he had no choice. He telephoned a JP who apparently lived not far away, and they spoke for a minute or two. I didn't want to know what was being said.

We waited. I rang Nora back, and she told me not to worry. The doctor filled up various forms, and because I had to do something, I made a cup of tea. By this time, it was round about one o'clock in the morning. Half an hour went by, and a car pulled up in the street outside. When the front door was opened, it revealed Charles Innes.

I think I was beyond embarrassment, but he was disturbed and upset. He hadn't realised - he would have suggested we called someone else. Eventually he was persuaded to go upstairs with the doctor, but after about five minutes they came down again. The magistrate was refusing point blank to sign anything that would compel Hugh to have treatment against his will.

'He's my friend,' Charles Innes said. 'And he's no danger to anyone on this earth.'

The doctor pointed out that he had to think about the patient's wife and child; in any case, Colonel Pollock was hardly going to recover without specialist care. Eventually Mr Innes said he would go back upstairs and talk to Hugh alone. When he came down again, some time later, he was able to tell us he had persuaded my husband to sign for himself.

I never saw Charles Innes again, but I have always remembered him warmly.

By morning, Ba and I were alone in the house. When I telephoned Nora Casey again, she was optimistic and encouraging - the worst was over now, and Hugh was in the best possible place. In the meantime, I could begin to think about sorting our lives out. I talked to Reggie and Aunt Dolly, and it was arranged they should come over the following day.

Aunt Dolly agreed to stay indefinitely, and without her I'm not quite sure how I would have got through the following weeks. Whether knitting, or playing with Ba, or singing *The Arab's Farewell to his Steed* while putting the kettle on, she made the world steady again. And Ba adored her.

For about a fortnight Hugh was allowed no visitors, and when at last I saw him the change was startling. The hallucinations, I was told, had gone altogether and he seemed to be feeling rather fit, if not in the best of tempers. Since he had responded so well, the doctors said he ought to be coming home fairly soon. Which meant I had a lot of thinking to do.

Hugh's superiors at the Cabinet Office had been understanding and supportive, and they assured me his job would be held for him. In the meantime our three month term at the Quality Street house was coming to an end, and I knew it must not be renewed. We had to find something else, a lot nearer to London. I went to an agent, and in no time had tracked down a cottage in Surrey. On the edge of Bramley village, near Guildford, Yew Tree Cottage was apparently crammed with old oak. It also had three bedrooms, a sitting room, a dining room and a playroom. It was to be let for a six month period, and it would see us through the summer. Without bothering to go and look at the place I wrote a cheque and signed the lease, then Aunt Dolly and I started packing things up. A few days before Hugh was due to be discharged, the four of us - Ba and I and Aunt Dolly and the cat - travelled to Bramley. When we left Quality Street, the antique mirror upstairs was still leaning with its face to the wall. I hadn't wanted to touch it. Whatever it was Hugh had seen that morning, I didn't believe it had much to do with the lurid hallucinations that came later on. When a human brain is on the edge of delirium tremens, various things develop - among them, I suspect, a heightening of psychic awareness.

Yew Tree Cottage was idyllic. The sitting-room had an inglenook fireplace, the garden had lawns and apple trees, a gypsy caravan and a cow byre. I was never quite sure what the cow byre was doing there, but it was picturesque. In front the garden was protected by a yew hedge and behind the house a grassy bank descended to a stream, beyond which lay miles of sleepy countryside. We had fallen on our feet again, and within a few days my husband would be home. Like many recovering alcoholics Hugh had developed a passion for cakes and sweets, so the night before his arrival I made a sponge and some shortbread biscuits.

The next day he turned up in a taxi, looking incredibly fit. He was sober as only a Scotsman who isn't drinking can be, and he was also in an icy temper. A plateful of shortbread biscuits disappeared within minutes, and he drank several cups of tea - unusual for him - but the frozen atmosphere persisted, into the next day and the day after that. And I understood quite well what it was about. Hugh had been through a period of stress and humiliation, and he thought that his problem - if he had one, which he probably believed was debatable - could have been resolved without any of that. I might have been in a position to prevent the humiliation happening, or so he imagined, but I hadn't done so. And he was furiously resentful.

It didn't last long, though, because our relationship wasn't like that. Within a few days the ice had started to thin. And then, suddenly, we were all right again.

*　*　*　*　*

XXI

Hugh had once come close to playing Rugby for Scotland and as a young man he had also been a tennis-player, but golf had been abandoned when a ball of his struck a baby in its pram (the baby had not been hurt, but Hugh's taste for the game had evaporated) and in middle age he was left with no active sporting interest. For some years he had not even possessed a garden of his own - the last had been Green Hedges. But he did love the business of growing things, and at Yew Tree Cottage this interest revived. A nice old man called Collier came to pull up weeds and tidy paths and mow the lawn, and the two of them got on well. While Hugh bought plants and seeds Collier put them in, and they spent a lot of time planning and talking about blight. A month after being discharged from hospital, Hugh returned to the Cabinet Office.

Aunt Dolly was still with us - because he liked her, Hugh had been happy for her to stay on - and I began to feel more relaxed. Ba was thriving in the summer sunshine, and Sally-the-cat was cutting a swathe through the wild life of mid-Surrey. (When we seemed not to appreciate a nestful of blue-tits deposited on the dining-room carpet, she took to climbing the honeysuckle outside our bedroom window and dumping field voles at the foot of the bed.)

And to my delight, Reggie had begun turning up for weekends. We gossiped and made silly jokes, and I felt as if twenty years had slipped away. Reggie had always felt like my brother, and now that we were older I realised just how much alike we were. We both had restless, irrational minds, we both felt at odds with the world around us. Together we could talk for hours, pouring out our thoughts and feelings. And he made me laugh. Emerging from the mists of a summer morning, he would park his bicycle beside the gate - Reggie couldn't afford cars, these days - and turn up outside our kitchen door, shoulders hunched and face contorted. 'Got any odd jobs, lady?' He was a powerful mimic, and if there had been more direction in his life might have made an actor or an impressionist. He sorted out our kitchen cupboards and slept in the gypsy caravan, and we all had a wonderful time - all, that is, except Hugh, whose jealous tendencies made it hard for him to accept the fact that my relationship with Reggie had always been innocent. He did keep his temper, though, most of the time. And for once I was determined not to worry. Reggie had recently turned to painting in oils, and though his style - which tended to involve sizzling skies and flamenco dancers - was not for me, it had put an idea into my head. I went out and bought myself some water-colours.

From the beginning I knew they weren't really for me, either. Ever since that time I have felt profound respect for anyone who *can* cope with what must surely be the trickiest of artistic media. But I had to do something, and much as I longed to start writing again I was still too frightened. So I sat in our cool, low-beamed sitting-room and tried my hand at a picture of Ba, calling her in every so often from the garden or the playroom next door. The playroom was a great asset and came in for a lot of use, the more so because Ba had made friends with a little girl called Patti, who lived just across the lane. Patti had a pet spaniel, and the two of them seemed to drift in and out all day, the spaniel and Sally-the-cat having evidently reached an agreement which involved pretending not to see one another.

Though she was still small and slight for her age, and her fair skin refused to pick up any tan, Ba was looking very well, which was a huge relief. Things really were beginning to work out.

Until one morning, when Hugh came hurrying down the highly polished, twisting staircase and fell, fracturing his ankle. It was a bad break and very painful, and it meant that once again he was going to be tied down, unable to reach his office in London. I knew that this was cruelly frustrating, and I was sympathetic. Even when his temper sizzled in the summer heat I tried to be patient, but it wasn't always easy.

In order to reach the Yew Tree Cottage bathroom everyone had to pass through the sitting-room, and when one or other of the children was involved they tended to come as a party. One morning, while I struggled with my fourteenth water colour effort and Hugh sat with his ankle propped in front of him, glowering at a newspaper, the playroom door opened and a small column emerged. Ba, followed by

Sally-the-cat, followed by Patti and the spaniel. Presumably Sally was tagging along to look after Ba's interests and keep an eye on the spaniel. Roughly five minutes later the column filed back again, and half an hour after that it re-appeared, once more heading for the bathroom.

'*Good God!*' Hugh exploded. '*What the hell do they think they're doing?*'

When I pointed out that it didn't really matter he became incandescent, so I picked up the saucer beside me, in the process tipping the water out, and aimed it - not at Hugh, but at the oak crossbeam above the fireplace. It hit its target with a satisfying crack, and fragments smashed on to the brick hearth below.

Hugh put his newspaper down, and looked at me. In the kind of voice his father might have reserved for addressing fellow Elders, he said: 'I do wish you'd try to control your temper.'

Eventually the ankle got better, and towards the end of July - by this time my aunt had gone home - we managed to get away for a few days, taking Ba with us. I think we went to Westgate in Kent; and after that Hugh returned to work. Soon afterwards, we were told that Pollock v the Eyre Development Company was now scheduled for some time the following spring. Because of this information Hugh may have started to worry afresh; I just knew that he was starting to drink again - socially, for the most part, but still too much.

What he needed, I thought, was a real holiday, something that would give him a boost, and an idea came to me. I had never been to Scotland in my life, and it was now seven years since Hugh had last travelled north of the Border. Surely, in all the circumstances, he could be granted one more week's leave. At first he seemed reluctant to ask for time off, but then it occurred to him we might spend a few days in Edinburgh, which was probably his favourite place on earth. While he fixed up the additional leave I made other arrangements, and Ba was told we were going to see the place where Daddy had grown up. Maddeningly, with a few days to go, he developed another chesty cold but the local doctor thought this should clear up fast enough, if treated with a course of M&B and a short spell in bed.

As I started packing, I was diverted from time to time by Hugh's stories of a mouse which had appeared in our bedroom. Apparently it was making regular round trips, emerging beside the fireplace and disappearing from view behind a chest of drawers. I wasn't particularly keen to see the visitor with my own eyes, but after a while

I did try to spot it and was puzzled that it never seemed to be visible when I was around. There weren't any mouse holes, either. I supposed it could be something Sally had absent-mindedly dropped, but when she appeared in the room she didn't seem to notice anything. The next day Hugh said several things that sounded rather strange; and with a sinking heart I telephoned for advice.

Though he was aware of Hugh's recent history, the local doctor didn't jump to any immediate conclusions. He spent some time alone with the patient, then he came downstairs. It was quite common, he said. A bit of a relapse. My husband was going to need further treatment, and that would mean going back into hospital, but it shouldn't be for very long.

There was a hunting rifle on display in the sitting-room, and in the dining-room a pair of antique cutlasses had been hung above a Georgian sideboard. These specimens had always interested Hugh, but they had never troubled me for one second. Now, with an awful sense of *déjà vu*, I watched as the Bramley GP thoughtfully took them all down. He suggested they should be lodged in some secure place, and I asked if he would put them in the spare bedroom, in a wardrobe that could be kept locked. I felt numb.

This time Hugh signed the necessary papers quite calmly and without argument. I cancelled the Edinburgh hotel, unpacked our cases and got another, smaller bag ready for him. The following day, as he sat waiting for the taxi that would take him back to hospital, he looked normal and endearingly attractive in an immaculate dark blue suit. Outside in the August sunshine Collier was digging, and Hugh announced that he would like to see the old gardener for a moment. A little hesitantly I called Collier in, and inevitably I heard part of their conversation.

'I've got to go away for a while,' said Hugh.

'Yes, sir.'

'The trouble is, someone has to look after things here. They're all round the place, you know. . . hiding behind the hedge. They've got knives and axes. I'd just like you to keep an eye on them. Make sure they don't get in.'

'Don't you worry, sir,' the old man said gently. 'I'll look after all that. Don't you worry about a thing.'

* * * * *

XXIII

Hugh was away for five weeks, and by the time he came home our six month tenure of Yew Tree Cottage was due for renewal. It wasn't difficult to make a decision. The cottage had been lovely - if not all that fortunate, from our point of view - but winter was coming, and Hugh would be better off without that daily journey. He got in touch with the proprietors of our old flat, and found they had something for us - the apartment next door, Number 83. After a little more than eighteen months in the country, we were on our way back to Chelsea.

Reaching London in November, we spent a few days at the Strand Palace Hotel. There was already a touch of smog in the air, and Ba promptly went down with bronchitis. It was the day of the Lord Mayor's Show, and a cheerful doctor called by the hotel suggested she should be got out of bed, wrapped up and taken to another floor so that she could get a good view of the passing spectacle. I panicked, and said no. She got better quickly, though, and we moved into 83 Beaufort Mansions. It was nice to have our things back - our furniture and pictures and books, and Hugh's old gramophone - and as soon as we were more or less settled Hugh went to collect Sally-the-cat, who had been lodged for a short time with the person who had looked after her before. At tea-time on a dull winter afternoon Ba and I stood by the sitting-room window, watching and waiting, and at last Hugh's taxi drew up outside. We saw him lift Sally's travelling basket out and pay the driver. But there was something wrong - he hadn't looked up at the window. I hurried to the front door, and as I opened it Hugh stepped across the threshold with the basket in his hand. Over the top of Ba's head, he looked at me and shook his head.

Sally was dying. She had contracted cat flu - distemper - and at that time there was no effective treatment. It had been suggested she might as well stay where she was, particularly as she probably hadn't got more than a few hours, but Hugh had wanted to bring her home. She was on some kind of medication, but he had been warned it could not be expected to save her.

That evening we placed her basket in the sitting-room, and every so often Hugh administered her medicine. She was dreadfully thin, lying in a corner of the basket, and her coat seemed white - she wasn't Sally-the-cat any more. By midnight I couldn't keep awake any longer, so I went to lie down for a while. When I went back around one o'clock Hugh was still sitting where I had left him, with the basket nearby. Sally had died a few minutes earlier. In the morning I broke the news to Ba.

After a time I suggested we might think about buying another kitten, but this time Hugh was adamant. London was no place for animals.

I felt rather lonely and desolate. Our old flat was now occupied by a youngish couple called Campbell - they had two small children of their own and at first Sally Campbell and I saw a lot of one another. We exchanged tea and coffee invitations and she tried to get me involved in a variety of things, but I had never fitted in with the young married set and on the whole I was happier gossiping with Laura, a cheerful girl who came in once or twice a week to help out around the flat. And I had started sketching. I practised for a bit, drawing Ba and the children next door, and the Peter Pan statue in Kensington Gardens, then I spotted a stunning photograph of Lichfield Cathedral and felt that I wanted to capture it. The result was good, I thought - reasonable, anyway, not bad for a beginner. Hugh surprised me by being visibly impressed, and so did one or two other people. To my astonishment someone even asked why I didn't try for the Royal Academy's Summer Exhibition. I hesitated, but Hugh made some enquiries and eventually I went ahead. I had my drawing framed in accordance with Academy regulations, Hugh packed it up and it was delivered to Burlington House. A few weeks later, it came back. This was not exactly a shock - what did surprise me was the fact that my drawing had apparently come through two of the three selection stages. Somebody said I should feel pleased with myself, I was only a beginner, after all. And I did feel pleased, for about ten minutes. It wasn't like actually getting into the Exhibition, though. Anyway, I was already bored with sketching.

As for Ba, having had several bouts of bronchitis she still wasn't considered strong enough to start school, so a vast quantity of home study equipment had been ordered and every evening, when Hugh came home from the office, her work was checked. Determined her education was not going to suffer he was very firm about this, and quite soon she started to do well.

Spring arrived, and two weeks before our case was due to come up in Court Hugh's solicitor visited the flat, requesting a sizeable advance payment for the barrister who had been briefed. Hugh wrote a cheque, but he was not happy about this development, and my uneasiness deepened. On the day of the hearing I left Ba in Laura's care, and went to Court with Hugh. I was wearing a dark blue suit and a small hat, the same sort of outfit I had chosen for my wedding day. Surrounded by murmuring barristers we waited for our case to be called, and eventually, moved to a space outside the court-room, we saw our Judge, be-wigged and robed, presiding over the closing moments of an earlier hearing. We were next.

With a few minutes to go Hugh's solicitor came to whisper something in his ear, and they disappeared together. When they came back, twenty minutes later, I was told that it was over. At the very last minute, the opposition had suggested a settlement. In exchange for five years' rent and the payment of all costs, they were prepared to tear up our fourteen year lease. Both sides had gone to the brink, but in the end they had been the ones who pulled back.

If we had gone ahead we might have won, but defeat would have meant an horrific bill and I knew Hugh had probably done the right thing. We would still be handing over quite a lot of money, but he said that we ought to be all right, just. He looked grey with worry, though. And I wished I had a firmer grasp of our financial situation.

I didn't want to take an ordinary job, not while Ba was still at home all the time, but I had to do something, so I started to think about trying to write again. I wouldn't begin with anything too serious or demanding. If the headaches were to get going again, I knew I would be put off for life. But I might try a lightish novel - all right, a romantic novel. An idea came to me, and I typed a few pages. I didn't get a headache, so the next day I typed some more, and still no headache. I carried on, and when I had completed a chapter or so I showed Hugh what I had done. He said that it was good.

'*Really* good?' I pressed pathetically.

He said again that it was good, and I should get on with it.

Everyone in Hugh's Cabinet Office team had been chosen for combining military experience with an understanding of literature, and among this exclusive set there was a Major John Boon. John's father, Charlie, had founded the publishing house Mills and Boon, and as Charlie was now dead the business had passed to his three sons. One day Hugh seems to have told John that I was working on a romantic novel, whereupon John suggested I should send something to his brother Alan. For the time being, it seemed, Alan was in charge of Mills and Boon.

Twenty years earlier I had taken a typescript to the office of Charlie Boon, and had been told to go home and write another. If I produced the second within a month, and if he found it satisfactory, he might - might - offer me a contract. I thought he seemed almost brutally tough, more like an old-fashioned factory foreman than a publishing executive. Actually he must have been a very clever man, but given a choice between scrubbing floors and writing for his firm, I think I'd have gone for the scrubbing brush.

His sons were supposed to be different, though. I wrote to Alan, and received a response that was businesslike but polite. When I had about half a dozen chapters to show, he'd be very pleased to take a look. I got back to work, but now that there was a publisher in view immediately began to suffer from writers' block. The story I had started was abandoned and I set to work on another, then another. I wasn't getting past the first few chapters and though there hadn't been a return of the headaches - so far - it was disheartening.

And Hugh was not himself. Worry - something - was getting him down and his other side was taking over, the side I didn't like; the side that had to be kept at bay. Perhaps, I thought, it would help if we got away for a few days. I persuaded him to ask for a week's holiday, the first that year, then I booked us into the Ship Inn at Swanage in Dorset. I chose Swanage because it was what Hugh wanted. He and Enid had liked the place, and he didn't see why we shouldn't go there. He was totally unsentimental about the Enid aspect, and anyway that didn't bother me. I never felt jealous of her. I knew, with absolute certainty, that I had no reason to be.

The *Ship Inn* had been bombed during the war and there was still a gaping hole at one end of the roof, but we were made very comfortable and the weather was good. We prowled about, spent time on the beach and took holiday snaps, just like any other family. And Hugh was drinking less. The backlash came, though, when it was time to settle our bill. His hands had begun to shake, and it took him twenty minutes to sign a cheque.

I had hoped the holiday might make a difference, but in the end there were too many problems. Back in Chelsea he developed another chest infection, and our GP remarked acidly that alcoholism - particularly in a family man - was contemptible. Outraged, I made some reference to Hugh's brilliant Army record, and the doctor observed that among his patients there were two VC's and a number of lavishly decorated senior officers, and they were 'always the worst'. (The same applied, apparently, to judges and senior barristers.) He asked me not to talk, in his hearing, about glittering records of achievement and he got his way because I didn't talk to him again. The next time we needed a doctor, I called a different practice.

Hugh recovered from his infection and went back to the Cabinet Office, but time was running out in that direction and one morning his boss, Brigadier Latham, got in touch with me by phone. Again and again he stressed the value of Hugh's contribution to what they were doing. How fond they all were of him, how much he, the Brigadier, personally admired the way Hugh had dealt with his 'various difficulties'. However, my husband's problems were now beginning to affect his work.

'I'm sure,' said the Brigadier, 'you understand what I mean. *Take him away, Mrs Pollock. . . get him sorted out. Then tell him to come back here and help us finish the job.'*

When Hugh came home, later in the day, he seemed bewildered. He had been sent upon a kind of compulsory sick leave, but he didn't seem to understand what his sickness was supposed to be. I tried seizing the opportunity to speak candidly, but I could see this wasn't going to work so I simply said they must have thought he was a bit run down. We could go away again, for a few days. It was summer, after all.

We had a week on the Kent coast, but the atmosphere was fraught and Hugh was drinking a lot. He must have known the reason for his suspension from the Cabinet Office, but it wasn't something he felt able to talk about. All his life he had been successful, sought after, and his present situation was biting deep. I kept thinking we might work something out, if only he would talk, but there seemed to be no chance of that.

And the damage wasn't only to Hugh's ego. Naturally enough his salary had stopped, and I knew this was a development we simply couldn't afford. Like many women at that time I didn't see my husband's bank statements, but I did know we had problems and I couldn't quite see how we were going to manage without any income. Naively, I suggested we might think again about running some kind of a business together. I wasn't sure exactly what sort of business I was thinking of, but I did have a lot of ideas. Of course, I *might* be able to write for Mills and Boon, but that was going to take time. Hugh said he was thinking the whole situation over, but apart from that he barely seemed to hear what I was saying. Then one day he told me he had written to his friend, Wendell Endicott, about the possibility of a future on the other side of the Atlantic.

I knew Mr Endicott had urged Hugh to give some thought to this idea, that he had said work permits and things of that sort ought not to be a problem, but I had never believed my husband would do anything about it, and I was stunned. I had always been ready for adventure, but this was something else. There was Ba, for one thing. If we did go to the United States it might mean she would be growing up into an American citizen, and I wasn't at all sure how I felt about that. Then there was Reggie, and Aunt Dolly - since my marriage I had needed them both more than ever, and I couldn't imagine how it would feel if we were all to be separated by the width of the Atlantic. Yet Hugh seemed to be taking the view that it all came down to a single decision on his part.

Looking back, I can understand how he felt. After years of effortless achievement, he now stood staring into an empty future. Enid had hacked away at the foundations of his existence, and because for some reason he couldn't help doing so he had taken the axe into his own hands and worked to finish the job. In America, he must have thought, it would be different. Over there, he might be able to go on achieving.

When Wendell Endicott's reply came, it was full of warm encouragement. In the States, especially if he were to choose New England, he would be given a great welcome, and a variety of openings would be made available to him. All he had to do was go over and get things sorted out, then his family would be able to follow.

So that was that.

In order to enter the United States it was necessary to obtain various vaccination certificates, and by this time one of Hugh's certificates was out of date. When he went for the requisite injection he suffered an unusually severe reaction, but after a day or so of fever and a swollen arm he had recovered enough to go and sort one or two things out with his bank manager. When he came back he said very little, then I realised that for half an hour or so he had been staring blindly at the newspaper held up in front of him.

The truth came out gradually. Hugh's bank account, it seemed, was empty. Furthermore, the overdraft that had been sustaining us was now about to be called in. Hugh had been aware of this situation, but he had imagined the overdraft would be extended so that funds could be made available for his American trip. After all, America had almost certainly been going to mean a hefty salary, and any initial outlay would have been money well spent, to say the least. But the Bank Manager hadn't seen it that way. Hugh's divorce settlement - aided by the Eyre Development Company - had brought him to the brink of ruin. With the loss of his monthly pay cheque, he had effectively been pushed over the edge.

The Bank Manager may not have felt able to go on funding an impecunious client who was now planning to live and work abroad, but I think he made a mistake. Once in the USA Hugh would undoubtedly have gained a highly paid post, and the Bank would have been well rewarded for its trouble. Without money, though, he couldn't go to America.

Of course there were recriminations. I probably said some hurtful things, but I think I kept them to a minimum. It wasn't the moment for that kind of thing. Hugh was broken and devastated, and I would have got no satisfaction from pushing salt into his wounds. Something had to be done quickly, though. I might have gone straight out to find a job, but I had a child whose health was still so dodgy that she couldn't go to school, and nobody in London to leave her with (Laura might have been ideal, but she could manage only four hours a week). First of all we needed to sell something, and that, I thought, shouldn't prove too difficult.

We had a lot of good Georgian silver, and with Hugh's reluctant consent I took some candelabra and set out along the King's Road. Within an hour I had sold the candelabra for sixty pounds, and we had won ourselves a respite. (Weeks later the purchaser sent a second cheque, saying he had offered too little. He can't have known how much we appreciated his staggering honesty.)

Now we had to get out of London. I bought the *Lady* magazine, and found just what I was looking for. The nursery wing of a Berkshire rectory, furnished and available for rent. Hugh did not want to become involved in tours of inspection, so taking Ba with me I discovered the village of Yattenden, wrapped in a late summer haze. The Queen Anne rectory was very big and had an air of uneasiness about it; the shadowy drawing-room and dining-room were no longer used, 'except when the Bishop came'. But the nursery wing was what we wanted, clean and comfortably furnished, with two bedrooms, a sitting-room that looked out on the church, a bright, well-fitted kitchen and a bathroom that had just been added. On top of everything else, it was cheap. Joyfully I went back to tell Hugh that it was perfect, that we had to take it, and he agreed. It was an odd feeling, not having to argue with him - well, not much. But Hugh had changed since that visit to the Bank Manager. He wasn't drinking, for one thing.

We sold a few more items, then most of our portable belongings were put into packing cases and placed in storage, together with our furniture, and as we arrived in Yattenden I felt a surge of optimism. We had come through a lot, but things were beginning to get better. We had a few debts, it was true, but Hugh's credit was good in most quarters and it wouldn't be long before everything was sorted out. Somehow or other I would manage to finish a novel for Mills and Boon. I had to get it right, though. In the meantime Hugh was writing to friends, just asking whether anyone knew of a suitable job. We weren't going to be that far out from London, and it would still be possible for him to commute.

In the meantime we were safe in a lovely village, and it was autumn. As Ba and I shuffled through piles of leaves I talked to her about the carriages that would once have rolled out of the coach house behind the rectory, and the gentlemen whose horses would have cantered past. Then while she got stuck into sums and exercises, I settled down to write – or tried to. The problem was I couldn't settle my mind, couldn't concentrate. Stress may have been partly responsible, but there was something else as well. For some reason, the atmosphere of the place was starting to get me down.

At about six o'clock in the evening Hugh usually walked to the village pub - he was always perfectly capable of drinking moderately - and during the half hour or so before Ba went to bed, she and I would go through a book, or play a game. As we worked through *Alice in Wonderland*, or played Contraband in front of the sitting-room fire, I tried not to notice the October darkness closing down outside, tried to ignore the noises. The snatches of whispering that weren't quite inside my head but couldn't be real, the sudden click of a door closing inside our own apartment. The Rector and his wife were out a good deal, and in any case their part of the house was so remote that we rarely heard a sound from them; but their Siamese cat quite frequently turned up in our midst, even when every door and window had been closed for some time.

Then one morning, as we came back from a walk, Ba asked if I had noticed 'the lady'. Apparently she had just walked down the main staircase. She had been wearing a very long skirt, but Ba hadn't seen her top half.

'Why didn't you see her top half?' I asked.

'She hadn't got one,' Ba responded with seven-year-old simplicity.

The next day I related this story to the Rector's wife, who seemed mildly diverted. '*Oh!*' she said brightly. 'She's found our little ghost!'

Their little ghost was evidently the shade of a well documented Victorian housekeeper. The Bishop had once spotted her mingling with a cluster of wedding guests on the lawn but her favourite 'haunt' was said to be the kitchen, where she could sometimes be seen lifting the lids from saucepans. Only a few months earlier she had formed the subject of a radio programme; the Rector's wife had been interviewed, and they had received a great many letters. This was intriguing, and I felt more relaxed about the whole thing. Until evening came, and the noises began again.

But by this time we had other things to worry about. With the first chill bite of winter Ba had developed a cold and this had turned to bronchitis. A local doctor observed that the rectory was rather damp, which meant it wasn't the best possible place for a child with chest problems. I wasn't happy in the house, and more importantly I couldn't work there. Hugh didn't mind either way, but in any case it was Ba's health that mattered. If Yattenden Rectory was doing damage to her, then we had to go. The Rector and his wife were very understanding. The only problem was, where were we going?

Just a few miles away, near Windsor, Aunt Dolly was living with Reggie and his wife. They urged us to stay with them for a week or two, so as soon as Ba was well enough we travelled to Eton Wick. From my point of view this was marvellous, but there was tension between Hugh and Reggie, and the dank river mists meant Ba was not much better off. She was now suffering attacks of asthma, and though they were fairly mild we were advised to get her right away, perhaps to the seaside. I heard about a guest house in the Sussex town of Eastbourne, and the owner, Bridget Garland, told me her house was in a quiet street half a mile from the sea. We would have our own sitting-room, and she would look after us. Her terms were reasonable and if we liked we could stay with her until the following April, when seasonal bookings would begin. I clinched the arrangement, and when we got to Eastbourne knew at once that I had done the right thing.

Bridget Garland was small and plump, with dark eyes and curly brown hair, and she was Irish. Very Irish. In fact, she claimed to be a cousin of the revolutionary Michael Collins, and I've no doubt this claim was accurate. Amazingly kind-hearted, she made a great fuss of Ba and looked after us all superbly. She also told remarkable stories, mostly about Ireland and her youth, and the distant, early Troubles. For her the IRA were a band of heroes - this was long before their 1969 re-awakening - but most of all she liked to talk about moonlit evenings in Killarney, and the dress she had worn for her first dance. And the young man who had kissed her . . . of course, just as an early haze came creeping through the trees. She was anger and pity, romance and laughter, in fact, the embodiment of Irishness. We all became fond of her, and as a writer I probably stored her away for future reference.

Though she couldn't face the wintry sea front without gasping for breath Ba soon seemed quite a lot better, and after a peaceful Christmas I began writing again. Settled in the bay window of our sitting-room, looking out on a neat front garden, I embarked upon a brand new novel and within three or four weeks I had completed half of it. The story dealt with an eighteen-year-old girl, fresh from boarding-school, being persuaded into a hasty marriage, and though it may not have been all that original it produced a favourable response. I was asked if I could go up to London, and have lunch with Alan Boon.

And Alan did not appear to be a bit like his father. Tall and rather heavily built, he had fair hair and light blue eyes that stared through you at something in another dimension. He was a public school product - thanks, perhaps, to his father's business acumen - and his manners were excellent. During the war he had been an officer in the Navy, but now he was devoting himself to the family firm. Light romantic fiction, women's fiction, had the potential to become big business, and he was well aware of this. He also knew the business had got to be handled properly, with due regard for such modern concepts as market research. Alan was intelligent, and well read. He believed in maintaining good literary standards, and he also believed that some of his authors had the potential to become household names.

Strictly speaking, he was not operating quite by himself. His brother John, who had once worked with Hugh, was part of the firm and another brother, Caryl, was in charge of accounts. But it wasn't difficult to see that Alan was the driving force. Numerous women are said to have been bowled over by his charm, and if I didn't immediately detect much of this I did think he was interesting. I soon realised his easy-going detachment was little more than a mask, and in fact he had one of the sharpest minds in the book business.* More importantly, from my point of view, he knew a great deal about publishing and so far he liked what he had seen of my work.

It was agreed I should complete my new novel, which was to be called *Mistress of Brown Furrows*. If the second half matched the quality of the first - and if I were able to produce two further, equally satisfactory beginnings - I would be rewarded with a three book contract, plus an advance which would amount to the sum of one hundred pounds. Mills and Boon were not yet in a position to pay anything like big money, but if Alan's ideas bore fruit, as it seemed likely they would, such a day would not be long in coming. Anyway, to me one hundred pounds seemed like rather a lot of money.

Travelling back to Eastbourne that afternoon, I felt as if I had climbed over a succession of hurdles. Now I just had to finish the course.

* * * * *

XXIII

The following day I was back behind my typewriter. I was nervous because this time it was vital to get things right, but I soon started making progress.

Then something frightening happened, Ba went down with a bout of whooping cough. There had been a few cases around our part of Eastbourne, but they ought not to have affected Ba, with her sort of background I should never have allowed her to pick up whooping cough. I was panic-stricken but the local doctor, a young Scotsman, was reassuring. Every year thousands of children developed whooping-cough, and in the vast majority of cases it was all over within a week or two. Ba's recent history might turn out to be a complication, but on the other hand it probably wouldn't make much difference. And miraculously - or so I thought - he was right. Ba suffered a week of feverish illness, followed by a fortnight or so of the awful, distinctive cough. She also had one or two mild attacks of asthma, but the GP looked after her well and within a month she was clear.

In the meantime I had been writing hard, and when my typescript was completed I sent it to Mills and Boon. Never had success been more important, but my confidence was at a low ebb. I waited uneasily for Alan Boon's comments, but they weren't long in coming, and they were hugely reassuring. *Brown Furrows* had passed the Mills and Boon test, and would be accepted for publication as soon as I had supplied a further two beginnings, each one to include a synopsis and three introductory chapters. I looked again at my old material, but none of it was quite good enough so I started afresh, quickly mapping out a plot. *The Black Benedicts*. . . . Three chapters were produced, and I searched my mind for another idea. Nothing seemed to come right, though, and again it was getting hard to concentrate. For one thing it was almost April, and within a week or two we would be leaving our home in Eastbourne.

At that moment money wasn't the most pressing problem. We had sold more of our possessions and if we were careful the amount raised ought to keep us for another six months or so, even if I did not receive any speedy payment from Mills and Boon. But it wasn't going to be easy finding somewhere to live, not with summer just around the corner. Then I went into an estate agent's office, and there it was. Someone had been converting an old barn in the nearby village of Herstmonceux, and the result, a two bedroom cottage, was to be let furnished at a rent of two guineas per week. Hugh and I went to see it, and were smitten.

The kitchen and bathroom were brand new, the sitting-room/cum dining-room contained a genuine grandfather clock. As for the bedrooms, they had sloping ceilings and windows that peered out from under sparrow-haunted eaves. And there was a wild, over-grown garden.

We moved in towards the end of April. Bridget promised to visit us and I was happy to know she wasn't going to be far away, but our first weeks at Barn Cottage were unadulterated joy. It was a dolls' house, but it was *our* dolls' house, and it felt like a home. Half the barn had yet to be converted and there were plans to enlarge the cottage by adding a big first floor sitting-room, but as far as I was concerned no further additions were necessary. And the garden was a source of wonder. Originally attached to a house that no longer existed, it contained arches swathed in honeysuckle, beds full of roses, and a giant fruit cage. Everything was partially obscured by sorrel and bindweed, but Hugh quickly began clearing and digging, and remarkable things started to emerge. The diversion was good for him, too. Despite intensive efforts he had not yet been able to find any kind of suitable work; he had approached his old bosses at the Cabinet Office but for various reasons that, it seemed, was over. It was a difficult time. But after long hours in the garden I saw some of the strain beginning to lift.

And Ba seemed very fit. As spring turned to brilliant summer she spent hours running wild in the garden, and because she took so much interest Hugh gave her a plot of her own. The area was alive with birds and she turned into a junior ornithologist, studying the movements of goldfinches and identifying fragments of egg-shell. There was a small private school in the village, and we arranged to enrol her for the autumn term. After everything that had happened I wanted her to have one more completely free summer. Now nearly eight years old, she had a reading age of ten and was doing well in almost every subject except maths.

As for me, I had managed one or two more sample beginnings, but still they weren't right. I was experiencing a block. I would overcome it, though, I would get there, if only because it was something I had to do. In the meantime, when I wasn't writing I played house. The school cat had a litter of kittens and we acquired one, a tiny speck of black and white which we decided to call Mr Dinwiddy - Dinny for short. Dinny played in the garden, getting lost in the long grass. And one day, washing up in front of the kitchen window, I decided this was the happiest and most peaceful summer I had known for what seemed like a very long time. Then one morning Hugh received an official-looking letter. As he read it I saw how his face changed, and I felt real fear.

He owed money to the Inland Revenue, and they were going to make him bankrupt.

* * * * *

XXIV

The shock was horrible. I didn't know much about bankruptcy, but I understood that it involved disgrace, and it was menacing. Hugh may have seen it coming for some time, but that didn't mean he was not shattered when it happened. It was explained to me that the Official Receiver would now be in a position to seize our remaining assets, which consisted mainly of furniture and Hugh's treasured books. Most of the stuff was being stored in London, and the bankruptcy authorities would need to be given details so that access could be arranged. I was angry and wanted to fight, but that wasn't possible. Even I saw that, in the end.

Later that day we went for a walk, Hugh and Ba and I, along the lane that ran towards Herstmonceux Castle. The Castle had just become the new Royal Observatory and as a result was ringed by security, but we turned aside through a bluebell wood, and suddenly the ground fell away. There below us was a romantic rose-red fortress. . . a fairy castle, a place for silk-clad ladies and armoured champions.

Later on, when Ba was in bed and Hugh lost in some General's autobiography, I listened to the wireless and thought about my latest synopsis. Another storm had broken over us, and it was unlikely to be the last. But if we took each one as it came, we were bound to get through.

A week or so later Ba developed a streaming cold, and despite increasingly warm summer weather I kept her indoors. Then when the cold failed to clear up I sent for the local doctor, a rather brusque young man called Colin Graham. Dr Graham decided Ba was probably suffering from hay fever and accordingly gave her anti-histamine pills, but the pills had no effect and early one morning I found her gasping for breath. It was the worst asthma attack she had experienced, and a few hours later it was followed by another, then another. Thinking some allergic reaction might have caused her to panic Dr Graham put her on a low dose of pheno-barbitone, but the attacks continued remorselessly and the pheno-barbitone was stopped. By this time, she was hardly able to move from one room to another. Various drugs were tried, with minimal success. Then one night, after a serious attack, she was given an injection of adrenaline. This halted the attack immediately, but left her white and shivering with shock. Colin Graham explained that adrenaline injections were not exactly the ideal treatment for a child as young as Ba, but the alternative could be worse. When she wasn't able to breathe, something had to be done.

Hospital, everyone thought, would do her more harm than good, but after a week or two she was taken to the Royal East Sussex for X-rays and allergy tests. The X-rays showed lung markings consistent with asthma, the tests revealed sensitivity to pollen, poultry feathers, sheep's wool, the hair of dogs, cats, cows and rabbits, house dust and 'horse dandruff'. It seemed this did not necessarily mean she would experience a reaction every time she was exposed to any one of the items listed, but one or more was almost certain to be responsible for her present problems, the most likely culprits being pollen and animal fur. In other words the garden, and Mr Dinwiddy.

It was barely a year since Sally's death, and it was difficult to believe she could suddenly have become allergic to cats, but we were told that allergies could be acquired and lost again. Mr Dinwiddy would just have to go. We couldn't take the risk of keeping him. As for pollen, the worst would soon be over.

Ba was upset by the kitten's departure, and if anything her symptoms grew worse. Doctor Graham said he would like her to be seen by a consultant who lived nearby; just at the moment this man was away, but it would only be a matter of days. I moved Ba into our twin-bedded room, and Hugh took her place in the room next door. Colin Graham had stressed that we must call him, if we thought it necessary, at any hour of the day or night, and on numerous occasions he came along at two and three o'clock in the morning. As the cottage didn't have a phone, Hugh invariably had to get dressed and walk to a nearby call-box, then when the doctor had gone I would make tea and we'd sit together at the kitchen table, talking and yawning in the greyness of first light.

154

I was particularly anxious about the fact that Ba was barely able to eat. Between breathlessness and nausea - caused by a choking cough - she didn't want to swallow anything and at one point was being kept going on little more than glasses of egg and milk. During the day she read and did jig-saws, and as she spent a lot of time poring over her *Observer's Book of British Birds* our landlord got into the habit of writing her little notes; about the woodpecker that lived in his garden, and the nightingale he had heard one night as he walked home through the woods. She liked poetry, and to divert her I reeled off the things I had learned by heart when I was growing up. '*It was about the lovely close of a warm summer's day. . . there came a gallant merchant ship, full sail to Plymouth Bay. . . .*' Sometimes, I read to her from a book of children's verse. It could be hard to carry on reading - perhaps in the middle of the night or while we were waiting for the doctor - but as soon as I showed signs of drying up a voice would gasp: 'Go *on*. Don't stop!'

I was tired and worried, but I still had my writing. It was something I had to do, and it was keeping me sane. Also, the third beginning was taking shape at last.

Someone - I think it was Reggie's wife - had sent me a magazine article about Switzerland and the treatments available there for TB and other chest complaints. It wasn't the sort of thing we could afford, not yet, anyway, but as soon as we had some money. . . .

On Ba's birthday every child at the nearby school made her a card, but she wasn't well enough to look at them and when the doctor arrived he banned the cards from coming anywhere near her. There had been a lot of infections drifting around, and from her point of view the risk was serious. She was allowed to see the cards, from a distance.

When the consultant turned up, he told us the child was simply a victim of *status astmaticus*, in other words chronic, unremitting asthma. This imposed a tremendous strain, particularly on an eight-year-old, but children were resilient and despite her fragile appearance she must be quite a strong little girl, or she wouldn't have been able to stand it as well as she had done. He said she would almost certainly grow out of her problems, probably when she reached the age of thirteen or fourteen. In the meantime, a spell in Switzerland or France might be very useful. Otherwise, we could only hope the winter would bring some relief.

A day or so later Ba needed two adrenaline injections within the space of twenty-four hours, and before he left in the early hours of the morning Colin Graham called us into the kitchen for a chat. It was true, he said, that so far she had stood up to things well, but she was only eight and there was a limit to the battering her small body could take. At the moment she desperately needed a respite from continual breathing difficulties, and though getting away for a few days might not make any difference there was just a chance it would do the trick. Probably we should be thinking in terms of the seaside - or London. All things considered, London might be the safer bet.

At last we had something on which to focus. It was August in Festival of Britain year, and London was rumoured to be full, but we could try. Hugh rang dozens of middle-grade hotels and guest-houses, starting with Chelsea, Kensington and the West End, then working outwards. There was nothing anywhere, but then I thought about Brown's in Dover Street. One of the most splendidly comfortable of all the old family hotels, it would be expensive, but for a few days we should be able to manage it. If they had any space left.

They had. For three days during the following week they could offer us a large double room, and they would be happy to include a bed for the little girl. Their rates were steep, but no steeper than we had anticipated. We didn't have a car of our own and it was impossible to contemplate getting on and off trains with Ba, so we contacted a local taxi service and negotiated a reasonable rate. I don't know whether Ba was frightened by the thought of the journey. If she was she didn't show it, but as usual she was very breathless and Hugh carried her out to the car. I was anxious because there were no drugs or inhalers capable of providing instant relief - just the endless injections - and if she developed a serious attack we might have to make for a hospital. But the female driver was kind and helpful, and as we headed north across Sussex Ba's breathing became noticeably quieter. By the time we were halfway to London it was almost normal, and when we finally pulled up in front of Brown's Hotel every trace of asthma seemed to have disappeared. Because she was so weak she had to be carried up to our room, but that night she slept well and by morning she was eagerly taking in every detail of her surroundings.

The staff were very kind, reminding me of the people at Claridges, more than ten years earlier. In fact, it was a remarkable three days. We didn't go out because Ba wouldn't have been up to it, but we slept and relaxed, and had the unimaginable satisfaction of seeing her able to eat, and walk about, without perpetually gasping for air. We weren't sure what this miraculous change implied about the environment at Barn Cottage, but at least we knew the asthma could be switched off, and that was a huge relief.

When we got back to Sussex she walked into our cottage and up the stairs without any help. I saw her into bed, and went to fetch her a glass of hot milk. When I got back, she was struggling with the start of an attack.

This was disappointing but not completely unexpected and over the next few days it became clear that a lot had changed. Perhaps because of London - possibly because we were now well into August, and the lushness of summer had passed - most of the attacks seemed less violent, also they *were* attacks, with definite gaps between them. She could eat normally again and do a little walking, and because she wanted to do so she started regular lessons.

It was like waking slowly from a long nightmare, but now I knew that we had to think seriously about leaving Barn Cottage. Idyllic as it appeared, in some way it was bad for Ba, so there wasn't any alternative. Colin Graham had so far turned out to be fairly accurate in his recommendations, and as he suggested we should move to a pleasant spa town - somewhere like Tunbridge Wells, where the risk of allergy problems would be minimal - I started to make enquiries.

In the meantime, Hugh's solicitor had written to let him know the bankruptcy authorities had committed themselves to an unusually generous gesture. Most of our possessions had now been listed for sale, but because of 'special circumstances' the Churchill first editions, some of which carried personal messages, would eventually be restored to Hugh. (For the time being, they were to remain in the solicitor's hands.) Hugh had borne all the loss and humiliation extraordinarily well, but I could see that this boosted his spirits. Putting on a sudden spurt I completed the two beginnings required by Mills and Boon, and suddenly the package was almost ready. One complete novel, and two beginnings accompanied by synopses. The only thing still eluding me was a title for the second beginning.

Towards the end of August, Ba developed an attack in the middle of the night. When Colin Graham arrived he gave her an injection then sat with her until she fell asleep, but he pointed out the attack was much milder than the kind of thing we would have seen a week or so earlier. If we could just hold on to this improvement, and guard against allergic reactions, we were probably winning. When he left it was about five o'clock in the morning. I made a pot of tea, and as we had done so many times Hugh and I sat facing one another across the kitchen table. Through a partially open window we could hear small birds chattering, and as we drank our tea early gleams of sunrise started lighting up the recently cleared garden outside. The tea was warm and comforting, and as he often did, Hugh said something funny.

Optimism rushed over me. Ba was very much better, and somehow or other we would work out a way of making sure she stayed like that. I was going to make a lot of money, and when that happened we'd get her to Switzerland, where she would have the best treatment available, and be cured.

And suddenly I had a title for my second beginning. I'd call it *The Gates of Dawn*.

*   *   *   *   *

XXV

I sent my package off to Mills and Boon, and this time Alan's reply came almost by return of post. He liked everything, and the letter was followed by a contract designed to cover three novels. Once the contract had been signed and returned I would be receiving a cheque for the sum of one hundred pounds. It wasn't the end to all our troubles. *Brown Furrows* wouldn't be coming out for something like a year, and I wouldn't be getting any more money until another manuscript had been completed satisfactorily. But I had both feet on the first rung of the ladder and all I had to do was keep on climbing. Besides, one hundred pounds - the equivalent of fifteen hundred in today's money - seemed like rather a lot to us.

Having stayed for a few weeks at a guest-house in Tunbridge Wells, we decided to rent a nearby Victorian gate-lodge. Ba's asthma was in suspension, and I began working hard to finish both *The Black Benedicts* and *The Gates of Dawn*. Having been asked to choose a pseudonym I had picked 'Susan Barrie', but at this distance of time I have no idea whether the name had any special significance. Just before Christmas I went to London for a second meeting with Alan, and he gave me a lot of useful advice. I was beginning to understand how the romantic fiction business worked, and this was vital, because the formula was rigid.

In each novel a couple had to meet, fall in love and - eventually - get together, but there was more to it than that. Heroines were supposed to be young and attractive, though not stunning, and essentially innocent. Heroes - older and usually richer - needed to be good-looking men of impeccable character (though a 'ruthless streak' and an incisive temper were believed to be popular with the readership). Having met in the opening chapter, this pair were supposed to work their way through sixty thousands words of agony and misunderstanding before finally achieving an emotional dénouement in the last few pages of the book. Children and animals could be part of the picture, as could fiendishly glamorous Other Women, comforting aunt-type figures, splendid country houses and exotic overseas locations. Above all, these were stories in the traditional mould, and each one had to be properly equipped with a beginning, a middle and an end.

Partly because of late twentieth/twenty-first century moral attitudes, romantic fiction has now ceased to be a respectable art form, which makes it rather curious that Jane Austen's *Pride and Prejudice* - that archetypal romantic novel - resonates even more powerfully today than it did in its author's lifetime. To some extent this phenomenon may be attributed to a brilliant TV spectacular and an actor called Colin Firth, but once drawn in, many women in particular are held by the fact that *Pride and Prejudice* places under a microscope that most significant of all human relationships, the life-long bond - physical, mental and spiritual - that can develop between one man and one woman. Real love is a phenomenon in itself, and in the end it's what romantic fiction is all about.

Even at its peak the romance industry was derided, but its principal crime had to do with the fact that it had *become* an industry. There were just too many authors churning out too many stories, and no artistic *genre* can easily survive mass production. While its boom lasted, though, romance was hugely successful – comparable, perhaps, to some sections of the modern pop industry - and a number of publishing companies jumped on the band-wagon, though none were ever to equal the success of Mills and Boon. M&B's triumph was to swell the list of publishing legends, and to a very large extent it was designed and crafted by one remarkable man, Alan Boon himself. Alan's brothers, John and Caryl, played their part but Alan had an extraordinarily analytical mind[*], and taken together with common sense and a wide understanding of literature this spelt out a recipe for publishing success. Unemotional - on the surface, at least - and certainly not over-chatty, he could be quite difficult to understand, but it didn't take me long to gauge the level of his ability, or to realise that I would be wise to take any advice he cared to offer.

I went to London just once while we were at the gate-lodge, but this was more than enough, if only because the exercise called for a bit

---

[*] Alan's son Julian has turned into a respected criminal psychologist

of organization. On that January day I had left Hugh and Ba with a lunch that consisted of beef stew and vegetables to be followed by rice pudding, and I had also left directions. When I arrived home, around six o'clock, it seemed everything had gone perfectly - they had had a nice day, and an enjoyable lunch. Hugh, it seemed, had dealt with food preparation, then Ba had taken charge on the washing-up front. The beef stew had been very nice, they said, and the vegetables. The rice pudding, though, had refused to heat through properly. Hugh said he had put it in the oven and adjusted the temperature as directed, but still the creamy mass had remained tepid. It seemed very odd until Ba followed me into the kitchen, where I was about to get started on supper.

'*I* think,' she said judiciously, 'Daddy ought to have shut the oven door.'

When spring came we moved to Winchelsea, a mediaeval hill-top village close to the border with Kent. Originally one of the guardian Cinque Ports it had once stood on a cliff over-looking the sea, but over six centuries the English Channel had receded until now it lay more than two miles away on the other side of a sheep filled, bird haunted marsh. At one time the village - officially a town - had been surrounded by walls, and though most of these had fallen away two original gates remained standing. The town of Rye, another Cinque Port, lay roughly a mile away to the east, but to the west and north there was only the deep tranquillity of eastern Sussex.

Built - so far as I remember - into the old south wall, our small rented house looked towards the sea. Ba's asthma had not so far re-appeared and though I did feel apprehensive, particularly as summer approached, I was determined to be optimistic. We had no pets, and the Winchelsea air seemed much fresher than the air at Herstmonceux. Somehow, it was going to be all right. We started going for long walks, sometimes across the marshes but mostly through fields and woodland, starting out from the old windmill that still stands near the village. Usually we aimed for some impossible goal. I remember wanting to reach Icklesham windmill, which beckoned from several miles away. . . we were never going to get there, not with an eight-year-old who still wasn't strong, but it was fun planning. Sometimes we took a picnic and as we ate our sandwiches, perhaps sitting on a log surrounded by new-born lambs, I felt as if the great difficult world had somehow started to pull away and leave us alone.

It hadn't, of course. Hugh's bankruptcy hearing was due in a couple of months' time, and every employment possibility still seemed closed to him. As for me, I had made progress with *The Black Benedicts*, only to be told that Alan would much prefer me to finish *Gates of Dawn*. *Brown Furrows* was due to come out in October, and that was something to look forward to. But money was short and I was finding it hard to write.

Our Winchelsea house was not particularly expensive, but it was too expensive for us. Reluctantly I wrote to the owner, a young barrister called John Reed, and asked if he would release us from the tenancy, which had been supposed to run for one year. In response, I got the kindest letter I have ever received in connection with a business issue. He told me not to give the tenancy another thought. Obviously I had enough to worry about. And he wished me good luck. I don't know whether John Reed ever became a judge, but in my opinion he ought to have done.

For a short time we went to stay with Reggie and his wife - not ideal from Hugh's point of view - then we moved into an apartment nearby. We had a little money left, and though my writing was still affected by some kind of block, I knew it would get going again. Anyway, when autumn came Ba really ought to be starting school, and after that I might be able to get some kind of part-time job, just to see us through until the book money started flowing in earnest. It wasn't what I had planned for Ba, I had envisaged a nice private boarding school. But life, as I had reason to know, doesn't necessarily work out the way you plan it. And the private boarding school might well come later on.

I started looking around at job possibilities, then one warm summer's afternoon Ba developed an asthma attack. I hadn't yet told her about school, or the possibility that I might be going out to work. She had seemed relaxed and happy, but it was high summer - and Reggie's wife Dora had a large tabby cat. During the previous months Ba had been in accidental contact with one or two cats and had seemed to suffer no ill effects. But it might just be that certain cats were different.

Because she had been so much better we thought the attack might turn out to be a one-off, but within days she was almost as bad as she had been at Barn Cottage, too short of breath to eat or move around, and once again surviving on a cocktail of drugs. I was desperately anxious - also, it was very unlikely that I would now be able to take a job.

One evening, as I sat talking to Dora, I mentioned the Trust Hugh had set up for the benefit of his older daughters. At one time it had occurred to me that this might be opened to include Ba, but Enid had control of the Trust and when approached through her solicitor had responded with a blunt refusal. Dora was shocked and incredulous about this. Surely Enid wouldn't continue to refuse, not if she knew all the circumstances? After all, her whole life revolved around children. Someone really ought to go and talk to her.

I recoiled. There weren't many possibilities I would not have contemplated just then, but an approach to Enid was one of them. Then Dora said that she would do it. Beaconsfield wasn't all that far away. She would go to see Hugh's ex-wife, and put the situation in front of her. It wasn't a question of asking for charity, we had a right to have that Trust opened up.

This was awful. I couldn't stand the thought of Enid being approached, and couldn't begin to imagine what Hugh would say when he found out. But we had so few choices, and Ba was a sick child.

When she was younger Dora had done quite a lot of amateur acting, and she had an actor's enthusiasm for getting mixed up in highly charged situations. She didn't drive a car, but she took a bus to Beaconsfield and walked the rest of the way to *Green Hedges*.

Told this woman on the doorstep was some relation of mine Enid may have felt a degree of curiosity, or perhaps she was drawn by the tenuous link with Hugh. Anyway, Dora was admitted. To begin with, I think, she was polite and conciliatory. Surely, she suggested, it should be possible to open up the Trust - after all, Hugh had established it for the security of his children. And his little girl, Rosemary, was very unwell.

Definitely not, said Enid - or words to that effect. The Trust had been set up for Gillian and Imogen, and she had their interests to consider. But now, Dora pointed out, Hugh had another daughter. Everyone was worried about Rosemary - alias Ba - and surely. .

'I don't care,' said Enid Blyton, 'if the child dies.'

I have no real idea what I thought when I first heard these words. I do know what I think about them now. As a very young girl Enid had been devastated when her father went off with another woman, and devastation had turn to nightmare when she found herself side-lined in

163

favour of a new half-sister. Then she had met Hugh. I have no doubt at all that her second marriage was genuinely happy and successful, but my husband was her first and to some extent probably her last love. The marriage ended and both moved on, but there is no doubt that Enid was hurt; in particular, perhaps, by the knowledge that Hugh had a new family. So when approached on the subject of Ba she reacted like the damaged child she was. I am sure she regretted what she said, and in fact the Trust was opened - eventually - to release two hundred pounds.

Enid's teenage sufferings - and their long term effects - serve to underline the point that parents, generally speaking, have an absolute duty to stay together. I always felt that Hugh and I were somehow meant for one another, but there never was a time when I wasn't troubled by the fact that in marrying me he turned his back on other commitments. He and Enid would almost certainly have broken up, even if I hadn't been around; and of course there had been another wife, and another child, before her. But I still regret having once been caught up in the nightmare of a divorce, and I particularly regret the fact that two little girls were involved.

Hugh's bankruptcy hearing can't have been easy, because these things never are, but once it was over we could at least begin to sort ourselves out. A doctor said he thought Ba should be taken further away from the river, so we found a little guest house in the Buckinghamshire village where long ago Thomas Gray composed his Elegy, and at first she seemed quite a lot better, though the improvement didn't last very long. Then one warm summer evening, as we were wondering what to do next, a young man in a trench coat caught up with us. He was a journalist from the *Daily Mirror*, and he wanted to talk about Hugh's bankruptcy.

Hugh had always refused to see any journalist and instinctively I wanted to follow this example, but the young man pointed out how useful a little publicity might turn out to be, particularly in view of the fact that Hugh was still seeking a job. Anyway, they would be writing something, whether we talked to them or not. In the end we let the reporter in, together with his cameraman, and there followed a brief interview. At this distance of time I can't remember exactly what was said, but I know I was uneasy - although the young journalist was certainly sympathetic, particularly on the subject of Ba.

And when the piece appeared, there was nothing seriously offensive about it. Depressingly, the paper received no calls from would-be employers, but a couple of days later they passed on to us a letter contained in a handsome cream-coloured envelope. The letter had been typed on notepaper belonging to the Dorchester Hotel, and enclosed within it there was a cheque for two hundred pounds - around three thousand in today's money. The letter and cheque had been despatched by an aide attached to the Sultan of Johore, who had been staying at the Dorchester. His Excellency, the letter said, had noted the newspaper story relating to Lieutenant-Colonel Pollock, and hoped the attached cheque would be of use.

This was like a miracle. I looked at the letter, and the cheque, and could barely believe they were real. Then I just felt dizzy with gratitude.

Hugh remarked that it was one thing to advertise one's misfortunes for the purpose of attracting employment, quite another to start accepting charity. We couldn't possibly take the cheque. We could, I said, because we had a sick child, and because most of our assets had been taken away. We hadn't any choice. He still hated the idea, but in the end he gave way. I wrote a thank you letter - short but sincere - and we cashed the Sultan's cheque. Within hours, the bankruptcy authorities were directing us to hand the money over immediately.

I may have been naive, but it hadn't crossed my mind they would do such a thing. The two hundred pounds had been exactly what we needed, and now it was being wrenched away. I got in touch with our solicitor, but he saw little chance of salvaging anything. He pointed out that Hugh had been made bankrupt by the Inland Revenue, which meant few concessions were likely to be made.

Phoning the Dorchester, I found the Sultan was planning to stay on for a further week or two, so I told Hugh I was going up to London. And I wasn't going to argue about it. I knew what I had to do.

I travelled the short distance by train, and when I got to the Dorchester asked if I might see his Excellency the Sultan of Johore, or a member of his staff. As I spoke, I tried not to look at the receptionist's face.

I felt low and worn out and humiliated. I sat in the lobby for a few minutes, then I was taken upstairs and shown into the sitting-room of an opulent suite, at which point I started to feel sick. This time I was left alone for a very long time, so long that it began to seem certain I had been forgotten. Eventually a man appeared - olive-skinned, and wearing a neat dark suit. One of the Sultan's aides. He fixed me with a cool stare, and I embarked on what I had to say. Having apparently read about my husband's recent financial problems, the Sultan had very kindly sent us a cheque for two hundred pounds, but now the bankruptcy authorities were going to seize this money, and I thought - I wondered whether the Sultan would be willing to intervene. The words were almost choking me, but I forged ahead. If the Sultan, or perhaps one of his staff, could just approach the British authorities and explain that the money had been intended for my husband's personal use. . . it might just make a difference.

The man was probably thinking that Hugh Pollock truly was unfortunate. On top of all his other problems, he had a wife who possessed no pride.

An approach might be made, he said stiffly. However. . . the British bankruptcy authorities had evidently made their decision already. Silence, and a shrug. Could I find my own way downstairs?

I thanked him, and left. I had done my best, but it hadn't been good enough. I was tired and bitterly disappointed.

I did feel better, though, once I was back with Hugh and Ba. We would manage somehow, we always had done. I might still succeed in getting a part-time job, or Hugh might. Two days later, we learned that the Official Receiver had reversed his decision. Following representations from the Sultan of Johore, Hugh could now keep the two hundred pounds.

*　*　*　*　*

XXVI

Days after this, I received a parcel containing six complimentary copies of *Brown Furrows*. My first Mills and Boon novel had found its way into print. Of course I had been published before, but not for fifteen years or so, and anyway this was my first hardback production. Its appearance might not be going to affect our finances - not for a while, anyway - but it did give me a lift. Reading it while I got the lunch ready, I felt as if it had been written by somebody else.

The book was a bright spot, but it was hard to remain positive for long, because apart from anything else Ba's asthma had not disappeared with the coming of autumn, or even winter. Helped by the Sultan's money we took her back to Sussex, where we found comfortable lodgings in the house of a charming Scottish lady called Mrs Stobart. Mrs Stobart looked after us well and I began struggling to write again, trying to finish *Gates of Dawn*, then as Christmas approached we took an apartment in the nearby town of Seaford. We hoped the Channel air might make a difference to Ba, but it didn't, and a doctor told us it was time she saw some kind of senior consultant. She had already been examined by two specialists, but it might, he thought, help if we went right to the top – perhaps, at this stage, to a paediatrician rather than a lung specialist. This was going to dislocate our desperately tight budget, but somehow or other we would manage. Recently the Officers' Association, having heard about Hugh's difficulties, had been in touch to ask if they could help with any specific, necessary expense - by this time Hugh had learned to swallow his pride, and he wrote to them about Ba. Not only did the Officers' Association agree to pay the consultant's bill, through medical advisers they managed to arrange the whole thing, and within a couple of weeks Ba and I were on our way to London, where we were to keep an appointment with one of Harley Street's most distinguished paediatricians, Dr Wilfred Sheldon (later Sir Wilfred). Dr Sheldon had recently become responsible for looking after the royal children, Prince Charles and Princess Anne.

It was one of Ba's better days but by the time we got to Dr Sheldon's consulting rooms she was pale and very breathless. She was told to lie down on a couch while the doctor checked her lungs, then she was taken to the door and instructed to go back down a long, curving staircase. At the bottom, on the right, she would find a big room where she must wait while the doctor talked to her mother. Dr Sheldon asked me a few questions about the medication she had been receiving, then he delivered his verdict. My daughter was chronically asthmatic – obviously – and at the moment she was in a fairly fragile condition, but by the time she reached her teens the problem might well have disappeared. In the meantime, we ought to find her a good boarding-school, preferably somewhere near the sea. The Welsh coast would be ideal. *'Then don't go and live near her'.*

Our own GP was bewildered and disappointed. At the very least he had been expecting a detailed analysis, followed by suggestions for treatment, and he didn't think Dr Sheldon's assessment had made much sense. Of course, the consultant hadn't seen her with a full scale attack. 'There isn't a school in the country,' the GP said, 'that would take her as she is now.'

Looking back, I'm not certain Dr Sheldon's view was necessarily wrong. He *was* a paediatrician, not a lung specialist, and he was looking at what might now be called the whole child. Probably he was right to point out that Ba stood a good chance of out-growing her asthma, the trouble was that she was still a long way from reaching that stage of development, and in the meantime she was a little girl struggling to cope with constant bouts of damaging and distressing illness.

One thing stuck in my mind, though. Dr Sheldon had mentioned the sea. The Sussex coast didn't appear to be doing much good, but maybe some other kind of coast. . . .

Christmas passed, and on a bleak January day I purchased the *Lady* magazine. And there it was, under 'Accommodation to Let'. A converted boat-house, situated in a Cornish village. Portscatho, on the Roseland Peninsula. If only we could. . . why couldn't we, though? The rent wasn't much, and our train fares wouldn't be too expensive. Dr Sheldon had talked about the Welsh coast, but why shouldn't Cornwall do just as well?

I arranged things, and on a day in early February we set out for London and the Cornish Riviera Express. Our journey had an anxious, uneasy start, but by the time we reached Paddington Ba seemed quite a lot better. At half past ten the powerful steam engine drew its long line of coaches on to a west-bound track, and my spirits began to climb. Soon after lunch we reached the red fields of Devon, then we were skimming the edge of the sea. The train threaded its way through arches made of fuchsia pink rock and by tea-time we were on Brunel's bridge, high above the Tamar River, then we were in Cornwall.

There were little fields and deep wooded valleys, and over to our right the scarred brown slopes of Bodmin Moor. Bits of Masefield's *West Wind* started running through my head: *'The west land. . . the old brown hills. . . .'*

We left our train at Truro and by the time we got to Portscatho it was already dark, but I could smell the sea and hear its voice. Ba was practically asleep on her feet and I had a cold coming on, but the boat-house was everything I could have hoped for - clean and bright and prettily furnished.

When I drew the curtains back in the morning, I found myself looking through a short alley-way into something like a stage set. There was a small harbour fringed by up-turned boats, and beyond that an expanse of pale, early morning sea. Just visible through drifting mist, I glimpsed a range of headlands. Apart from the wailing of sea-birds, everything was deeply quiet.

And Ba's asthma had disappeared. She had caught my cold and I waited anxiously for that to produce complications, but nothing developed. Within three or four days we had both recovered and on a warm, still morning I took her down to look at the beach, where our feet sank into yellow sand. Steam was rising from the rocks and floating along the shore and we walked beside it, watching the red-legged oyster-catchers that paddled at the water's edge, and gathering up empty cowrie shells. It was magic, and yet it was real. For the first time ever, a place had gone beyond what I expected of it.

And Ba continued to be free of asthma. Her strength returned quickly - as it always seemed to do - and we began walking, the three of us, as we hadn't been able to do since Winchelsea. We walked along the shore and over the green cliff-top, and down the shuttered lanes until we reached a hamlet called Treloan - I went back to Portscatho a few years ago but although I searched exhaustively

169

Treloan appeared to have vanished. I wanted, very much, to reach St Anthony's Head and the miracle-working chapel that was said to have been built by Joseph of Arimathea, but they were just too far away.

Within a fortnight, my writers' block had evaporated and I was working on another novel - not *The Gates of Dawn*. While Hugh did the shopping, occasionally taking a bus to Truro, I sat in our little sitting-room and made rapid progress with a story I had decided to set in southern Cornwall. *Hotel Stardust*. To this day, when I look at its opening pages I am back in that little room, gazing out at the harbour, and the Nare Head beyond.

Alan Boon liked *Stardust*, in fact he liked it very much, but he was insistent that I must finish *Gates of Dawn*, then if I liked I could complete *Stardust* in place of *The Black Benedicts*, on which he had never been all that keen. After that - if everything was satisfactory - we would be looking at another contract. In the meantime money was running short again, and realistically it was going to be some time before my literary efforts started to produce more cheques. We wanted to keep Ba in the West Country, but this time one or other of us really needed to find some kind of job. Perhaps, I thought, it could be both of us. I was a reasonable cook - no, quite a good cook - and Hugh was a competent gardener. There must, surely, be people who would pay us to do their cooking and gardening for them. We might even find something that would provide us with accommodation. In my spare time I could go on writing, and eventually our problems would be solved. It would have to be in the West Country, though. I couldn't take Ba back east again, not just yet.

I talked my plan over with Hugh, then looked down the *Lady's* Situations Vacant column and found just one possibility, in Devon. A senior teacher - female - who lived in the coastal village of Shaldon, beside the Teign River, was searching for a gardener and cook-housekeeper. She could offer comfortable, spacious quarters and a reasonable salary. She also had no objection to 'one child'. There was an exchange of letters, and we spoke on the telephone. I explained that neither of us had done this kind of thing before, but that Hugh was a keen gardener and I was an experienced cook. No references were demanded, and it was agreed we should start as soon as possible.

I hated leaving our boat-house, but it wasn't as if we wouldn't be coming back, to Cornwall at any rate. It wasn't good-bye.

Tucked away behind a tree-covered promontory known as the Ness, Shaldon was – still is, I believe - a village full of fat cream-coloured cottages, most of them covered in thatch and surrounded by roses. Our destination turned out to be a large 1920's family house with a substantial garden, and I wasn't surprised its owner needed help. As promised our accommodation was roomy and comfortable, with two good-sized bedrooms and a large sitting-room that seemed to be full of books - Ba was thrilled to discover something called *Green's History of England*, which apparently ran to about twenty volumes.

As for our employer - I'll call her Miss X - she appeared rather taciturn. She took no notice whatsoever of Ba, which, considering she was in the teaching profession, seemed rather odd. Her detachment might turn out to be a good thing, though, if it meant we were going to be left with more time to ourselves. I didn't think the garden would be a problem. Hugh knew what he was doing, and it seemed unlikely he would suffer much from interference. I was nervous, though. The housework didn't bother me and for some considerable time I had known I could cook - false modesty confuses things - but I had never before been paid to cook, and Miss X's first supper was a nightmare. It seemed to go down well, though, in more senses than one, and after a few days Miss X pronounced herself satisfied with my work.

So this was going to be our life, for a while, at least. Ba was feeling well and studying hard. And Hugh was always happy enough to spend his days in a garden.

Then one morning Miss X came to see me in the kitchen. Apparently she had something important to say, and at once I felt uneasy.

She said that she was still pleased with my efforts. In that direction, she had no complaints at all. My husband, however, was another matter. Twice she had seen him smoking a cigarette when he ought to have been working. Furthermore there was a large bed, full of weeds, that had not yet been dug. True, my husband had done some planting and sowing, but what use was that kind of thing when the whole place was so untidy? I would have to speak with him, make him understand he needed to do a proper day's work. Otherwise . . . she would be sorry to see us go, but really there would be no alternative.

I was extremely angry. I told her I would not be asking my husband to do anything at all, but that need not concern her because

171

we wouldn't be staying. She said she was sorry I had decided to take such an attitude; she still had no fault to find with me, but she needed a gardener as well as a cook-housekeeper. It was agreed we should complete one calendar month - so far, we had been with Miss X for about twenty-one days - and that we should receive payment for the period we had worked.

Later on I asked Hugh why on earth he hadn't cleared the over-grown patch, and he said he had been getting around to it. He thought, actually, that I had been a bit hasty, and said he would sort things out with Miss X. Oh no, he wouldn't, I said. For one thing, I had no intention of continuing to work for a woman who talked about my husband as if he were some kind of sub-standard labourer.

There were campsites beside the river bank, and I promptly went out to see if we could rent a caravan. Most, I discovered, were reserved for holiday lettings, but as it was still only April the place was deserted, and I secured a small van without much difficulty. In those days caravans did not usually have either piped water or mains drainage; water was collected from a standpipe, and waste was carried away in buckets - if you were lucky, you might find a toilet block nearby. But our little caravan was pretty and clean, and Ba was thrilled to bits with it. As for me, it was what the French call a *coup de foudre*. I fell in love with the whole concept of caravanning, and that passion was to remain a part of my life, re-surfacing at all kinds of peculiar moments. Even today, the sight of a caravan lifts my heart.

And Hugh quickly found another job, this time as gardener at an hotel about two miles away. Every day he travelled there by bus, and I was left with time on my hands. I tried to write, but it felt like fiddling while fire took hold of Rome. I wanted to be doing something active, something that might help to turn our present situation around. I noticed a small shop to be let in the village, and thought of all the things we might do with it - could do with it, if only we had a little capital. I talked this over with Hugh one night, and he started thinking about the Pollock family book business, a valuable concern which would have been his if he had not many years earlier urged his father to settle the whole thing on Fred, who - unlike Hugh - had always been happy to centre his life on Ayrshire. Fred had put a lot of work into Stephen and Pollock, and it was perfectly fair and reasonable that in the end he should have acquired undisputed possession; Hugh had inherited a smallish sum of money, which I think had gone into the Trust set up for Gillian and Imogen. But the business had been his birthright, and with some reluctance he now decided he might ask Fred for a loan. Just enough, perhaps, to set us up in something like a small shop – or tea-room - some kind of business. The Official Receiver, after all, would not have any control over borrowed money.

The letter was written and posted. Hugh set off for his gardening job, and later that morning Ba and I walked up over Torbay cliff-top, looking for the place where he worked. It was a warm May morning, and when we found him we threw toffees over the hedge. A few days later, Fred's reply arrived.

It was a deeply unpleasant letter, or so it seemed to me. Apparently he might have been able to help, but his three children were all getting married and as a result he was in the process of buying three new properties. Anyway, he was a little surprised his brother had the nerve to ask. *After the way he had treated poor Enid.*

Years later I was to be told that Fred, a kind and reasonable man, had regretted but understood the far-off childhood trauma that had seemed to turn his brother against him. Maybe, just maybe, Fred really was kind and reasonable. I do know he had lifelong health problems. I also know that he had once been quite close to Enid, and like half the London publishing world had eagerly accepted her side of the story.

Hugh was never again to be in contact with his brother - who sadly died the following year - but on his side at least I don't believe there was real bitterness.

And we had other things to worry about. There had been a lot of rain that spring, and the river was beginning to rise. We were in a vulnerable corner of our site and needed to move, at least to one of the other caravans, but by the time things began to look seriously nasty it was late afternoon, and a Saturday afternoon at that. All the other vans were locked and their owners proved impossible to contact. It was suggested we might spend the night inside Shaldon's village hall, but – crazily perhaps - I was afraid this might not be good for Ba. Also the caravan was our home, our refuge, and I didn't want to leave, not to sit all night in a public shelter, as if the war had come back to claim us.. At dusk Hugh went to look at the river, studying it with the experienced eye of a country-loving Scotsman. If the Teign were to over-flow it would roll over the top of a protective wall and descend on to the roof of our caravan. But it was still nearly three feet from the top, and in Hugh's judgment it was not going to rise any further.

We didn't go to bed. The police, I think, watched all night, and by morning the level had gone down, very slightly. Finally putting in an appearance, our landlord moved us to another caravan in a safer corner of the site, then someone told me there were more vans on the opposite side of the river. They were in open countryside a mile or so up-stream, and they belonged to a farm. They were also said to be a good safe distance from the river bank.

After Hugh had left for work, Ba and I set out to walk over the long bridge that separated Shaldon from the town of Teignmouth. These days the town has probably stretched itself some distance up river, but on that morning fifty years ago we simply turned left on to the Newton Abbot road, and within minutes the narrow suburbs had been left behind.

It was a spectacular morning. The sun was shining, the hedges were full of primroses, the trees were breaking into leaf. I felt - or half of me did - that I was setting out on a wild, pointless errand, but at the same time a bubble of hope was urging me along. We walked about two miles, then on the left-hand side of the road I spotted a farm track sloping away towards the river. I could see what appeared to be a large, square white house, and I could also see the caravans, tucked away in a small field next to an orchard. This was almost too good to be true.

We made our way down the track and round the edge of a farm yard, until we reached the house. The front door was opened by a lady whose name was Mrs Coaker - a widow with four children, she had somehow managed to keep the farm going after her husband's death and was being helped, now, by her nineteen-year-old elder son. As for the caravans, they just brought in a little extra money. We could have one, if we liked (my spirits rose). But if we were going to stay for a while she could do better than that. She could give us rooms inside the house. Originally a manor-house built partly in the seventeenth century, the farm had proved too big for the Coaker family's requirements, so several rooms had recently been turned into an apartment designed for seasonal visitors: two bedrooms and a bathroom, a large sitting-room - once the main dining-room - and a small, neatly constructed kitchen. The apartment was already booked throughout August, but for the next ten or twelve weeks it was ours if we wanted it.

The rent, I thought, was certain to be too high. It wasn't, though, it was hardly more than we had been paying for our caravan in Shaldon.

The walk back to Shaldon took some time, but Ba seemed all right and I barely noticed the distance. When Hugh came home I gave him our news, then a few days later we called a taxi and removed ourselves to Wear Farm, in the parish of Bishopsteignton.

Life was easier, and I could dare to look ahead. Hugh carried on with his gardening job, and Ba made friends with nine-year-old Anna Coaker. As my block cleared away I got my little portable typewriter out - I had come close to selling it - and started working to complete *Hotel Stardust*. When this was finished I sent it off to Alan, then I started on something fresh, this time telling the story of a tragic young girl in love with a high-flying barrister. *Carpet of Dreams. . . .* To my own astonishment this was completed inside a month, and I sent it off to join its predecessors.

It was the summer of 1953, and when Coronation Day came we listened to the ceremony on an ancient wireless set. The following week I took Ba to Newton Abbot to see the whole thing on film, and as the sunny days went on she and Anna seemed to spend half their time playing coronations along the wide south terrace; at least until they got bored and went hurrying off to help collect the day's batch of new-laid eggs. I remember hoping desperately that Ba was going to be all right - it was high summer after all, and we were living in a lush environment - but the asthma stayed away. And she was doing well with her 'schoolwork'. Wildly enthusiastic about history, she was getting into the works of Arthur Bryant, and seeing her anxiety to read anything and everything I also steered her in the direction of Jane Austen's *Northanger Abbey,* which she adored. (Afterwards she took it upon herself to dig out a copy of the much more grown-up *Persuasion*, which she liked even better.)

Hugh, on the whole, was pleased with her, but he wished she would take more interest in maths.

Early in July, I received a letter from Alan Boon. *Brown Furrows*, he said, had been well received and I was due a small royalty payment. As for *The Gates of Dawn*, that was to be published shortly. In the meantime he had now read the completed *Hotel Stardust,* and also the brand new *Carpet of Dreams* - both were 'excellent', and I would be receiving advances to cover them. In fact, I would be getting three advances, because he knew I had already started something else. I would also, of course, be receiving a second three-book contract.

Shortly afterwards, *Gates of Dawn* was published in hardback. I got my complimentary copies, my new contract and a cheque. I think the cheque was for something like six hundred pounds - approximately nine thousand in today's terms. And this, I had been assured, was only the beginning

*   *   *   *   *

XXVIII

I had always known that things would change for us, that somehow or other we would get through. Our lives had broken up and we had walked into a kind of wilderness, but since that crucial day three years earlier Hugh's drinking problem had disappeared, and though Ba had been ill she now seemed to be fit again. As for me, I was happier and stronger than I had ever been.

But we needed to find a home, if only because our corner of Wear Farm was to be let from the first week in August. I got in touch with an estate agent, and was shown pictures of a nice modern house in the village of Bishopsteignton. It wasn't particularly exciting or romantic, but it was beautifully furnished and equipped and it had a garden full of shrubs and fruit trees. We signed up for a period of twelve months, and then we began to think about something else. Mrs Coaker had decided Anna should go away to boarding-school, and she believed she had found the ideal place. Well run and not very large, it seemed to be set high above the seaside town of Salcombe. She asked if we would be interested in looking at the school's prospectus, and as soon as I saw it I knew this was something we had to do for Ba. '*Send her away to boarding-school. . . somewhere not far from the sea*'.

We visited the school together - Ba and I, Anna and her mother - and my initial impression was confirmed. It was a small place, but it took girls from the age of seven right through to eighteen. The two Principals were extremely understanding about Ba's health, and they promised she would be carefully supervised. Having had a chat with her they felt she was way ahead in certain subjects, and would no doubt catch up quickly in other areas. (It wasn't every day, after all, that you found a ten-year-old hooked on Jane Austen and Arthur Bryant.)

I asked Ba what she thought, and she seemed happy with the idea. After all, she and Anna would be together, even sleeping in the same room. And though she was shy and reserved she didn't seem nervous at the prospect of school. We booked her in, Hugh gave up his gardening job and a week or two later we moved to Bishopsteignton.

As soon as we were settled I started work again, but that was all right because it was what I wanted to be doing. At the same time, it was fun playing house again. Polishing furniture and baking cakes, making sure the apple green carpet stayed as immaculate as the day we moved in. I was getting Ba's school things ready, too. Hugh seemed relaxed, and I remember him making us laugh, one afternoon over tea, with his impression of a Scottish country boy calling at the Manse. It was the sort of thing he was good at, when he felt like it.

Then one evening I noticed Ba was short of breath. She said she was all right, but the problem worsened rapidly and by morning she had fully blown asthma. The attack did not clear up, and when I called a doctor he gave her adrenaline at once. As usual this brought relief, but the asthma didn't go away - not then, or the next day, or the day after that. Once again, it was continuous and incapacitating.

I asked her if she had been worried about starting school, but she shook her head. No, she hadn't been worrying about school. Perhaps, I thought, she might be allergic to something in the house, and I found that the beautiful green carpet, which ran into every room, had recently been cleaned. The doctor wanted to know whether any particular chemicals had been used and our landlord very helpfully supplied details, but in the end it seemed unlikely the cleaning agent could have triggered anything. After three or four weeks, we knew there was only one thing for it. Our rooms at Wear Farm were free again and we would simply have to go back there, at least for a while.

Back at the farm Ba did seem a little better, but only a little. After a few days she developed a temperature, and late that evening I called for help. The doctor, a pleasant young woman who had been dragged away from a dinner-party, told us Ba was on the edge of pneumonia; because she had been too breathless to climb the stairs she had not yet gone to bed, and the doctor felt it would be best just to tuck her up on the sofa in the sitting-room. She was given M&B, and the doctor promised to be back first thing in the morning. It was an awful night, but by morning her temperature was down and the following day we were told she was no longer in immediate danger of pneumonia. Checks did suggest that one of her lungs might have collapsed, and though a hastily arranged hospital X-ray revealed this was not the case, it was agreed she could not, at that moment, be sent away to school. For the time being she needed careful handling, and a healthy environment.

We took her back to Cornwall, this time to the north coast. I found a house at Treyarnon Bay near Padstow, and in November we settled in. This time our windows looked out on the surge of the Atlantic - when the sun was shining it was a view coloured in blue and white, when the December gales began creamy-grey spume settled in drifts on the cliff-top, startling the huddled sheep, and our kitchen linoleum billowed as if the sea itself were underneath. It was exciting, and I loved it. While Hugh did most of our shopping, setting out across the cliff and walking miles to a village called St Merryn, I wrote, and wrote and wrote. And Ba was better. For the time being at least, she was no longer dependent on drugs or injections. Treyarnon was too wild for her, though - because the wind took her breath away, she could hardly go out at all. We were in the wrong place, and when spring came we moved again, this time to the village of Coverack, on the Lizard Peninsula, where the air was warm and humid.

When we arrived the daffodils were already out. Our rented cottage was newly furnished and equipped. . . . And almost as soon as we got there I knew we had made a terrible mistake, because Ba was very much worse. A local GP fixed her up with the new anti-asthmatic inhaler - fuelled by something called Rybarvin, it had a mild palliative effect - but he didn't believe in giving adrenaline. Shocked by her inability to get out and about he did suggest making temporary use of a wheel-chair, but his partner felt this was too drastic and might have a devastating effect psychologically. I was inclined to agree with this.

But there were some bright moments and on calm, warm days Ba was able to get out. Once, we took her down on to the quayside to see a new lifeboat launched. And local people were very kind, in particular an old fisherman called Sam Hewett, who brought us fresh mackerel and told extraordinary stories, mostly about the Coverack of fifty years before. On one occasion, according to him, the authorities had arrived to seize a consignment of ship-wrecked brandy, only to discover that it had apparently de-materialized. 'There was one 'ouse had four bottles in the harmonium, an'ee still played lovely'. Mr Hewett's only son was part of the lifeboat crew, and he had no daughters. 'I'd give'ee a thousand pound,' he told us one morning, 'for that li'l maid'.

One evening, before going to bed, I went to check on Ba and found her sitting up, gasping for breath. There were tears rolling down her cheeks, and she whispered that it wouldn't stop. '*Why doesn't it stop . . . ?*'

This was almost more than I could bear. I told her that very soon now it would all go away again, as it had done on other occasions. That one day, when she was a little bit older, it would go away and not come back. But I couldn't get her words, or the tears, out of my mind. One Sunday evening I went to the Methodist chapel - I remember there was an excellent female preacher - and prayed as I had never prayed in my life.

In the meantime Hugh and I had been talking about what we ought to do next. The West Country didn't seem to be helping Ba any more, and now that my career was developing steadily - a third novel, *Marry A Stranger*, had been launched in May - I ought occasionally to meet up with Alan Boon. It was time, we decided, to think about moving back east. Again the *Lady* was consulted and again she produced something, this time a seventeenth century cottage half a mile from the village of Ashmansworth, on the borders of Hampshire and Berkshire. The place had three bedrooms, a bathroom, a sitting-room, dining-room and kitchen. It also had a large, well established garden and a telephone. What it didn't have was mains electricity. For the time being any occupant would need to be content with oil lamps, candles and open fires; but the cooker and fridge were powered by Calor gas and of course one could always purchase oil heaters.

We didn't hesitate. When we arrived at Newbury station I stepped out on to the platform, slipped and fell to my knees - it felt like an omen. But by the time our taxi stopped beside the gate of Wych Pits Cottage, it had been forgotten already. The owner, a young woman who worked in London, was waiting to check the inventory and hand over the keys. Her mother was there too, I think. But they were soon gone, and it felt peaceful. Ba had come through the journey well, and while I got supper ready Hugh went to inspect the garden. A long lawn, edged by borders and watched over by a tall yew tree, a vegetable patch, an orchard. In front the windows looked on to a quiet lane, on the other side ripening cornfields sloped towards Highclere Castle a mile or so away. Looking into the distance, we could see for thirty miles.

As we settled in Ba seemed much better than she had been in Coverack, and at least she could spend time in the garden. Hugh got to know people, and one afternoon the local Master of Foxhounds dropped in. He had with him a busy little hunt terrier which he left outside in the garden, and when he took his leave half an hour later the terrier was found to have struck up a cordial relationship with Ba. I was alarmed, mainly because dogs had long been on our 'banned' list; the MFH, on the other hand, was impressed. His terrier bitch was supposed to be a bit dodgy, particularly with children. He wouldn't have left her to run around, if he'd known our little girl was in the garden. The child obviously had a way with dogs - ought to have one of her own.

Quickly I explained the reason for our animal-free situation, and he stuffed the terrier back in his Land Rover. He said he'd telephone later, just to make sure the dog had done no harm. If there *wasn't* a problem, though, would we allow him to do something? The little terrier had a family at home, four six-week-old puppies. They had all been booked for some time, but one at least could be unbooked, and if Ba wanted it she could have it. If the pup did cause difficulties - anything at all – he'd arrange to have it picked up immediately.

I was uneasy, but Hugh thought it was an excellent idea and seeing the look on Ba's face I knew we probably hadn't got much alternative. The terrier's visit seemed to have produced no ill effects, so two weeks later, on a warm Sunday morning, a glossy black puppy was delivered to our door. For the next few days I kept a close eye on things, but it was easy to see the puppy was not going to be a problem. These days Ba's asthma never quite disappeared, but the little dog's arrival certainly wasn't making things worse. We knew that cats were a problem, but it was beginning to look as if we might be able to strike dogs off the danger list.

Tosh - I have no idea why we called her that - was a delight. Half Jack Russell and half whippet, she believed in getting about by herself, and however many times Hugh blocked gaps in the hedge she always found another way through. Fortunately she had a sweet tooth, and a certain kind of scarlet chocolate wrapper, waved high in the air, would bring her back from three fields away.

It was nice having an animal in the house; and there were other nice things about life at Wych Pits Cottage. For one thing we weren't all that far from Eton Wick and it wasn't long before Reggie came to see us; then he brought Aunt Dolly and she stayed for two months.

Autumn came and the evenings lengthened, filling up with the glow of oil lamps. The barley fields turned to pale stubble, and the Highclere gamekeeper started bringing us pheasants, I think in recognition of the fact that we had been repeatedly shot over. A few days before Christmas Ba went to bed early - she was getting over a slight cold - and a band of carol-singers, having tramped all the way from the village, grouped themselves underneath her window. They sang *Away in a Manger.* Overhead the sky was full of stars, and I was in the kitchen, making mince pies. It was a moment that was to become fixed in Ba's memory. It's an intense experience, living at the heart of rural England. Or it used to be.

When February came we were walled in by snow, and as several cars got stuck on the hill below us Hugh went to help dig them out. But it felt very cosy inside the cottage, and our only problem was that as the snow thawed cracks began to appear between the roof tiles. Water dripped through steadily and we all spent several nights downstairs, sleeping by the sitting-room fire. It was fun, though, and it didn't appear to be doing Ba any harm.

By April, though, the asthma was worse again. This time we knew it wasn't linked to the house we were living in, or to the district, or to the time of year, or to the presence of an animal - as far as I could see, it wasn't even linked to psychological pressure. It was completely random and unpredictable.

That month I went to London, where I saw Alan Boon. My latest story, *Moon over Africa,* had turned out to be a little more exotic than anything I had so far produced, and Alan suggested it might be time for me to think up an additional pseudonym. Susan Barrie's books had so far been strongly romantic but also slightly wistful in character, and her readers would be likely to expect more of the same, so if I wanted to vary my approach it might be better to make use of more than one pen-name. This tactic, of course, is still used by publishers of commercial fiction.

I promised to think up a fresh name, and then we got on to other subjects. I told Alan about the recurrence of Ba's asthma, at the same time explaining my absolute belief that if only I could get her to Switzerland. . . . Another two or three novels should do it, but three novels might take me another six months, and I had been wondering. . . .

Alan looked at me thoughtfully, then he picked up the menu. The lemon meringue looked nice. Only from his point of view it might not be advisable.

Before we parted, he said: 'When I get back to the office, I'll see you're sent a cheque that will cover five advances. Stop worrying, and take her to Switzerland.'

* * * *

XXVIII

For more than three years I had hung on to the address of an hotel in the Swiss mountain village of Reuti-Hasliberg. The address had been given to me by a lady in Tunbridge Wells, and I had always felt the place it represented would be ideal for us. The Hotel Viktoria was a *Christliche* establishment - which meant, among other things, that it didn't serve alcohol - but it also seemed comfortable and very modern, and it was right in the middle of the Bernese Oberland. When I wrote to the Manager he immediately wrote back, offering me two rooms for the first three weeks in May. We were almost there.

In the mid 1950's flying was still very expensive, and anyway I had read that air travel could make chest problems worse, so on a morning in early May we crossed to Calais by means of the Channel ferry. The sea was a bit choppy but this didn't affect any of us, and before long we were on a train, heading across France. A long journey stretched ahead, but night came quickly and we slept. Ba had always travelled well, and in spite of everything she came through without any particular difficulty. Early in the morning we reached the frontier city of Basle, and there we changed to a Swiss train. And I realised that everything was different. The French train - like the station at Calais - had been grubby and crowded, grubbier even than British Railways, but the Swiss train was spotless. It was also of a type that would not be seen on British tracks for something like another fifteen or twenty years.

We climbed aboard and settled down, and the sleek train glided into Switzerland. There were green slopes and musical box chalets and neat, dark strips of woodland, and everything looked as if it had just been vacuumed. It was all very wholesome. But somehow it wasn't Switzerland, not the Switzerland I had been expecting. The mountains couldn't be far off, I supposed, but when an hour or so had gone by and nothing had changed I did begin to wonder. This was starting to look like a bigger - and more incomprehensible - disappointment than Morocco. Hugh had been nearly everywhere, or so it had always seemed, but he didn't know Switzerland, so he just said the Alps must still be some distance away, and went back to his book.

About lunchtime we slipped into the capital city of Bern, and I noticed some fine medieval buildings. Which was something, but not what I was looking for. Then on the other side of Bern we came upon a glittering sheet of water, and the train started running beside it - and I spotted, in the distance, what looked like a line of broken meringue, all creamy and glistening in the noonday sun.

The mountains came nearer, until they were brooding over us, and the train rolled into Interlaken. Someone pointed out the spreading, snow-capped bulk of the Jungfrau, looming above the town. *'Gazing down on the Jungfrau. . . .'* (But was that possible?)

Past Interlaken the train skirted another lake, Lake Brienz, and we began cruising forward across a flat green plain. On either side of us rocky walls rose, shutting out the sun; these walls were something like three miles apart but they were also a thousand feet high, and they cast large areas of the plain into shadow. Somewhere up above, though, we could glimpse the shining peaks.

We came into Meiringen, where Sherlock Holmes hunted for Moriarty, and in the small, quiet station switched to a little mountain train. Pulled by powerful cables we climbed into the hot glare of afternoon. Now Meiringen was a toy village spread out on the floor of the valley, and we could see the shoulders of the Alps. We left the train at Brunig-Hasliberg, and took a taxi. There were three villages spread out along the Hasliberg ridge, and Reuti was the last of them. It was a journey of about seven miles. We were all tired by this time and I was concerned about Ba, but we were driving across a green plateau in the heart of the Alps, and the experience was spine-tingling.

And the Hotel Viktoria was even more comfortable than I had expected it to be. In fact it was almost luxurious, and its *alkoholfrei* character didn't seem to be worrying its reasonably sophisticated clientèle (it's true that Hugh and some of the other male guests got around any inconvenience by paying occasional visits to a nearby wine bar).

After Ba had gone to bed, Hugh and I watched sunset creep across the mountains. The *Alpenrose*. . . I had written about it.

And I felt a huge sense of relief. After four years we had at last got to Switzerland, and anything was possible.

* * * * *

XXIX

There was no time to be wasted. The following morning I told a receptionist that my daughter needed a doctor, and she said she would send for someone. Dr Stadler, who lived in Meiringen. He should be with us by about eleven o'clock.

Dr Stadler was tall, smartly dressed and rather good-looking. As he appeared in the doorway I felt a moment of sudden anxiety, but he smiled reassuringly.

'It's all right. I speak English.'

He examined Ba, and we went out to the verandah for a talk. Judging by the state of her bronchial system, Dr Stadler said Ba was one of the worst cases of childhood asthma he had ever encountered. She might grow out of it eventually, but even that wasn't certain. In the meantime, her young life was being ruined and her body placed under considerable strain. If we agreed, he would start by giving her some medicine, a sort of linctus that ought to clear the bronchial tubes within a day or so. After that, he would put her on a new drug called AM 49. Apparently AM 49 had been developed in Germany during or just after the recent war, and perhaps because of this had not so far caught on as it might otherwise have done. He told me that it was based on a sort of gold extract, and that it worked by re-lining the damaged system.

Suddenly wary, I asked if he could be sure this new drug was safe, and Dr Stadler looked straight at me.

'Shall we just say. . . if I had a child as sick as this one, I wouldn't hesitate.'

We didn't hesitate. For two days and nights, Ba's eyes and nose streamed as if she had a heavy cold, but when this stopped her breathing seemed to be clearer. Dr Stadler was satisfied, and the treatment began. Four pills a day - two with meals, two in between -

to be taken for a period of three months. At first I was convinced there were bound to be side effects, but nothing happened, except that for the first time in a year and a half Ba seemed to be free of asthmatic symptoms. She had a lot of ground to make up and once she almost fainted in the Alpine heat, but there were no breathing difficulties and no coughing spasms. She was able to walk, and to eat, without gasping for air. We stayed for three weeks, then Dr Stadler told us the treatment was taking effect. There were most unlikely to be any attendant problems. . . if we wanted to do so, we could now go home.

For all sorts of reasons, my first experience of Switzerland had been wonderful. And one day - *one day* - I would come back.

In England again, we spent a few days on the Sussex coast. I kept expecting Ba's miracle cure to evaporate like Cinderella's ball-gown at the first stroke of midnight, but this didn't happen. We went to see Pevensey Castle, we even walked along the breezy cliff-top, and she was fine. We were approaching the height of summer, though, and the test would come when we went home to Wych Pits.

We collected Tosh from her boarding kennels, and arrived home on a warm June afternoon. I kept thinking about Barn Cottage and the evening, years earlier, when we had arrived home from London. But Ba slept well, that night at Wych Pits Cottage, and when morning came she was still a normal, healthy child. Switzerland had worked, just as I had always believed it would.

* * * * *

XXX

Almost immediately, I started writing again. I had debts to clear for one thing, but also I was beginning to suffer withdrawal symptoms. I needed my work. As for Hugh, he had the garden and through the long summer days he worked tirelessly, once again encouraging Ba to develop her own patch - on this occasion she produced a remarkable crop of beetroot.

In the evenings Hugh and I talked a good deal, and we also talked over breakfast. One warm August morning we sat for rather a long time chewing over a letter I had just received from Alan, who had begun offering some of my novels for advance serialisation in magazines such as *Woman's Weekly* and *Woman's Own*. Ba and Tosh had gone out into the garden and Tosh, never one to hang around, had promptly squeezed through the hedge, hurried across the lane and disappeared into the meadow beyond. Ba called her back. She did not expect much response because Tosh was a dog who did not believe in coming when she was called, but perhaps because it was Ba - and they were good friends - Tosh decided to turn around. She raced back across the meadow, towards the lane and her gap in the hedge, and as she did so a heavy grain lorry came lumbering down from the village. Ba saw the lorry go past, then she saw it jolt as if it had struck a bump in the road. For a moment she was afraid, but the heavy vehicle went on down the hill. . . until she heard it stop and begin to reverse back up. She ran outside; but when she came into the dining-room, a moment or two later, she couldn't bring herself to say exactly what she had seen. She simply told us Tosh was lying in the road.

Hugh jumped up and went outside. There was a sound of voices, and he came back into the house. Quietly, he told us Tosh was dead.

Ba just kept saying 'No'. She said it again and again, and again, then she screamed. Outside I could hear the unfortunate lorry driver talking to Hugh. *'I'll get the little girl another dog. . . .'*

By this time Ba was crying and shaking. I made her drink some hot, sweet tea but it didn't seem to have much effect, until Hugh came back.

'You can come and see her now,' he said.

He had brought Tosh in and covered her with sacking, so that only her small, undamaged head remained visible. He suggested Ba should give her a pat, then said they would look for somewhere to put her. In the garden, not far away.

They placed her under a hazel-bush, near the edge of the barley field, and Ba picked some flowers to put on the grave. When they came in I could see she was calmer, that the worst was over. . . as always, in a desperate situation, Hugh had known what to do.

That afternoon Ba didn't want to see anyone and there was nothing she wanted to do, so in the end she and I just went for a very long walk, through the quiet village of Ashmansworth and on through the ancient lanes, until we were tired. Then we went home to supper.

Poor Tosh. She had a short life - if a fairly merry one - but she was much loved and was to be long remembered. If I went back to *Wych Pits Cottage* now, and stood in the garden on a summer morning, I'm sure I should see a little dark shadow skimming through the cornfields - pausing, now and then, to sniff the air for chocolate bars.

*   *   *   *   *

XXXI

We knew that we'd have to get another dog, for Ba's sake particularly, but also for us. This time we might buy a pedigree puppy, perhaps the dachshund I had been wanting ever since I caught one studying me from under a chair in the Burford Bridge Hotel. Then one day the local RSPCA man stopped outside our gate. He lived in the village, was acquainted with Hugh and had heard our sad news, which was why he had come to visit us in his RSPCA van. I was in the garden, and he held something out to me, over the gate. It was creamy yellow in colour, had a long, limp-looking tail, and two kinds of coat. Smooth at the front, curly at the back. It was an abandoned puppy, and was due to be destroyed the following day. Ba came over, and the RSPCA man seized his moment.

'So this is the young lady who likes dogs. . . .'

Of course she hadn't yet got over Tosh, but this was a small animal in need. I looked at the yellow puppy, and knew I couldn't send it away. Hugh was out and wouldn't be back for some time, but I could talk him round - probably. Within a month the Inspector would call back, just to make sure everything was all right. In the meantime Ba and I fed the puppy, introduced her to our garden and decided to call her Penny. When Hugh came home, he took one look and remarked that we were not keeping that. 'She's lovely', I said. 'She's a freak,' said Hugh. We pointed out that she was hovering on the edge of destruction, whereupon he retreated behind his newspaper.

Ba and I did our best for the new arrival. We groomed her, took her for walks, trained her and advised her - audibly - not to take any notice of hurtful comments. Then one afternoon she sat in front of Hugh, gazing at him admiringly. He lifted his book a bit higher, but the following day she was back again, this time with one paw resting delicately on his foot. The book was put aside, and he looked at her.

'I think,' he said, 'you're getting uglier.'

The next day she was there again, and all at once Hugh stood up.

'That damned animal,' he observed, 'needs more exercise. I'll take it to the village.'

Of course, she turned into Hugh's dog. Ba and I were treated cordially, even with affection, but we knew our place. One day, I thought, I'd have my dachshund puppy.

Not that I had much time for thinking about anything apart from work. By the following spring I had covered my obligation to Mills and Boon, and gone some way beyond it. I now had three pen-names. Pamela Kent (exotic backgrounds) had been followed by Rose Burghley (French and Spanish locations), and I had been told that Mills and Boon would be prepared to publish six or eight of my titles in every year. The trouble was that I was producing more than that, and they were beginning to be stacked up.

I did my homework. I studied library shelves and read all the women's magazines, and I knew that several other publishers were now getting into light romance. So long as I continued to give Mills and Boon as much as they wanted, why shouldn't I try to find an additional outlet?

I talked to Alan about it. We were having lunch at an attractive Austrian restaurant, and he stared at the tablecloth for a very long time. I always had the feeling that more went on inside Alan's rather large head than was ever likely to be seen on the surface. It would, of course, be very unusual, he said at last. But he understood I needed to consolidate my financial position. Just so long as Mills and Boon would always be assured of taking precedence, could be certain of receiving at least six novels in every year . . .then well, all right. Going further, he said I really ought to have an agent, just to help me deal with the other firms. So long as I understood that never, *ever* would Mills and Boon agree to operate through any kind of formal representative.

This was satisfactory. But I was sure I could pick up one or two extra publishers without bothering about anything as cumbersome as an agent, and it turned out that I was right. I approached a firm called Wright and Brown, and within days they had accepted *The Black Benedicts*, the only one of my original 'beginnings' that Alan hadn't really wanted. They gave me a four book contract and I turned my attention to Ward Lock, who at that time were a major publishing house. One of their senior executives, a nice man called Colonel

Shipton, took me to lunch at the Berkeley Hotel, and soon another contract had been signed. I wrote them a novel set in Ireland. . . *Haven of the Heart*. I cried – unusual for me - when I was working on *Haven*, and to this day it's still one of my favourites. Ward Lock employed a young woman editor whose name was Bertha MacLennan; dark-haired, attractive and thirty-ish, she actually *liked* romantic fiction, and this was a bond between us. Alan understood the genre better than anybody, and he was also expert at turning it into money, but being a man I don't suppose he ever enjoyed reading the stuff. Bertha, on the other hand, did. Often, apparently, while listening to the music of Sibelius.

All this was involving me in an increasingly heavy work load, but I could do it. Not only that, I loved doing it. Every morning, from Monday to Friday, I got up at seven o'clock, made early tea, got dressed and cooked breakfast - usually porridge, followed by eggs and bacon. Over breakfast Hugh and I usually chatted for a while, then I washed up, did some dusting and laid the foundations of lunch, after which I drank a cup of coffee and got down to the serious business of the day, stopping just in time to complete the task of preparing lunch. Afterwards Ba and I sometimes washed up together, then I'd snatch a short rest before starting work again after tea. Invariably I stopped at a quarter to seven, when the *Archers* came on.

On Saturdays I did extra housework, and sometimes I went shopping, but several tradesmen delivered and given an adequate list Hugh was so efficient that I didn't often need to bother. On Sundays, I cooked lunch and then relaxed. I had been brought up to believe that you didn't do unnecessary work on the Sabbath, and now I could see the practical purpose of this rule. Without the enforced break, I might not have carried on as easily as I did. When I was finishing a novel I did often work longer hours, occasionally getting up at five o'clock and certainly working on Saturdays. But I don't think I ever - at that stage - abandoned the rule that meant Sunday had to be kept free.

And as I stood in the kitchen, making pastry or washing up, gazing across the fields towards Beacon Hill - a wooded slope that lay a mile away - I constructed plots and wrote endless pages of dialogue. I rarely bothered with hand-written notes, just as I never produced more than one draft of a novel. Sometimes I might re-type a page or two, but on the whole everything I wrote came out of my head and having landed on the type-written page tended to remain there, more or less unaltered, until it arrived on a publisher's desk. Not many people work like this and perhaps it isn't the best way, but it always was the only way for me.

Once a typescript was completed, it was out of my hands. Hugh would separate the top copy from the carbon, punch holes in it and place it in a binder, then he would do it up in a parcel - always finished off with sealing wax - and post it off for me. When the proof arrived, two or three months later, he would check it for mistakes while I waited anxiously for comments or signs of approval. *('How d'you like it?' 'I don't know, I'm looking for littorals.' 'How far have you got?' 'Page ninety-two.')*

By the summer of 1956 I had got myself on to the list of yet another company. One of my recent Mills and Boon novels had been - they thought - a little *risque*, too *risque* for them anyway; so I sent it to Collins, where it was promptly snapped up. I'm still fond of *A Nightingale in the Sycamore*, but looking through it today I can't for the life of me work out where the shocking bits were supposed to be.

I now had five publishers, and knew that I really needed an agent. Briefly I worked with someone called Peter Lewin, but before very long I switched to A.M. Heath, where I was signed up by someone called Mark Hamilton. Young and enthusiastic, Mark would many years later become a President of the Literary Agents' Association. He had at that time dark hair, a gentle manner and - I think - one or two young children. I liked him. I still believed I was perfectly capable of handling publishers for myself, but he would be very useful for processing their contracts.

Every few weeks, on average, I travelled to London to see one or other of my publishers, but I hated leaving Ba and Hugh and sometimes we all went together. When that happened, we stayed for a night or two at Durrant's Hotel in Manchester Square. While I did whatever it was I had to do Hugh took Ba around the museums and art galleries, then later on we sometimes went to the cinema, or perhaps the theatre.

Now thirteen years old, Ba was interested in many things, but she didn't want to think about school, and just at that moment I was afraid to push her. Unable to forget what had happened the last time we booked her into an educational establishment, I had made up my mind things would have to be managed differently. We would wait for another few months, perhaps a year, then send her to school in Switzerland. That way, if problems did arise she would be in the best possible place. In the meantime she was still studying hard. Hugh, I realised, disliked the fact that she was being allowed to get away with taking so little interest in science and maths - he had done his best in that direction but he wasn't a professional teacher, and he was afraid this hole in her education might, as she grew older, prove to be a handicap. I just thought that she could and would catch up if she needed to do so. In ten years of formal education I had not, it seemed to me, picked up very much - most of my learning had been done at home, and I hadn't done all that badly. Ba could construct conversations in German and answer profound questions on the Wars of the Roses; she also read everything she could get her hands on and was mad about poetry. If at some time in the future maths or science were to become important in her life, she would somehow get to grips with them, I had no doubt of that. Anyway, she would soon be going to school. A good school, I hoped.

In the meantime, every day at Wych Pits seemed precious and untouchable. Ba was well again, Hugh seemed happy and at peace, and I - I was writing books and getting them published. And I was getting Readers' Letters.

Writing is a lonely business. Even when you're being read quite widely you don't, as a rule, come into direct contact with any part of your audience. You see your books - your mind's children - going out into the world, but you don't really know how they're getting on out there. It's a bit like having grown up sons and daughters but never, ever, meeting any of their friends. Then a letter comes, forwarded by the publisher, and you see that somebody has taken to your child. *'I just couldn't put it down . . .'* *'I loved your heroine (the little boy, the dog, the house'*). Most telling of all: *'It took my mind off things'*. One of the first letters I ever received stuck in my mind more than any other because it came from a lady who told me she had recently lost her husband, and my books had got her through. Another, in the Australian Outback, had felt she wanted to 'do something to say thank you', so had knitted me a magnificent pair of bed-socks. I kept those bed-socks for a very long time. Rather more oddly, I once heard from a male surgeon attached to the Royal East Sussex Hospital. He said that he read my books to keep himself calm between operations.

We went away quite a lot, to Windsor, Eastbourne and other places as well as London, but coming home was always wonderful. In summer the garden was idyllic, and during long July evenings we played croquet on the lawn. And there were other distractions. The field mouse, for instance, that swung by its tail from the gas pipe

195

beside the cooker - it looked so relaxed, when I first caught sight of it, that I wasn't particularly startled. And the ghosts.

Aunt Dolly stayed with us frequently, and one morning she woke to see a hunched, crone-like figure walk across her bedroom, leaning on a stick, and disappear into the wall. The figure didn't show itself again, but my aunt was very certain about what she had seen and wasn't to be shaken on a single detail. On another occasion Hugh was walking back from the village when he saw a woman, dressed in blue, pass through the garden gate ahead of him. I was standing nearby, and there was no woman in blue. Then one quiet autumn night, as Ba was sitting up in bed reading by candlelight, she heard a sound of frenzied banging, coming from the room beyond her own. Too scared to move she called out, but as I climbed the stairs - she said later - the banging ceased. All the windows were closed, and anyone entering the inner room would have had to walk past Ba's bed. Lying on one of the ledges, though, there was a metal stay-bar which had broken away from one of the windows and hadn't yet been replaced. When used to strike the window frame this object evidently made exactly the sound Ba had heard. She wasn't upset for long, though. If there were ghosts at Wych Pits Cottage they didn't, somehow, feel menacing.

But the outside world was pushing closer. In the Lake District for a short holiday we planned to go on into Scotland; but for the second time since my marriage to Hugh Scotland had to be abandoned, this time because the magazine *Woman's Own* was about to serialise one of my novels, and the Editor unexpectedly decided to give a small party in my honour. After we got home they sent a photographer down and there was a write-up in the magazine, as a result of which I was telephoned by a glossy, gossipy publication known as *Woman's Pictorial*. The *Pictorial's* Editor wondered if I would agree to have a chat with one of his journalists. . . just a few questions about the romance industry. How I felt about it. How I put my books together, etc, etc. I telephoned Alan and Mark Hamilton, and they both approved strongly. Within days, a young woman journalist was on her way to see me at Wych Pits.

The journalist's name was Susan Curtis-Bennett, and I realised afterwards that she was the daughter of a well-known QC. She was a pleasant, attractive girl, and diplomatically she arrived bearing flowers. We spent an hour or so chewing over the things she had come to talk about, and then Hugh joined us for lunch. After he had gone away again she said what a delightful man he was, and feeling quite relaxed by this time I told her about the sadness he had suffered as a result of being separated from his older daughters. Susan was extremely sympathetic. She was also a good journalist, and she knew exactly how to extract the details of a story. Within the space of half an hour or so she probably knew all she needed to know about Hugh's marriage break-up, and the situation regarding Gillian and Imogen. I hadn't meant to talk so much, but she was a good listener - naturally. At one point I realised she had real tears streaming down her cheeks. We got back to the subject of my work, and by the time she left to catch the London train she was saying she had an excellent story. Within a few days she would be sending me a draft of the piece she intended to produce.

Susan was as good as her word. Only when the article arrived, it was not exactly what I had been expecting. The first half, and the last few paragraphs, were concerned with me and my literary work. The remainder dealt almost exclusively with the treatment Hugh Pollock had suffered at the hands of his former wife.

I was horrified, and Hugh was furious. I immediately got Susan Curtis-Bennett on the phone, and told her how we felt. She sounded surprised, and a little upset. She told me she had taken a lot of trouble with the article, and there was nothing in it that could possibly reflect badly on my husband, or on me - nothing whatsoever. It was a story that needed to be told, and I must see that. My husband must see that. Privacy was one thing, allowing this sort of tragedy to drag on forever, without protest, was quite another, and it was time Hugh's daughters understood their father had not deliberately abandoned them. She told me she had talked to Enid on the telephone and had challenged her on most of the issues involved. There had been no denial, so she had told Miss Blyton exactly what she, personally, thought about this kind of behaviour. Enid had talked about going to a solicitor, but that wasn't really relevant because we were dealing with inescapable fact. Anyway, Susan - and the Editor - were committed to getting this story out.

I said that I had to respect my husband's principles, and his feelings. Unwisely, perhaps unfairly, I had told her certain things in confidence, and that confidence would have to be respected. In any case, I had not expected her to concern herself, in print, with aspects of my husband's former life. When the Editor telephoned I repeated what I had already said to Miss Curtis-Bennett, and he expressed himself more bluntly than she had done.

'*Mrs Pollock, you received one of my journalists into your home . . . you personally supplied her with the information we're talking about. It's a good story. We've checked it out. . . . And it's not in any way damaging to you or to your husband.*' He said he was sorry, but they intended to print. And that was that.

Hugh and I talked to our solicitor. More to the point, perhaps, Enid talked to hers and eventually the magazine backed down. Alan Boon was not an insensitive man, but I'm sure he thought this a criminal waste of good publicity. Judging by things I was to hear later, I don't think Enid suspected for a moment that Hugh had lifted a finger to stop the story being printed, in fact, she may have thought he was behind the whole thing. Which shows how little she really knew about the man to whom she had once been married for seventeen years.

* * * * *

XXXII

Life started to settle down again. Or it might have done, if one day the post hadn't brought a startling letter from the owner of Wych Pits Cottage. She was about to get married, and she wanted her house back so that her mother could live in it. Our lease had been due for renewal in three months' time, so we had just twelve weeks in which to find another home. This was a shock for all of us, but for Hugh, I think, it was devastating. Ba had her life in front of her, I spent much of my time in places of my own creation, but for Hugh Wych Pits had been both a refuge and a source of hope.

We'd find something else, though, perhaps even nicer. There must be hundreds of cottages around, just waiting to be snapped up. We couldn't afford to buy, not just yet, but we might find something unfurnished, something needing a bit of attention, and that would be fun. Unfortunately, the reality was disappointing. There seemed to be hardly anything available just then, and time wasn't on our side. In the end, faced with a choice between something square and newly built, on the outskirts of Newbury, and a period house in the little town of Hungerford, we plumped for Hungerford and started packing up. We had taken the period house for six months, 'with an option to continue'.

We left Wych Pits just as spring was beginning, not an ideal time. Ba said afterwards that it didn't feel as if we were leaving, when we finally drove away, because it wasn't possible we would not be going back to Wych Pits. We hadn't been there all that long - rather less than three years - but for us that was rather a long time.

Hungerford was pleasant enough, though, and the local people were friendly. Our new house was an interesting old property - '*John of Gaunt*', the landlord said mysteriously, pointing down into a murky cellar - and like most of its neighbours it had a pretty, straggling garden. In the little towns of England there must be literally thousands of similar gardens, but that doesn't detract from their charm.

And we were back in the world of electricity. We had said good-bye to our oil lamps and candles.

I had two novels to finish quickly, and thankfully found that I could work in the new house. Ba started regular music lessons, and Hugh adjusted as he had always done. The gardens behind the houses filled up with apple blossom, and on May Day the town was taken over by an ancient tradition; mainly, this seemed to involve a group of young men going from house to house, looking for girls to kiss - Ba fled in terror. And as summer got under way I began to work out how many books I might be able to get through before the end of the year.

So far we weren't rich by any means, but more and more money was coming in, and I was beginning to receive advice about tax. I had no particular desire to dodge the Inland Revenue, but I was warned that within a year or so I could be facing unreasonably heavy demands; in other words, it might be an idea to start thinking about a home abroad. I had made some enquiries about Swiss finishing-schools - we wanted Ba to go over there when she was about fifteen - but Switzerland wasn't going to be much use for tax purposes. Hugh and I would need to think about moving somewhere else. Spain, perhaps, or the Balearic Islands. Alan - or Mark, or somebody - was quite keen to push the Balearic Islands. Anyway, nothing had to be decided just yet.

Like lots of young girls Ba had become a follower of magazine tittle-tattle. Taken to the Berkeley for lunch on her fourteenth birthday, she had been excited to find that deb-of-the-year Henrietta Tiarks, later Duchess of Bedford, was sitting nearby with an escort. And it was Ba, I think, who first picked up the story that her half-sister Gillian was planning to get married. Gillian's future husband was a promising young TV producer called Donald Baverstock, and the ceremony was to take place at St James's Church, Piccadilly. There were to be six attendants, and of course the bride's famous mother was expected to be present. At this stage I don't believe any mention was made of Gillian's 'real' father.

It would have been wrong to keep this news from Hugh, even if it had been possible to do so, and of course he was shocked. In one part of his mind Gillian was still the ten-year-old girl he had last seen at Beaconsfield Station in 1942 - the child he occasionally talked about.

But in reality Gillian was almost twenty-six years old, and there must have been moments - I had almost seen them happening - when Hugh paused to think about that, to wonder what she looked like and what she thought of the world. What sort of young men had begun to hang around her, what kind of choice she might eventually make. That choice had been made now, and he had not even known anything about it. I was angry and hurt on Hugh's behalf, but there was nothing much that I could do.

Days later, a London newspaperman turned up on our doorstep. Hugh happened to be alone in the house, and because of his poor hearing he didn't realise someone was ringing the doorbell. The reporter pushed our front door open and walked inside, then finding Hugh at the back of the house he asked without much preamble if Gillian's father had any intention of attending her wedding. At first Hugh refused to comment. He had no desire whatsoever for contact with the Press, and in addition he was furious over what he saw as an outrageous intrusion, but in the end he was pressed into making a short, blunt statement.

'I haven't seen Miss Blyton for fifteen years, and I don't want to see her now'.

After this he asked the reporter to leave. The following day his words were quoted in the Daily Mail's gossip column, and I could see how much this upset him. Since the day their divorce went through, he had refrained from making any sort of public comment on the subject of Enid Blyton, and though what he had said might not seem very shocking today - to most people it didn't seem shocking then - it was a public statement, and he loathed seeing the words in print. Anyway, what was Gillian to make of it? The implication was that he would have refused to attend her wedding, even if invited, for the simple reason that he didn't want to encounter her mother. If he had been invited, I'm not absolutely sure what he would have done. But I know he hated the idea that Gillian might read what he had said and perhaps imagine her happiness meant nothing to him.

On the day before the wedding, I think he said that he wished he had written her a letter. It was a sudden observation - like most men in such a situation he hadn't so far wanted to talk about any of it - but it gave me an idea. Why didn't he ring her up? He still had the Green Hedges phone number. It might have changed, of course - if it had, and if he couldn't obtain the new number, than that was probably that. But it was worth a try.

He got through, and found himself speaking to a young woman who told him she was a secretary. Though he hadn't seen her or talked to her since she was six years old, Hugh knew at once that this was Imogen. At the same moment, she seems to have realised the man on the telephone was none other than her own almost unknown father. Hugh asked if he could speak to Gillian - though he didn't know it, she was apparently sitting a few feet away from her sister. Imogen said Gillian wasn't there, she was out. And that was that.

I was desperately sorry, and remember wishing I hadn't urged him to make the effort. He offered no comment on the inevitable newspaper reports that followed the wedding, and so far as I can remember never again made any unnecessary reference to either of his older daughters.

Imogen Smallwood is a deeply honourable person who has inherited her father's generous, sensitive spirit. She has long regretted what happened on that August afternoon, but she has no reason to reproach herself. Enid, apparently, had developed a paranoid belief that Hugh would somehow attempt to disrupt the wedding, that he would 'make a scene', and her entire household had been placed on alert. (Many years later her literary agent, George Greenfield, was to reveal that he had been asked to place guards at the door of St James's Church.) In spite of all this, on the morning of her wedding Gillian looked around the church, hoping against hope that her father might, just possibly, be somewhere among the guests.

Round about this time Hugh and I received a letter from Enid's solicitor. The letter, which requested that we should never again discuss Miss Blyton with the Press, was so bizarre and unreasonable that our own solicitor wasn't sure, at first, how to handle it. In the end, he simply wrote to say that we had no immediate plans to talk about Enid Blyton, but that we could not and would not allow our actions to be dictated by her. We heard nothing further.

All this seems to have coincided, more or less, with the onset of Enid's tragic illness, and there may have been a connection, but I'm inclined to think her attitude had more to do with the blunt observations of Susan Curtis-Bennett. Once again Enid had been faced with the reality of her former husband's existence, and the injustices he had suffered. Enid Blyton lived for another eleven years, but we never again heard from her, or from her solicitor.

It isn't necessary for me to point out that Enid gave a huge amount to the world. She brought delight to millions of children, and not only to children, for the books we love when we're very small tend to remain with us forever. When she was dying, I believe she said that she was going to see her father - at least, she thought she was. I hope, very sincerely, that she found him.

*   *   *   *   *

XXXIII

The trauma of Gillian's marriage passed, and a few weeks later I received a call from the Daily Mail. Alarm bells rang inside my head, but this time it was the office of Olga Franklin. Born in pre-Revolutionary Russia, Olga had used her humour and skill with words to blaze a trail that would later be widened out by stars such as Jean Rook and Lynda Lee-Potter. She said that she would like to interview me, about myself - my work, my ideas on romantic fiction, how I had got my career going, and so on. I wouldn't, I told her, say a word about Enid Blyton. No, no, that was fine. She wouldn't ask me to. Honest.

Olga Franklin came down to Hungerford, and she was as good as her word. Though she naturally asked a few questions about my husband's career, that was as far as it went. As it was a cool day I had lit a small fire in the sitting-room, and when Hugh eventually appeared I asked him to bring some more coal, whereupon she seized the opportunity to observe that he was attractive, but still she resisted the temptation to ask further questions.

I told her nothing about my own supposed links with Russia - I never told that to anyone - but before she left I asked about her own family, mentioning the fact that my fourteen-year-old daughter had recently become keen on the idea of learning Russian. Olga Franklin shrugged sympathetically. *'Well, young people today. . . .'*

When I repeated this to Ba, she was extremely cross. She wasn't remotely interested in the speeches of Lenin, or the forward march of the Soviet Socialist Republic, she was simply in love with Tolstoy and old St Petersburg. Which, now that I come to think about it, was oddly significant especially as I hadn't yet told her anything about the likely identity of her maternal grandfather.

Olga Franklin's piece appeared a few days later, in a column which bore the label 'Frankly Yours'. It was frank, too. So frank that briefly I was rather annoyed. For one thing I had been portrayed as a bubbly chatterbox, and that wasn't me (was it. . . ?). Unexpectedly, too, the piece was accompanied by an Emmwood cartoon in which I was depicted as an Edwardian heroine apparently on the edge of being abducted by an Arab Sheikh. Hugh, in Indian Army uniform, was shown walking by with a coal-scuttle. Fortunately Hugh was philosophical about this, and actually it was rather funny - Alan, etc, thought it was marvellous. We were presented with the cartoon original, but rather sadly it has since been lost.

I was supposed to complete another two typescripts before the beginning of October and I got them done, but then I started to feel tired. I had developed one or two minor health problems, so I went to see a doctor and he told me I was exhausted. Shattered, in fact. Ideally, I should do no more work for a period of at least three months, and at the very least I needed an immediate break. A holiday. Obviously this looked like a good time to check on the Balearic Islands, so I booked us in for a three week stay at an hotel in Palma de Mallorca, and we left almost immediately.

Arriving by steamer from Barcelona, we found temperatures soaring into the nineties. We also found that our luggage, which was being handled by Thomas Cook, had somehow disappeared from view. We had seen it in Barcelona, but now it was nowhere to be found. Dockside officials were sympathetic about this, as were the shipping line and the local representatives of Thomas Cook. But it was now after sunset and practically everybody was just about to go off duty. In the morning, they told us firmly, our belongings would be discovered.

I supposed we could manage for one night. Anyway, we didn't have a lot of choice, so we accepted the assurances of Thomas Cook and the shipping line and departed by taxi for the Grand Hotel Calamayor, a long white building that was discovered sprawling seductively in front of the Mediterranean. Here we received a warm and courteous welcome, before being told that there had, most unfortunately, been some confusion over our booking. It was, the management conceded, entirely their fault, but we were not expected until the following week.

This contretemps, I must admit, was handled with consummate skill. Not only were we offered the Proprietor's private guest villa, we were also assured that we might retain it, if we wished, for the entire three weeks of our stay (I think there was also a bottle of some remarkable wine, which did nothing for me or Ba but cheered Hugh up quite a lot).

In the morning, after breakfast, we went straight down to the harbour and Thomas Cook, where we were told our luggage was still not available. It wasn't available because it wasn't there, and it wasn't there because it was still in Barcelona. Of course, there would be another steamer coming in that evening, and our stuff was certain to be on board. This was infuriating to say the least, but there was nothing we could do about it, so we bought one or two things to wear and went off to look around Palma.

In spite of everything I was feeling a lot better than I had done for months, but I wasn't at all sure how I felt about Mallorca. I had been expecting something like Andalucia transferred to an island in the Mediterranean, but the real Mallorca was being squashed already under the requirements of tourism, and I didn't think I would ever want to live there.

It was very much a Spanish island, though, and tourism or no tourism was also very much under the control of General Franco. Heavily armed police - *guardias civiles* - seemed to be patrolling wherever you looked, and they tended to turn and stare at you. (It was rumoured that imprudent British visitors were not infrequently bundled off to the cells.)

Anyway it was colourful, and we were on holiday. And bits of what I was seeing would certainly find their way into a book.

The following morning we returned once again to the docks, and once again we presented ourselves at the office occupied by Thomas Cook. A young man with the face of an *hidalgo* went behind the scenes to check, before coming back with the latest news. Our luggage had not arrived.

I couldn't believe it. It wasn't possible. *'Why not?'* I asked.

He didn't know.

My temper was beginning to bubble. *'Well, will you please try to find out?'*

He went away and apparently telephoned someone, then came back to say that there had been a delay in Barcelona, but it had been sorted out. By the following morning, our luggage would have arrived.

The next day we went back early and again we waited, only not for very long, this time. It wasn't there.

'*What?*'

'Your baggage,' the *hidalgo* repeated helpfully, 'has not come.'

'*Why not?*'

A shrug. 'I don't know.'

I told him what I thought, exactly. About the people in Barcelona, about him personally, about the Spanish style of management. I was comprehensive, and as I got angrier I became increasingly lucid. Behind me, an American woman started to clap. When I had finished, the *hidalgo* turned and stalked away. Possibly, to summon the *guardias civiles*. Two or three minutes later, he was back again.

'It is here,' he said shortly.

I don't think there was an explanation, or perhaps I just wasn't listening. For a moment I was stunned, then relief spilled over into nonsensical gratitude.

'That's wonderful!' I said. 'I'm sorry I. . . you've really been very helpful.'

The *hidalgo* stared blankly at a spot above my head. 'I know what I am,' he said with the dignity of an Armada captain about to go down with his galleon. '*You tell me what I am.*'

We settled down to enjoy the remainder of our holiday, and on the whole it was very pleasant. Every evening, about halfway through dinner, the electricity failed and staff rushed around gathering up candles from two large chests kept strategically in the wide entrance lobby; as it was usually about an hour before power was restored, we invariably finished dinner by candlelight. We were told that this phenomenon was caused by the effect of tidal movements on a vulnerable underwater cable. I am sure this no longer happens, which does seem rather a pity. Progress can be very boring.

I wasn't enthusiastic about Spanish food - in Barcelona I had been confronted by a large raw egg, floating on top of a bowl of soup - but I adored the sweet croissants, *ensaimada*, that turned up every morning on our breakfast table. And I liked the people. I realised eventually that within the Spanish character there lies a partly hidden sweetness, and I made up my mind that I would write a lot more stories set within the Iberian Peninsula. I still didn't want to live there, though.

As for Hungerford, our six month term was almost up and none of us particularly wanted to stay on. For the winter we went back to Treyarnon Bay, renting the very same house we had occupied four years earlier, when Ba had been a sick and fragile ten-year-old. Now she could walk in the wind by the sea, worrying only about the possibility that Penny might one day chase a seagull over the cliff edge. When spring came we moved for a month or so to a house on the Point between Treyarnon and Constantine Bay, then we took a luxuriously furnished farmhouse on the edge of Dartmoor. This time it was three months with an option to continue; and it was different from anything I had known. The great brown moor lay all around us, and we hadn't been there long before police rang to tell us a prisoner had escaped. Penny lay all night growling by a French window, and when morning came they found the wretched fugitive in a barn not far away. We were in a fairly lonely situation, but the nearby village was friendly and it wasn't long before I was being asked to open a local fête - I had always imagined I would loathe this particular sort of recognition, but when it happened I enjoyed it.

By this time I was completely well again, but I was working hard and knew that I probably needed to take on a cook-housekeeper. For one thing, she would be some kind of company when Ba was no longer at home. I remembered, very well, the time only five years earlier when I had been looking for such work myself, and made up my mind that the successful candidate would be offered a happy, welcoming home. Again I turned to the *Lady* magazine, but this time it was to place an advertisement. I received just one reply, but this came from a lady who sounded both interesting and competent - she was, apparently, a Cordon Bleu cook. She came for an interview, and I noted the fact that she was alarmingly elegant. Perhaps too elegant. She told me she would be happy to arrange flowers, and plan my dinner-parties, but of course, no housework - and she would need an assistant in the kitchen. Quite definitely, our three times a week daily help would not be enough.

I told her I didn't think we would be good enough for her, or words to that effect, and went back to the *Lady*, but by this time I was beginning to wonder if my idea had been such a good one. For one thing, our dog Penny was turning into a problem. Her coat had evened out, her tail had settled down and she was a good-looking animal - the image, somebody told us, of a well-bred Irish Terrier. But she had a bit of Alsatian in her, or so her RSPCA guardian had once said, and now she was entering upon her prime the Alsatian bit was starting to come out. Always Hugh's dog, she had now begun snarling at any stranger who had the nerve to come near him, and it didn't stop there. She growled at the daily who came in from the village, and at our elderly part time gardener. She took a violent dislike to the grocer, and she even formed the habit of swearing at anyone who ventured near her food dish. Realistically, if a stranger came to live in the house there was going to be trouble.

Then I had an idea. We would buy another dog, a pedigree puppy, the dachshund I had always wanted. It would bring out Penny's maternal instinct, and be company for her. She had been turning into an introvert, but another dog would sort her out. And almost immediately I found a litter of smooth-coated, black and tan dachshund puppies. They had been bred not far from Chagford, and would be available within a week or two.

We went to see the puppies, and I chose one. His name, on formal occasions, was Minutist Peppercorn, and he was the most incredibly beautiful living thing I had ever come across. He wore a black velvet coat, his paws were tipped with gold and there were spots of gold above his eyes. He had that air of wistful fragility that hangs around certain baby animals. And he was going to be ours. We took him home, and named him 'Rudi'.

Penny was intrigued and diverted. She seemed to get a lot of pleasure out of knocking him down, but then his mother had probably done the same thing. We thought it was very likely going to be all right, but Penny's temper showed no immediate signs of improvement.

In July, Mark Hamilton came to stay with us. Mark was getting more and more concerned about my 'single-minded' obsession with romantic fiction and he wanted me to widen out, to stop piling all of my eggs into one basket - five baskets, actually, but it came to the same thing. I told him I would widen out when I and my family were financially secure, but at the moment I couldn't spare the time, or the energy, needed for playing Hamlet. Hugh took little part in this discussion - despite his wide experience he rarely, if ever, interfered directly between me and my book world contacts. Ba was shy and remote, and while Rudi scampered around making himself irresistible Penny retreated to the kitchen, where she mounted guard over our refrigerator.

Mark had children at home and he decided they ought to have a puppy, preferably something like Rudi. But he was a likeable, decent sort of person, and like all decent and likeable Englishmen he was anxious not to ignore the under-dog, who in this case appeared to be Penny. Finding himself at a loose end he formed the habit of following me into the kitchen, something which rapidly turned into a source of stress, at least from my point of view. I had no objection to discussing the vagaries of Collins' list - though not, ideally, while whipping up a complex meringue topping – but Mark seemed determined to become Penny's best friend, and this, to say the least, was distracting. Though he had been warned he didn't seem to notice the low growl or the quivering lip, nor did he appear to realise that Penny's main aim was to stop him getting near the fridge. (If a literary agent were to be bitten by an author's dog, I wondered as I basted the roast potatoes, would it affect the level of his commission?)

Mark, I'm happy to say, escaped without a scratch. He went back home, and bought a Corgi puppy for his children. Others, however, were not so fortunate. Just a few days later Rudi stumbled cheerfully into Penny's dinner-bowl and she promptly bit him through his glossy black nose. The wound was centimeters from his left eye, and as blood poured on to the kitchen floor he screamed like a hurt child. In panic I rang the vet and he came immediately - vets did things like that in 1958 - and while he dealt with the damage poor Penny was shut away in a little study behind the kitchen.

The vet said Rudi ought to be all right, though he had had a miraculous escape. But as for the other dog - no healthy, youngish bitch ought to savage a ten week old puppy. We would never be able to keep the two of them together, and he knew which one he would choose. Appalled, I said Penny had been part of our family for years - anyway, she was my husband's dog - and after thinking a bit the vet said there might be just one possibility, another vet who lived not far away and who had done considerable work in the field of canine psychology. He might be worth a try.

We called the dog psychologist, and he agreed to put Penny up for a few days. During that time, he said, he should be able to work out what was going on and whether or not anything could be done about it. Hugh took Penny over, and less than a week later the psychologist telephoned to ask if he could go back for a chat.

When Hugh returned that afternoon he asked me to call Ba, then he told us Penny had bitten the psychologist on the mouth. She had also attacked a chronically timid spaniel. In the vet's opinion something in her ancestry, perhaps that bit of Alsatian, was now beginning to come out; it could happen when a dog got to Penny's sort of age. He didn't think it was a psychological problem as such, therefore it was hard to believe there could be any treatment. Probably Ba and I were safe and it was unlikely she would attack Hugh, but essentially she was dangerous. Perhaps very dangerous. The next step, of course, was up to us - but very sadly, he knew what he would advise.

I said that we would find a home for the puppy, then somehow we would make sure Penny didn't get a chance to attack again. We could manage. But Hugh said we couldn't. Sooner or later someone - possibly a child - was going to get bitten seriously. He had argued with the vet, but not for long. At twelve noon the following day, Penny was going to be destroyed. The time lapse was simply because the vet felt we needed a chance to talk things over. But Hugh had already made up his mind

I felt like a murderer. If I hadn't bought a dachshund puppy none of this might have happened. Penny was the scrap I had taken in at Wych Pits, she was part of us - we couldn't *do* this. Before being taken away finally she had sat on Ba's lap, one paw on each shoulder, licking her face. It was awful, and Ba was distressed. But Hugh simply said very firmly that he believed there was no alternative, and in the end I knew he was right.

At a quarter to twelve the following day, Hugh announced he was walking to the pub for a drink. It was a hot August day and the pub was a mile and a half away, but I knew he needed to take his mind off things, and I didn't start to get worried until some time after two o'clock. At half past two I telephoned the pub, and the landlord said my husband had set out to walk home at least an hour and a half earlier.

Ba and I started walking along the winding road that led to the village. I didn't know what we would find - if anything - but my legs felt heavy with dread. It was, I remember, desperately hot.

We found him sitting on the grass beside the road, about half a mile from the village. Although quite conscious, he seemed dazed and said he didn't know how long he had been there. I didn't think, somehow, that he had been drinking heavily. A passing farmer drove us all home, and a doctor was called.

The doctor said Hugh had suffered a minor coronary spasm. It wasn't a good thing to happen, but no serious harm appeared to have been done and within a few days every trace of the event would probably have disappeared. He might need to adjust his lifestyle, though. If a recurrence were to be avoided he would need to give up smoking, for one thing, and also stick to a sensible level of drinking. And he could do without the burden of too much stress. On this occasion, there had obviously been a link with the fact that his dog was being put down.

Within a day or so Hugh was more or less himself again, but I had had a shock, and I knew I had some thinking to do. Within the last four or five years I had seen forty of my books published and distributed by five different companies. Our financial position had been stabilised, and life was fairly comfortable. I loved seeing my stories come out, and I loved being involved with publishing, with the book world in general. But where, exactly, was I heading? Where were *we* heading. . . ? We had all been happy at Wych Pits, but that was in the past. It had been a bright bubble, but like all bubbles it had burst in the end, and now it could not be re-captured. Hugh's health was weakening, and Ba was growing up. Who could say how much longer we three might have together?

I asked Hugh how he would feel about going abroad - to live, or perhaps just to wander about for a while. We could start out in Switzerland, so that when Ba joined her finishing-school we would be on hand. Then we might just drift on. . . . As for the puppy, he was family now and he would come too. After all, we would be away for some time.

Hugh liked the idea. I think it came as a kind of relief. And Ba was thrilled to bits. I wrote to the Hotel Viktoria, and though they were fully booked until late autumn they gave me the address of a lady - Fraulein Ella Huggler - who had some beautiful apartments in the village of Goldern-Hasliberg. I got in touch with Fraulein Huggler, and an apartment was booked. Then I told our landlord we would not now be requiring the farmhouse for a day longer than three months.

On August 25th we arrived in London. We had decided to stay at Durrant's for a couple of nights, and on the first day I had lunch alone with Alan. We talked about work for a long time, then our conversation turned to the adventure ahead and he wished me luck. If I needed anything, he said, I must get in touch with him. I knew that he was a friend, the best I had ever had, and was sure I could trust him.

In the meantime, since I was going abroad for some time, Alan said the firm would like some fresh publicity photos. They had booked me a session with Baron, a society photographer well known for being closely associated with Prince Philip, and the following day I went to his studio. Rudi, who had accompanied me to the lunch with

Alan, also came to be photographed and I think he appeared in every picture - what photographer in his right mind would miss the chance to include a three month old dachshund in a publicity shot?

The next day we left for Switzerland. I knew that just ahead there lay a completely new bend in the road, and I couldn't wait to find out what lay beyond it.

* * * * *

CPSIA information can be obtained at www.ICGtesting.com
Printed in the USA
LVOW01s0022131213

365131LV00013B/412/P